A Fair Cop

Michael Bunting

FRIDAY
BOOKS

The Friday Project
An imprint of HarperCollins Publishers
77–85 Fulham Palace Road
Hammersmith, London W6 8JB
www.thefridayproject.co.uk
www.harpercollins.co.uk

First published by The Friday Project in 2008
This paperback edition published by The Friday Project in 2009

A catalogue record for this book is available from the British Library

ISBN 978-1-906321-92-5

Interior Design and Typesetting by Maggie Dana
Badge icon by Carrie Kabak

Printed and bound in Great Britain by Clays Ltd, St Ives plc

Mixed Sources
Product group from well-managed
forests and other controlled sources
www.fsc.org Cert no. SW-COC-1806
© 1996 Forest Stewardship Council
FSC

FSC is a non-profit international organisation established to promote the
responsible management of the world's forests. Products carrying the FSC label
are independently certified to assure consumers that they come from forests
that are managed to meet the social, economic and ecological needs of present
or future generations.

Find out more about HarperCollins and the environment at
www.harpercollins.co.uk/green

A Fair Cop

Mum and Dad –
You went through hell, and words can never describe my
eternal gratitude.

Helen and Stuart, Adam and Oliver, and Nan.

And my girl, Rach –
When no one else would listen, you were always there,
night and day – I love you, babe x.

Acknowledgements

I would like to thank all those who supported and believed in me over the past ten years. And especially:

Tim and Cath – the best friends I could ask for. We never got the party after the trial. Can we make it for the book launch instead?

My friends in West Yorkshire Police – you know who you are.

The police officers who gave evidence for me despite efforts to stop you – you showed great moral courage, which will never be forgotten.

The Napa gang – once again, you know who you are. Thanks for keeping my chin off the floor on the July '99 tour weeks before I was sent to prison.

Everyone at BBC Radio Leeds – I'm humbled and hugely grateful for your support over the last few years.

The *Sunday Times*, the *Yorkshire Evening Post*, the *Press* and *Birstall News* – many thanks.

The Management Team at the Asda Store, Morley – the shelf-stacking job was very much appreciated, as was your support during my term of employment.

Roy and Paul at UK Workout – you have made a real contribution to my new career.

Norman Basson – you have been and remain an inspiration.

The chaplain and the doctor at Armley Prison – you both contributed to my survival.

Clare Christian – I cannot begin to express what your enthusiasm and belief means to me and my family - a special thank you to the whole team at The Friday Project.

Everyone else who helped my family and me either directly or indirectly – there are lots of you and I'm indebted to you all.

God – You found me in my prison cell and never left my side.

The Beginning

8th September 1999

Within minutes of receiving a four-month prison sentence for common assault, I was given my first taste of being locked in a cell alone and I had already received my first death threat. Prisoners had daubed their names on the walls along with short messages, most of which were obscene. Little had they known that I, a serving policeman, would end up in the same cell as them. I would be transported from Leeds Crown Court to Armley Prison very shortly. I knew the prisoners would make my life hell when they realised I was living amongst them. I sank to the floor, buried my head in my hands and began to shake. My worst nightmare had come true.

I remember one message in particular. It read, *The Ointment are back.* The Ointment is a gang of hard villains from Yorkshire. I had dealt with one of its members before. He had been owed money from a drug deal and when the deadline for paying the debt had passed, he used a machete to cut off the debtor's arm at the elbow. He even paraded the injured man up and down the street while he was bleeding profusely, demonstrating what the outcome would be for other would-be defaulters. I was now in the same cell that was once occupied by one of this notorious gang. He had used human faeces to write the message. The stench was nauseating. I was in their world now, and I was petrified. There was a bench bolted down to the concrete floor, which was damp. A metal cage welded to the ceiling protected the light bulb. I took this personally. Did they really think I would damage the light? Society was against me now. At least that was how it felt. I was being treated in the same way as the hundreds of criminals I had arrested over the past six years or so. I would not allow myself to think that I was one of them, though, and I saw my conviction as a miscarriage of justice. I hoped it would be corrected.

There was also a musty odour, a smell I was familiar with, as most police cell areas are like this. I could hear the voices of the court cell staff. They joked about something they had seen on television the night before, and discussed who was to do the sandwich run for lunch. Everything was normal for them. Occasionally, I'd hear an officer's radio in very close proximity to my cell door. Each time I heard the jangling of keys, my hopes would be raised that I'd be let out. I had only been locked in the cell for about twenty minutes and already felt unbearably oppressed by the size of it. It seemed strange that I was sitting in such surroundings in my best suit. I knew that every stitch of my clothing would be taken from me at HMP Armley, the notorious category B prison in Leeds, home to hardened criminals, rapists and murderers. I would be known to them, as I was a serving Leeds officer and my case was in the media. This increased my fear as I consciously tried to stop the shaking. The consequences of being sent to a category B prison could, realistically, be fatal.

After another ten minutes or so, though it seemed like hours, my thoughts were interrupted by the sound of a key in the lock of my cell door. As it opened, an old-looking Group 4 security officer greeted me. He was short and slightly built. His hair was grey and greased back, his fingers were stained yellow, and he smelt of tobacco. His shirt was dirty and displayed the parts of his breakfast he'd failed to get into his mouth. Opening the heavy steel cell door seemed a real effort for him. Despite all of this, he was kind-faced and he spoke with a soft, compassionate voice. 'Come on, kid. Let's get ya downstairs.' He placed his hand on my back, not as a gesture of authority but one of sympathy. I immediately liked him and, in my vulnerable state, I needed him. 'Bet you didn't expect this, did you, lad?'

'I knew,' I replied. 'The bloody judge told me five weeks ago he was sending me down. Can I see my brief before I go?'

'It's all been sorted. He's waiting for you down there, kid.'

'Cheers,' I said.

As I arrived at the basement level of the court building, I was taken to the booking desk. There was an abundance of Group 4 security staff and a distinct lack of other prisoners. It explained why I had been kept in the holding cell for an unusually long time. This had given the officers the opportunity to get all the other prisoners locked away. They would surely have heard the news of my sentence by now, especially if it had been announced in the news bulletin on the local radio, as all my other court appearances had. Information travels fast amongst inmates and an imprisoned policeman is big news; news that would inevitably unite them so that they could plan exactly what they were going to do about it. All of the officers looked at me with serious expressions, yet I felt they were sympathetic.

I arrived at the desk. The officer there was also quite old. He looked at me and shook his head. 'I can't believe they've done this to you, lad. What the hell is this country coming to? Are you okay?'

'It hasn't sunk in yet, if I'm honest.'

'The other prisoners know you're here, so we'll sort you out with separate transport to the prison. I'm not letting the bastards at you in the sweat box.' (A sweat box is a large vehicle used to transport people in custody, and on long journeys they get warm, hence the name.)

My safety was being taken seriously, although really it was a case of *when*, and not *if*, the prisoners would find a way of getting to me for my introduction to prison life. I'd heard of policemen getting sent down before and they rarely got out in one piece. I knew that a lot of prisoners at Armley had very little to lose, so doing a copper would mean nothing to them. As the officer filled in the paperwork for my records, it seemed highly ironic when he asked me for my occupation. He hesitated, looked deep into my eyes, shook his head again and then proceeded to write the words, *police officer*.

When he'd finished, one of the younger officers walked me to another cell. I was already feeling institutionalised and so I just followed him, without even knowing why or where I was going. My barrister was sitting at a desk in this cell, seemingly hiding behind his opened briefcase. He held his grey wig in one hand and opened the top button of his shirt with the other.

'Michael, I'm sorry,' he said as I walked in. 'We never stood a chance with that judge. You're going down because you're a policeman.'

'I didn't bloody well do it. I want to appeal.'

'We will appeal, Michael, but it will take time. There's plenty to go at. I can also try to have you released pending appeal, if you want me to.'

In the five weeks from my conviction to the date of my sentence, I had considered very carefully what line to adopt if the worst happened, as it had done. There were two possible options. The first was to appeal immediately against conviction and to request bail pending my appeal, which would have meant I would not have served my sentence at this time. If, however, my appeal was unsuccessful, then I would face doing my time in prison at a later date. The second option was to serve my sentence with the appeal pending, meaning that my sentence would have been over by the outcome of the appeal.

The list at the Court of Appeal was a very lengthy one, so yet more waiting was inevitable. The stress that the two years leading up to my conviction had placed on my family had been unbearable, and my mother hadn't coped well at times. I don't think she could have held out for much longer. She had seen the threat of a prison sentence hanging over me for those two years so I didn't want to prolong it any further. I had already made the decision not to request bail. I looked at Mr Stewart, my barrister, and I felt that this was now a test of nerve. I imagined my reception at HMP Armley, and then stopped myself. I had to condemn myself to four months in prison; it was the right thing to do. Four months may not sound like a long time, but if the first twenty minutes in the holding cell were anything to go by, it would feel like a lifetime. This was without doubt the toughest decision that I have ever had to make in my life, but I remained true to my plan to serve my sentence immediately, for Mum's sake. I had made the decision in the comfort of my own home, but carrying it out had proved much harder, now that I was actually standing in a cell.

I resigned myself to doing my full stretch in prison. I swallowed. It was painful, as my mouth was dry. I felt like someone who was trapped in a maze and, after hours of searching, seemed to have found a way out, only to realise it was yet another dead end. It was very frightening. I tried to stay focused and in control. I failed. My breathing became laboured and I had to sit down. I buried my face in my hands. 'They'll bloody well kill me in there. You can't send a copper to Armley.'

Mr Stewart closed his briefcase, ready to leave the cell. He told me that he would work hard on my appeal. This was little comfort to me, as it had paled virtually into insignificance. My short-term welfare became the priority. For the first time in my life, I felt completely helpless. I was now in the hands of the prison service and the inmates at Armley. Anything could happen in there.

He slammed the door shut as he left. The lock was bolted into place making a loud metallic clunk which echoed down the cell passage. It was a sound I was to become all too familiar with whilst serving my sentence. Hearing anything similar today is a stark reminder of those very dark times I spent in prison. The silence in the cell was in stark contrast to what I had just heard and, once again, I was left with my own company and my autobiography of Tony Adams, the Arsenal and England footballer. My mum and dad had given this to me the day before as a birthday present. It was the only item I had taken to court with me, in the hope I'd be allowed to take it with me. I loosened my tie and opened the top couple of buttons of my shirt. The optimism which had been my main strength for the past two years had deserted me. I felt physically sick, as I really didn't know how I would cope in prison. Throughout my whole service, I had been so proud of being a police officer. Now it was the worst thing in the world for me to be, but I was one, and I couldn't change it. My fear of how the other inmates would treat me intensified. I began to think of my mum and dad. I hadn't had the opportunity to see them since being given my sentence and I desperately wanted to speak to them, so that I could tell them that I was okay, even though I felt far from being so. I couldn't begin to imagine Mum's reaction. I knew that Dad would now be feeling the strain, too. He's a tough character and had worked his way up the ranks in the police service through hard work. He's self-educated, with few formal qualifications, which goes some way to show what a remarkable achievement it was for him to get to chief inspector, a rank that nowadays is often held by under-experienced academics with very little practical, hands-on knowledge. Dad was now Mum's only hope of surviving the forthcoming months. I knew I could rely on him. I'd have to. I exhaled slowly through my lips. The loss of my identity had begun.

'Boss, can I have a phone call?' someone shouted from a neighbouring cell. (Criminals call law officials 'boss' when they are locked up.) This was the kind of question that I'd been asked whenever I worked in the police cell areas. I knew that, from now on, I would be asking it. I would have to ask for everything for the next four months, even a drink of water. I certainly wasn't 'boss' now.

I tried in desperation to think of something positive. I failed, so I listened intently to what was going on outside my cell. I still hoped someone would open the door and tell me that a huge mistake had been made. Of course, this wasn't going to happen. All I heard was a relentless jangling of keys and the distant slamming of cell doors. The place seemed very busy, yet in my cell I felt abandoned and alone. It was as though the world had forgotten I existed. My cell walls seemed to close in, and this prompted me to start walking around. In just a few paces, I had walked its length. I desperately searched for something to occupy my mind because I knew that worse was to come. I knew, with dread, that the fight against the boredom was going to be as hard as the fight against the conditions and other inmates. I needed to develop a strategy in order to get through the long days ahead.

I sat on the bench and tried to think as I flicked through my book. Even Tony looked frightened on the front cover. I didn't know what to do, so I stood up again and put my face right up to the closed hatch in my cell door in the hope I'd be able to see out. I couldn't; it was too dirty. Then suddenly, the hatch fell open with a loud bang. Two eyes appeared at the slot. 'Stand away from the door,' came the forceful command. I complied and stood at the opposite side of my cell. My experience as a police officer had taught me just how daunting entering a cell is when it's occupied by an unknown quantity, which is how I would be being viewed by the officers. As the door opened, an overweight individual confronted me. His uniform clung tightly to his bulging belly, but he had a pleasant demeanour. He had an air of superiority over me because he could go home and I couldn't. He took me out of my cell to a door which led to the outside world. Two other Group 4 security officers waited for me. One of them was spinning a pair of handcuffs around his index finger, joking with his colleague about something. This made me very uneasy. I was relieved when his expression became more serious as he saw me walking towards him. I knew that he had probably been laughing at something entirely unrelated.

He looked at me. 'I'm sorry, mate, we're gonna have to put these on,' he said as he held out the handcuffs. The reality of the situation hit me again and I really did not want to be restrained. I had no intention of trying to escape and to think that I was a risk to the safety of the officers was ludicrous.

The officer handcuffed me with my hands to the front and a second pair of handcuffs was used to handcuff me to the second officer. I felt like a gangster. I looked at the officer. 'I'm not gonna kick off, mate,' I assured him.

'I know, but we have to do this,' he said.

'I know you do, but I'm here for a common assault that I didn't even do. I'm a bloody copper, for God's sake.'

'I've got to, mate. Sorry.'

I wasn't annoyed with *them*; they were just doing their job. 'Sorry, mate. I'm just pissed off about all this now. It's been going on for two years and they've fucking stitched me up because I'm a bloody policeman.' I realised that I was beginning to get a little too vocal. 'Sorry,' I said again, 'it's not your problem.'

With this, there was a buzzing sound and a green light lit up on the door handle, indicating that the officers could open it. One of them put his thumb up to a camera over the door. I assumed that he was thanking a colleague who had remotely unlocked the door for him. 'Come on then,' he said.

As the door opened, I saw a Group 4 car waiting. Large metal shutters surrounded the yard. Another officer sat in the driver's seat and the engine was running. The two officers led me to the car. We all got in, with me in the middle. It was very cramped and finding a comfortable position with my hands chained together was impossible. The driver switched on the radio. It was as though I was being given my last taste of civilisation, freedom and the outside world. The song, *How Do I Live Without You?*, by Leanne Rhymes, was playing. I find the irony of the song title quite amusing now, given the position I was in between the two guards. If I ever hear it, though, I feel physically sick, too. Every so often, the officer I was handcuffed to would glance at me. 'If it's any consolation to you, we're all on your side,' he said. 'You should have a medal for what you did; you shouldn't be getting this. It fucking stinks.' I didn't tell him, but it *was* a consolation, a big one.

The drive to Armley Prison took about ten minutes and I cherished every second. I wasn't a free man, but this was the nearest I'd get to freedom for a while. People driving their cars had no idea how lucky they were to be free. It seemed that way, anyway.

Then, the sight I'd been dreading was in front of me. Armley Prison is an old stone building, blackened with pollution, and it looks similar to an ageing castle. It's massive; it has to be, as it holds over a thousand inmates, some of the nastiest criminals in the UK. It stands as a visual representation of institutionalisation and is an enormous warning to anyone contemplating a crime. The walls are high and topped with about three feet of closely coiled barbed wire. There is no way out of this place. Stunned, I shook my head in despondency. The driver pulled up in front of two large doors. They were about ten feet tall and looked Victorian. We waited. I saw scores of prison officers coming and going, as there had obviously just been a shift changeover. They all seemed so intent on what they were doing, clutching their empty lunch boxes and pacing to their cars to go home and get on with their lives. Again, I felt abandoned. No one seemed bothered about me. Why should they be? When the doors eventually opened, I was horrified by what I saw. There were about fifteen prison officers standing around. Some stood with their hands in their pockets whilst others casually smoked cigarettes. Several others swung large bunches of keys on long chains around their fingers, just as the Group 4 officer had done with the handcuffs.

'They always fucking keep us waiting here,' said the driver, indicating his distaste for the prison officers. There had always been an antagonistic relationship between the Group 4 officers and the staff at Armley Prison. I didn't know why.

One of the officers approached the driver's window. 'Who've we got here then?' he asked.

'Ummm what's his name, lads?' asked the driver to the officers sitting either side of me.

'Bunting,' came the reply.

'Bunting,' said the driver to the prison officer.

'Okay. You'll be in, in a minute,' said the prison officer. He seemed to enjoy his power of being able to keep the Group 4 men waiting, but sure enough, after a couple of minutes the shutter finally began to open slowly. We entered the prisoner reception yard, which was about the size of a football pitch and surrounded by high walls, which led to the main building where all the wings were. There was a door in the far corner.

The driver took us towards it and parked. He turned off the engine. 'Bloody useless. Where are they now?' he shouted. With this, the officer who I was handcuffed to began to escort me out of the car.

'Get him back in,' came a bellowing voice from inside the

building. 'Bloody well get him back in. He's a fucking v.o.' (A v.o. is a violent offender.) At this moment, a prison officer charged out of the building with a German Shepherd dog on a lead. He approached the car. 'For God's sake,' said the driver, 'I think they're expecting bother from you, kid.'

The dog jumped up at the side of the car and left damp patches on the window where it had pressed its nose against the glass. It opened its mouth and displayed a jaw full of lethal looking teeth. I cowered away like a child, pulling the officer with me, until we were allowed out.

As I alighted, the prison officer gave the lead more slack and so the dog was able to come right up to me. It frantically sniffed my leg. I was scared and knew that if I made a sudden movement, the innocent sniffing would turn into something a lot more sinister. I felt resentment towards this officer; I was to have similar feelings again.

He marched me to the prisoner reception door and unlocked the handcuffs. Both of the Group 4 officers shook my hand and wished me well. It was brief, but emotional. *I* found it emotional, anyway. I suspected that the prison officers weren't going to be quite so understanding. I was placed into yet another holding cell, as there were about six or seven other prisoners waiting to be booked in. This cell shocked me just like the Crown Court cell had, except this one made the one at court seem like a room at the Hilton. There were puddles of urine all over the floor and I had to pull my jacket over my face in order to breathe without wanting to vomit, due to the stench. The familiar writing on the walls was also present in abundance. The prisoners outside my cell sounded rowdy and aggressive. My being placed into the holding cell so quickly must have been unusual, as I heard two or three asking whether or not I was a *beast* (a prison term for paedophile or rapist). *Beasts* are very vulnerable when inside, as other prisoners see it as their duty to give out their own form of punishment, usually in the form of violence. I would rather the prisoners knew I was a policeman than for them to think I was a *beast*. Neither option was ideal, but in prisoners' eyes, there is nothing worse than a *beast*.

Fortunately, the questions soon passed and the other prisoners' initial interest in me subsided, as a prison officer tried to combat the rowdy behaviour by threatening the prisoners with a 'nicking' or a reduction to basic status. This was followed with a chorus of 'Sorry, boss,' from the prisoners. Losing standard status in prison to basic status is a massive punishment to any person in custody.

There are four different statuses in prison: basic, standard, enhanced and super-enhanced. The privileges a person receives whilst they are serving their sentence are related to their status. For example, someone with super-enhanced status may get a paying job in prison and therefore will spend much of the day outside their cell. They have more money to spend on food, cigarettes, and phone cards. Super-enhanced prisoners can even get a television in their cell. Basic prisoners, on the other hand, get nothing other than the statutory one-hour exercise period each day and the bare minimum to spend on luxuries. Basic status is avoided at all costs and therefore encourages good behaviour in prison. Every prisoner enters with standard status and, following a minimum of four months good behaviour, he can then be offered enhanced status and eventually super-enhanced.

I continued to look around the cell. It was lit only by a small amount of light which penetrated the filthy window at the top of the far wall. These walls had never been decorated. They were bare brick and appeared damp. The light on the ceiling had been ripped off, despite a once-present protective metal cage. The bench was completely covered with cigarette burns, so I didn't sit down. Saliva dripped down the walls. I was now living with the animals I had dealt with in the years I had been a policeman.

I was hit by nausea and I felt involuntary contractions of my stomach begin to take hold. This time I *was* going to vomit. I banged on the cell door with the side of a clenched fist in the hope that I would attract the attention of a prison officer. I wouldn't have made the cell any dirtier if I had vomited on the floor, but I didn't wish to add to its sordid state.

A prison officer opened the door. 'What?' he shouted.

I must have looked as ill as I felt, because he immediately pointed down the corridor to the nearest toilet. I managed to get there just in time. I was violently sick for several minutes. I looked round for something to wipe my mouth on, but there was nothing, not even any toilet roll, so I used the sleeve of my suit. My legs felt shaky as I walked towards the desk where the prisoners were being booked in. I was told to wait, as it was my turn next.

The last remaining prisoner looked hard-featured. He was stocky and had a mass of tattoos all over him, including a picture of a dagger stabbing into his neck with blood dripping from the blade. He intimidated me just by his appearance. I dared not think of why he was in prison. I was trembling uncontrollably. It was cold and I already felt weak and I added to the stench of the place with the remnants of vomit on my jacket. The man stared at me, ignoring questions from the prison officer at the desk. He looked disgusted by my presence.

He took a pace towards me, meaning we were about an arm's length apart. His eyes were piercing. He breathed rapidly through his mouth, making a panting noise as he did so. He smelt of alcohol. He screwed his face up in another look of disgust and edged even closer. He began making noises with his mouth as if he was accumulating saliva. Before I had chance to retreat, he spat in my face, and phlegm landed right on my cheek. I immediately began to wipe it off with the vomit-ridden sleeve. The officers made no reaction; in fact, they stopped asking him questions as if they were happy to let him do as he pleased. I looked towards the one behind the desk and, using facial gestures, expressed my bewilderment at the situation. The officer looked wary. I was completely baffled by what was happening, as it seemed like the man had taken control of the area he was occupying. Just as I finished wiping my face, he spat again, this time towards my feet. He opened his mouth and, with a flick of his tongue, removed his top set of teeth. I stepped back. As I did this, he raised his arm and with a swift movement punched me in the face, causing an immediate popping sensation in my nose. He laughed in my face. I felt a salty taste in the back of my throat and blood started to pour from my nostrils. I stumbled back, too scared to react other than to put my hands in a defensive position over my face. The man laughed again and said something under his breath, I don't know what, then he turned away and walked off. With no fuss, a prison officer quietly led him away.

I bent over at the waist to prevent the blood getting onto my shirt. It dripped onto the floor and splattered onto my shoes. One of the officers approached me and unceremoniously gave me some toilet roll. My nose was riddled with pain and tears streamed down my face. I daren't even complain to the prison officers. I hadn't worked the place out and I didn't want to make more enemies than I already had in there. There was seemingly little concern, though, and no repercussions for the man who had assaulted me. I saw the custody sheet on the desk. He was in for manslaughter. I wiped my nose and looked for a reaction from the staff. There wasn't one. The next four months were going to be hell.

'Right, Bunting. Clothes off!' came the order from the officer at the desk. His attitude took me aback. I began to get undressed, but I found it rather embarrassing as there was no screen, and I was in full view of all of the officers in the area. There were also two cleaning ladies present, but they didn't seem to take any notice. I guess they had seen it all before. I carefully placed each item of clothing onto the desk: my tie, my dirty jacket, my shirt, my trousers, my socks and my blooded shoes. In contrast to the care I had taken with my clothes, a prison officer then crammed them into a small box, wearing medical gloves. I wanted to ask him to be more careful with my property, but that might well have been counter-productive. This was prison, and *I* was an inmate.

'I thought I said take your fucking clothes off,' he said again.

'Sorry?' I asked. He pointed to my underpants, which I had left on. Surely they would allow me to remove these in private?

'Off,' he said. I couldn't believe it. Another prison officer approached him and whispered something. I don't know exactly what he said, but it instantly transformed his attitude towards me. 'Oh, you'll find a robe in that box,' he said quietly. His behaviour generated a large amount of sympathy in me towards other prisoners, something which I never thought I would feel.

I placed my underpants into the box with my other clothes.

The prison officer gave me a name board with my details and prison number on it: *Michael E. Bunting. d.o.b. 7/9/73. DK8639.* That number would become my identity for the whole of my sentence. I held the board up to my chest and, with a blinding flash of light, an officer took my photograph. Following this, I had my fingerprints taken. It was a terse task and the officer didn't speak to me as he grabbed each finger and rolled it into the ink and then onto the paper. When he'd finished with me, I was covered in ink up to my wrists. I felt like a piece of meat. He told me to wash my hands, and I was sent to the supply room where I was given my prison clothing. The boxer shorts I was given were bloodstained. I cringed as I put them on. The T-shirt was so tight it seemed to almost squeeze the air from my lungs, and the jeans were so loose I had to hold them up to prevent them falling to my ankles. I remember there was a large drawing of a penis on the front of the left leg, drawn in ink by a previous inmate. The jumper had *HMP ARMLEY* written across the front of it. I wasn't exactly likely to forget where I was, but this served as a constant reminder. One of the inmates working in the storeroom then gave me my bed pack, which comprised two blankets and a pillowcase. I clutched them under one arm, as I held my jeans up with the other. It was hard to accept that just minutes earlier I had been wearing my smart suit. Now I was wearing a degrading prison uniform, which already had splashes of blood on it from my injured nose.

A prison officer then took hold of my shoulder and led me away. He was younger than the others and seemed far less robotic. He spoke to me as we walked through the door to the main prison, telling me I would be placed in a cell in the hospital wing, the wing where inmates with severe health problems were detained. I was being sent here because I was a policeman and therefore posed a security risk to the prison due to inmates' reaction to me. I wasn't sure whether this was being done as a result of what had just happened.

Armley Prison is huge and our journey to my cell was a long one. Every corridor was secured with a locked door and the officer would keep reaching for the keys on a chain around his belt to unlock and then re-lock each one. Prisoners stared at me as I walked through each wing. They were all going about their normal business of cleaning out their cells or reading newspapers, nothing much more. I had already been warned by the officer not to look back at them. That, in his words, would result in my first 'kick in'. I corrected him and said it would be my second. I tried to keep my head down, but this wasn't easy, as I thought that at any moment someone else would realise who I was and try to hurt me. I got the impression that if that happened, the officer wouldn't intervene, as this would result in him being attacked, too. I was relying purely on the fact that word had not yet got around that I was a policeman. I didn't know either way. I was petrified of an immediate attack, but tried to blend in as if I was a normal inmate. I felt my heart thumping in my chest, and I felt breathless.

Several corridors and many hard stares later, we arrived at the hospital wing. I was placed in my cell. It was tiny and mundane. There was a small desk and chair, a bin, a metal sink and, of course, the bed, which was more like a thin mattress on legs. My hopes of a lively ward of caring people faded fast. This cell was as bad as the other two I had been in. The moment I stepped into it, the door slammed shut behind me. 'You'd better settle down for a bit, mate,' said the officer, as he peered through my cell hatch. I was still clutching onto my book. I sat on the bed and gazed straight ahead. I knew that once word got around that there was a policeman in the cells, my safety was in jeopardy but I lay back and tried to calm myself down, as the thudding in my chest increased. I had officially started my prison sentence; the next four months were going to be a game of survival for me. I didn't know what was going to happen. One thing I did know, though, was that it was not a case of *if* I got my next beating, but a case of *when*.

I looked up to the ceiling and began my first ever plea to God.

Part I

*Police Constable 451
Michael Bunting*

Chapter 1

Early Days

29th March 1993 (six years earlier)

'Take that smile off your face, Bunting!'

It was, I have to say, not as I had expected. I had waited all my life for this moment and I was finally here, standing motionless in my brand new uniform on a freezing cold and wet drill square with ten other recruits. I certainly wasn't smiling. My first day at West Yorkshire Police training school had started.

He was a large man, well over six feet tall, and his smart appearance was dominating. The crease in his trousers appeared to be razor sharp and his boots shone like glass. His flat cap was placed so far down his forehead that you couldn't see his eyes. Every step he took echoed around the square. I knew that *I* would have to look like this one day, and soon. I still dared not move. I was intimidated by his presence, but this feeling temporarily subsided to relief, as occasionally Sergeant Wright would allow his emotionless face to show a smile. He walked behind the line in which I was standing and as he went out of sight, I closed my eyes tight. I felt his pace stick thud down onto the top of my helmet. The noise was deafening. 'Stop smiling!' he bellowed as he came nose to nose with me. I couldn't understand this; I wasn't smiling. I tried not to move, but I felt my helmet falling from my head and so I instinctively tried to catch it. 'Bunting, stand still!' His voice was penetrating and I immediately rose to attention as my helmet bounced off into a puddle. I had only had it about an hour and already it was filthy. It would be spotless again by the following day; it would have to be.

The initial training period was to be residential. One bed, one wardrobe, one sink and one metal bin were all that filled my tiny, lifeless room. I noticed a Bible purposefully placed on the pillow. I sat on the bed. My suitcase filled the only remaining floor space. I stood up and I saw myself in the full-length mirror. I could hardly believe what I saw. I was only nineteen years old and the uniform seemed to highlight my tender years.

One of the other recruits walked into my room. Richard was older than me but we'd queued for our uniform together and we were already relying on each other for support. 'Do we go to lunch in full uniform?'

'I think we'd better,' I replied cautiously. I had one final look at myself and then looked down to each button on my tunic. I had to make sure that the Queen's crown was perfectly upright on them all. It was the very first thing that Sergeant Wright had told us and I wasn't going to forget.

Richard approached me and pinched my back. 'Hair,' he muttered, as he held his index finger and thumb up to the window for a closer inspection of a stray hair.

'Cheers, mate,' I replied, knowing that he had just saved me from another reprimand from Sergeant Wright.

We all congregated in the television lounge on the landing. There was an uncomfortable silence, but that was only to be expected. We didn't know each other and we had all just spent four hours on a cold and wet drill square. This had come as a shock. After all, we had been on 'civvy street' at breakfast time. I had felt the effects of this massive change the moment I put on the uniform. I can't describe the feeling; it was just surreal.

The silence continued as we walked across the yard to the canteen. I thought we all looked immaculate. Before today, I had only seen groups of police officers like this on the television; now I was part of one. I smiled. My dream was coming true. This was all I'd ever wanted since seeing my dad in his uniform for the first time when I was about four. I remember he'd come home for a few minutes on Christmas Day to see my sister and I open our presents. Letting the neighbours see that you were a police officer wasn't as much of a problem in the seventies.

As we walked into the canteen, I immediately noticed the noise of the clanging cutlery. I joined the back of the long queue. No one else was wearing a tunic or a helmet. I noticed several groups of officers looking over and laughing. I realised that tunics and hats were not required in the canteen, yet I dared not remove mine. I looked into the eating area. It was full. I noticed a raised platform with tables on it. There were neatly arranged flowers, jugs of fresh orange and baskets of bread on these tables. A dominant picture of the force crest hung precariously on the wall. I figured that this was the area for senior officers, as the other tables simply had a jug of water on them. With extraordinary curiosity, my eyes wandered around the room. I saw a large portrait of the Queen. This was strikingly significant. She seemed to be staring at me even when I moved. It was as if the picture had been put there deliberately to make me realise where I was. I was now a servant of Her Majesty. A large gap had developed in the queue as the person in front of me strode on. I had to make a conscious effort to close my mouth. I was in awe of everything. I was living my dream, and it was impossible to hide the fact that this was my very first day as a policeman.

When I sat down to eat, I noticed that even the serviettes proudly displayed the force crest. I opened mine out and stared fixedly at it. I noticed that one or two others in my group were doing exactly the same. I began to eat and contemplated the forthcoming afternoon. We were due in the classroom at 1.30 p.m., but I didn't know what to expect. It was only twelve o'clock so I wanted to take advantage of the bit of free time. I needed to unpack my suitcase, the one my mum had packed. Mum seemed miles away now. I was on my own, about to enter the real world.

Despite these intentions, I didn't manage to do my unpacking. The free time was consumed by my stupefaction at my surroundings. I also knew that I needed to 'bull' my boots and press to perfection my trousers and tunic sleeves. I had already realised that impressing Sergeant Wright wasn't going to be easy, especially at seven o'clock in the morning, which was when we were next due on the square.

I sat in my room and carefully took off my uniform. The aloof authority around the place made me feel wary of creasing it, even when I was on my own with no one looking. I opened my boot polish and put some water into the lid. I took my cloth, wrapped it around my finger, dipped it into the water and the polish so I could shine my boots. As I did so, I listened intently to every noise. I could hear distant laughter from other rooms and, at this moment, hearing it was very daunting to me. How could anyone dare laugh here?

Richard knocked at my door and came in. 'We're all in the telly room, Mick. Doing our boots together, mate.' I picked up my boots and polish and walked the short distance down the corridor to join them. I was a shy nineteen-year-old and had been out of school for less than a year. The others were older than me, and just joining in with their conversation was unnerving. I would have preferred to stay in my room but that wouldn't have gone unnoticed. I had to make the effort; I wanted to fit in. I sat down. Everybody was doing exactly the same thing. Each had a cloth covering the index finger in one hand, working in a circular motion on the toecap of the boot held in the other. Occasionally, someone would raise the boot to their face, then open their mouth and breathe heavily onto it. It felt like the army to me.

'It's gonna take bloody hours, is this.' Diane was a slender young lady who was clearly frustrated as her boots were still dull. She kept going. I sighed. My boots were dull, too, despite almost an hour of continual 'bulling'.

We all began to talk, and spent the next couple of hours getting acquainted. This was interrupted only by the occasional gripe about the task in hand. I soon felt more comfortable as I learned that I was in the company of a wide range of people, from a former professional footballer to a check-out operative at a supermarket. One of the guys had been an undertaker before he joined the police and his stories about the situations he'd found himself in helped to pass the time. He'd been involved with the Valley Parade Football Ground disaster in Bradford in 1985, which I found disturbing, as some of my friends had been killed in the fire.

By about 9 p.m. there were ten pairs of pristine boots on the floor. My finger was stained black, and it appeared pruned from the damp cloth. Everybody looked tired but the atmosphere was more relaxed and the talking continued. The boots remained untouched for the next few hours. We had been driven only by the fear and anticipation of Sergeant Wright. Who would bear the brunt of his annoyance tomorrow? Not me again, I hoped.

The next few days consisted of much of the same. I soon realised that none of us would ever satisfy Sergeant Wright. One of the recruits had been told off for tying his laces using the wrong type of knot. It was his job to find fault, but I was determined to make his job as hard as possible. He was going to get the best from me. We all had to look flawless by Thursday. This would be the swearing-in ceremony to be held in front of our families and friends. Perfect appearance would be essential.

It was an early finish on Thursday and so there was no

excuse not to get it right. I returned to my room at about 4 p.m. I had got used to its size and its inanimate aura. There was just three hours to go. I tried to visualise Mum and Dad watching me being formally accepted into the police service. My stomach knotted with nerves. I laid on my bed, put my hands behind my head and closed my eyes. My whole body was shaking uncontrollably, and I felt cold. I could smell the dirty burning odour: the same smell I had noticed every evening as the heating system started. I could hear some men playing a game of football outside. They didn't seem to have a care in the world, not like me. Somehow, I dozed off.

The distant sound of a radio and the sound of hurried footsteps on the corridor were audible as I began to wake up. My mouth was dry and my eyes felt heavy. I was irked that I'd fallen asleep. I reached onto the floor for my watch. It was ten past six. I'd been asleep for two hours! Panic-stricken, I leaped from my bed and opened the door. I looked down the corridor and saw my colleagues nervously pacing up and down in full uniform as if they were rehearsing for later. I slammed the door. 'Shit.' I must have said this quite loudly as I heard a few chuckles from the others. The sound of the footsteps got louder.

'Get a move on, Mick, we're going in twenty minutes,' someone said.

'No probs, I'll be right along.' I tried to sound convincing, but as I said this I was hopping around the room, hurriedly taking off my trousers. Loud bangs rained onto my door. The others seemed to be enjoying my predicament. I ran out completely naked, clutching only a small towel and a bar of soap. The laughter was inevitable, as were the mocking wolf whistles. Fortunately, there was no time to think of the embarrassment. I didn't have long but I would make it. I had no choice, and by 6.30 p.m. I was standing in front of my mirror again. The work was already done on my uniform and it hung exquisitely. My boots gleamed. I placed my helmet on my head slowly and precisely. I looked at myself for one last time, took a long, deep breath and walked out onto the corridor. I felt contented but still very nervous.

The television lounge swarmed with anxious-looking new police officers. Everyone was on his or her feet and moving around, seemingly without purpose. Periodically, someone would pat themselves down with their hand bound with inverted sticky tape, in a frenzied attempt to remove the last remaining bits of fluff from their tunics. Richard looked at me and shook his head. He didn't need to say anything. I knew how he was feeling. These silent exchanges continued for a few minutes. The awkward silences were interrupted only by the reverberation of an object being repeatedly blown by the wind onto the metal flagpole just outside.

Phil, the ex-footballer, pushed the button for the lift. Being recruits, we were on the top floor and descending by the stairs would have been both time-consuming and tiring. The bell rang and the lift doors parted. One by one, we squeezed into the tiny space. I entered last. The doors closed and everyone looked downward. It was a game of skill not to stand on anyone's perfectly polished boots. The silence remained unbroken. I desperately wanted to speak. I didn't know what I wanted to say but I felt oppressed by the silence. I glanced across at

Phil. He was a tall, solid figure of a man and was known for his sharp wit as the class joker. He spoke with a gentle Irish accent and could have the class in hysterics with just a couple of carefully chosen words. He had done this all week. Phil's humour was certainly needed now and he responded to my glance.

'Tommy, what the hell is that?' Phil thrust his finger into Tommy's hairy nostril and pointed to something quite horrible. Everybody laughed. Tommy produced a handkerchief in an instant and wiped away the source of our amusement. This jovial moment had temporarily diverted my mind from the forthcoming reality. The bell rang and the doors opened.

The lecture theatre, which was being used for the ceremony, was a short walk away. We had to go outside. There was driving rain and a howling gale, conditions which threatened the appearance of our uniforms. I pushed against the door. It was, for a time at least, a test of strength: me versus the wind. Eventually, I won the battle. I buried my head into my tunic, closed my eyes as much as possible and began the journey. I was now faced with a dilemma: did I walk and risk a complete soaking, or did I run and risk splashing the back of my trousers? The scene to any onlooker must have been amusing as we all waddled like ducks in a vain attempt to prevent the splashing. Nevertheless, we all arrived at the lecture theatre seemingly none the worse for our ordeal.

Once there, I was bewildered by the sight that greeted us. The theatre was a phenomenal size, yet every detail was intricate and minute. Each seat exhibited an elegant nametag in enduring expectancy of each guest. Ten written declarations of the oath were on the front row. I figured that we would be sitting there. Flamboyant silk curtains decoratively circled the entire room, leading to the focus, a large white screen at the front. Alluring velvet strips draped yet another portrait of the Queen. She was looking to the side this time, but her presence was compelling. I thought she could sense my nerves.

'This is bloody posh, innit?' said Tommy. No one replied. I saw Richard read a copy of the declaration. I did the same. This wasn't a time for mistakes or tripped words. Several others quickly joined us. Two colleagues felt the need to read mine over my shoulder, yet their own copies were only inches away from them. The nerves had removed all rational thinking. A number of voices speedily whispered the words on the card.

'Does anyone know what we have to do?' someone asked. Again, there was no reply.

Then the inevitable came. I heard voices coming from outside, and the sound of high heels on the floor confirmed that the first guests were arriving. Whose family would it be? Tommy grimaced. There was a knock at the door. Whoever it was felt subordinate enough to seek permission to enter and this instantly gave me a feeling of confidence and control. Didn't they know it was only *us* in the room? They didn't need to knock. I realised again that I was a policeman and this was my first encounter with the public as such. *I* hadn't changed, but people's reaction to me had.

By the time the theatre had filled with our loved ones, we had all taken our seats. My hands were sticky and from time to time I would frantically rub my palms together in order to rid them of the sweat. I puffed out my cheeks and released a long breath through barely parted lips. The others remained still. The magistrates and college commander would arrive any minute. Sure enough, they did: with a ceremonious entry, a mass of grand-looking senior officers and court officials entered the room. The formal opening began.

I knew this was going to take a while, which exacerbated my nerves. I placed my hands on my lap and tried to listen. I continued to look around the room, but did so with the minimum of movement because each move that I made was the focus of everybody's attention, or at least that's how it felt. I began to think of my friends from school. I couldn't believe where I was. I wondered what they were doing at this very moment. They would never believe this if I told them – Michael Bunting, a police officer? Then my turn to be sworn in arrived.

'PC Bunting, please,' came a voice, out of the blue. I looked at the front and the officiating magistrate nodded his head and smiled at me. It was as if he sensed my anguish. I stood up and tentatively approached him. I looked over to my mum and dad before taking the oath. My formal acceptance to the service was complete. I had even been given my dad's old West Riding Constabulary collar number, 451. As a chief inspector of the same force, he looked on with the pride I had expected. I'd done it.

I spent the next fifteen weeks at the Police Training School in Warrington. On the final day, after having studied law in the classroom, done riot training on the drill square and performed role play scenarios in mock streets, I completed the passing-out parade with hundreds of other recruits from five different police forces. Once again, Mum and Dad came along with my grandma and grandad (Dad's parents) to join the crowds of proud onlookers as these new police careers began.

My life's ambition to become a police officer was complete. I wondered what the next thirty years had in store for me.

Chapter 2

Rich Man Hanging

My first memory after my initial police training is the sudden and unexpected death of my grandma. Just two weeks after she had proudly watched me in the passing-out parade, she suffered a fatal stroke, chilling in its timing. All she ever wanted was to see me become a policeman, just like my father had in the sixties. My grandma had enjoyed good health all of her life. Her death seemed cruel, especially to my grandad, who relied heavily upon her as he was partially disabled from a gunshot wound sustained to his right arm during the Second World War. On reflection, and having seen both my grandfathers suffer long illnesses before their deaths, I feel Grandma's death was a dignified conclusion to her life. She had enjoyed it to the full, right to the end and I now realise that this is something for which we should be grateful. As a result of losing Grandma, the relationship between Grandad and me became even stronger.

For the last four years of his life I visited him regularly. For months, he would accidentally call people 'Lucy', my grandma's name. It was heart-breaking. You could feel his loss.

Unfortunately, it soon became clear that death was a thing that, as a policeman, I would have to get used to. Having almost fainted during a day attachment to the mortuary, I knew I didn't like dealing with the deceased.

I remember being sent to my very first sudden death. I was with my tutor constable, Gary, when the call came over the radio. I looked at Gary. It was four o'clock in the morning, and it was cold.

'You okay with this, Mick?' he asked.

'Gotta get my first one out of the way, mate.'

Gary began to drive the car. 'Check to see if we have a Form Forty-nine, will you?' (A Form 49 is the paperwork used by West Yorkshire Police for sudden deaths. It usually involves interviewing the doctor and family members of the deceased. The mention of this form is guaranteed to make most police officers feel at least a little uneasy.) I found the relevant paperwork and told Gary that we were okay to attend. I tried to imagine the sight I was about to face. I sat quietly in the car. I didn't want to speak. I had to prepare myself. People at the scene would expect me to know exactly what to do and to be able to handle the situation without showing any emotion at all. After all, I was a policeman. The thought of a dead body was daunting, though. I hadn't been trained to deal with the emotional side of death; this could only come with experience. I opened my pocket notebook and began to jot down the address.

'What number house is it?' I asked. My mind was preoccupied now and the relevant information had escaped.

Gary repeated the whole radio message virtually word for word. He wasn't fazed. We pulled onto Barnsley Road and saw an ambulance halfway down. 'That'll be it, lad,' said Gary, with a look of concern on his face. 'You sure you're okay?'

'Yep.'

'Let me do the talking at this one and you learn as we go. I'll do the form as well. They're a nightmare when you haven't seen one before.'

'Okay, mate.' My mouth was dry, and I felt cold. People had gathered in the street. We were the sole focus of their attention as we drove towards them.

'Coppers are here,' I heard one person say.

I took a deep breath and got out of the car. A young couple approached me and pointed to the house. 'It's there, officer.'

'Okay, thanks.' I noticed they were still wearing their slippers. I found this rather strange. One of the ambulance crew walked out as Gary and I approached the door. He shook his head and said, 'Hi lads. There's nothing we can do here. He's dead. Doctor's been called to confirm death. We'll have to leave it with you, I'm afraid.'

'No probs, mate. Thanks a lot,' Gary replied.

We walked into the hallway. To the left was a half-open door leading to the living room. I could see the man's legs. He was lying on the floor. I tentatively pushed the door open and looked at his face. He was an elderly gentleman and he lay in an unnatural posture on the floor. His face was white and his mouth was wide open. The ambulance crew had placed his dentures next to him. I noticed he had a wet patch on his trousers and the dreadful smell indicated he'd had a substantial bowel movement upon his death. His fingers were purple and curled round into a partial fist. His hair looked immaculate. It was a really bright white colour, parted perfectly and styled seemingly with precision and pride. It looked unaffected by his death and this recovered his dignity despite the soiling of his trousers. I noticed photos of children on the fireplace. I assumed they were his grandchildren, or even great-grandchildren. I also noticed an old-looking black and white photograph of a woman dressed in old-fashioned clothing. A cross with some religious prose hung over this photo. I assumed it was a picture of his deceased wife. I sensed his loneliness.

Gary walked over to the window and began to inspect it. This baffled me. 'What you doing that for?' I asked.

'When we go to deaths we have to check the place for forced entry, signs of a struggle, anything nicked and stuff like that. You never know, one of these could be a murder and your feet wouldn't touch the ground if you missed it and let the scene go.'

'Oh yes. I see. This isn't a murder, is it?'

'No, mate. Poor old sod has seen enough of this life. Looks like a heart attack to me. Their mouths always stay wide open like that when it's a heart attack. We'll have to strip the body too, Mick. We have to check for bruises.' Gary seemed to know exactly what he was doing and this filled me with reassurance. 'Have you got your surgical gloves on ya?' he asked.

'Yeah, they're in the car.'

'You'll need 'em for this bit, mate.' Gary looked at me and gave me a forced smile.

'Right.'

I went outside and noticed more people had gathered. I felt very self-conscious and made a deliberate effort not to show any expression on my face. 'What's happening, officer?' asked the same man who had spoken to me earlier.

'I'm afraid I can't tell you.' This seemed to be the right thing to say but I wasn't sure whether it was or not. I knew that I wasn't allowed to tell people much so it seemed to be the best answer. I walked back into the house and unwittingly took a deep breath just as I entered the living room. The smell had worsened, as Gary had moved the man's body, causing more excrement to leak out. I turned my head back in to the hallway and took another deep breath.

I walked over to the body and robotically began moving it into positions that made removing the clothes as easy as possible. Rigor mortis hadn't set in and the body still felt warm. The dead weight felt weird: so heavy and floppy. I pulled my jumper up over my nose, as the excrement had smeared onto the carpet and all over the man's buttocks and legs. The stench was unbearable. I tried to remain expressionless, but I don't think I managed.

'You'll get used to this, Mick. This is a clean one. You want to smell 'em when they've had a few weeks to decompose.'

'I'm quite happy having this to break me in,' I replied, feeling alarmed at the thought that I'd eventually see far worse.

We lay him down again and as we covered him with a towel, a small amount of urine leaked out to add to the mess. It was then that the man's doctor arrived. He was quite old-looking himself. He strained his eyes, looking tired and dishevelled. He had obviously been woken up to attend this death.

'Now then, Ernest, what are you doing dying on me at this time of night?' Even though the words may have sounded quite unfeeling, he spoke with a sensitive tone and I sensed he was sorry about the death.

'I couldn't get him into hospital. He's been very ill.' The doctor held the man's arm for a couple of seconds and then shone a torch into his eyes.

'Goodbye, Ernest,' he said, as he placed his arm back on the floor. He turned to me. 'Certified dead, five fifteen a.m.' I looked at Gary who immediately wrote this down. Without being prompted, the doctor gave Gary the other details which we, as the police, needed. This had an ominous feeling of habit about it.

The undertakers didn't take long to arrive and by six o'clock, Gary and I were back in the station ready to finish the shift. I had dealt with my first sudden death and felt a little shaken by it. Gary put his jacket on, collected his sandwich box from the canteen and headed for the door. 'See ya tonight, Mick.'

'See ya, Gary.' I left the station, scraped the ice from my car windows and began the drive home. I could still smell Ernest in the back of my nose. A similar stench exuded from my clothes. I opened the car window and spat out a mouthful of saliva. I knew from this moment on that I'd never be comfortable with sudden deaths.

My days off after that particular week were most welcome. I met up with a couple of old friends from school. They listened with intrigue to my story about Ernest.

As a young man working long and varied shifts to make a living, the thought of being a multi-millionaire was nothing but a dream. I thought that having that kind of money would be the key to a life of happiness. At twenty years of age, this pre-conception of contentment was completely eliminated when I attended the most gruesome death that I would ever face. It made the scene at Ernest's death seem tame.

When I arrived at work that day, the sun shone gloriously

and the sky was beautiful and cloudless. I was working an early shift, known as early turn, which started at 6 a.m. and finished at two in the afternoon.

On this particular early turn, I was eating a bowl of cereal at the station when the call came through at about 7.30 a.m. I hadn't worked many early shifts, but I'd soon realised that, generally, there were very few calls before 8 a.m. After then, we would be hit with a surge of calls as people woke up to find they had been the victims of burglary.

I pushed the bowl aside and set off to a call that had been described to me over the air as 'an elderly woman in distress'. This description didn't reflect in any way the incident I was about to face. I had only been out of the company of my tutor constable for a couple of weeks, but I felt that an 'elderly woman in distress' was well within my capabilities, which is why I decided to go alone. Such was my complacency that I continued to appreciate the sunshine whilst I hurriedly made my way to the scene.

I arrived. The outside was strikingly similar to the one of Ernest's death. People had gathered, some with traumatised expressions on their faces. I was drawn to the magnificence of the house in question. It was large, with a number of tasteful extensions attached. The garage looked as though it would fit two, possibly even three cars in it. A brand new Mercedes was on the drive, sporting an extravagant personalised number plate. The house seemed repellent; no one was inside. I saw an old lady being comforted by a younger woman who looked to be in her fifties. Both women looked too numb to cry. I approached them.

'It's my brother,' said the younger one quietly, 'he's killed himself.' The shock of these words briefly sent me in to a state of near panic. I was alone and about to have to deal with a death. I instinctively asked where her brother was.

'He's hanging from the loft over the stairs,' she replied. With these words, I felt a surge of adrenaline shoot up my back, as the shock of what I'd just been told hit me. My inexperience was now being publicly exposed and I tried to not to let it show. I took a deep breath and gave myself a couple of seconds to come to terms with what I had heard. My mind raced. I tried to remember the protocol for dealing with deaths. Who should I inform? Did I need help? What would the body be like? Would I have to deal with it alone? Fortunately, this heightened mental activity anaesthetised my emotions and I cautiously entered the house.

I saw the staircase immediately on my left. I looked up. My view directly upwards was partially blocked by the underside of the landing, but I could see something dripping from directly above. The drops were different colours; some were red, others were white and frothy. Thoughts of Ernest came back to me as an identical stench hit me. I was unprepared once again. I stood on the bottom stair, pressing myself against the wall so as to avoid the dripping saliva, urine and blood. I looked up and saw the soles of the man's feet about six feet above my head. His body rotated very slowly and sinisterly: half a turn one way, then half a turn the other. It's extremely difficult to clearly describe the feeling that overcame me as I stood there, only that it was very unnatural and uncomfortable. I climbed a couple more stairs. I couldn't take my eyes off the feet above me. I felt scared, and I was quite out of breath. As I walked up a few more stairs, I began to see more and more of the man's body. He continued rotating. As I got to the top, he was positioned with his back to me, but I knew it would only be a couple of seconds before he would rotate to face me. I braced myself, as I knew I was about to see his face. What I saw next lives with me to this day as the most frightening sight I've ever experienced.

He was hanging with electric cable cut from his vacuum cleaner, which he'd looped over one of the beams in the loft. On the floor underneath him was his stepladder, which had fallen over, presumably as he'd hung himself. The cable dug so deeply into his neck that the top of his head almost pointed downwards towards his feet. His neck was broken. The pressure had caused blood to ooze from his nose and ears. The groove which the cord had made was so deep that his whole neck had turned dark purple. His eyes were wide open. As he rotated round and faced me, he seemed to look at me. His eyes looked alive; his tongue was hanging out of his mouth and had inflated to almost half the size of his head. A mixture of blood and frothy saliva dripped out with chilling slowness. His hands were white and his fingernails were blue. The television in his bedroom was still on and, strangely, made me feel very uneasy. I was scared and had seen enough. I went back downstairs and out of the house.

I wasn't at all surprised to be the focus of everybody's attention as I walked out. I couldn't even pretend to look unaffected by what I'd seen. A woman in her forties approached me and asked if I was okay. I instantly liked her; she appreciated that I was human, despite the impression a police uniform could give. 'It's a bit of a mess in there,' I said.

I immediately realised that this was not the best thing to say with the man's family in close proximity. I used my radio to ask for supervision to attend the scene, as this was procedure for any suspicious death, which was how I was treating it until it had been confirmed as a suicide. I needed assistance in any case. I went back into the house and did everything that I could remember to do. I checked all the doors and windows for signs of forced entry. I wasn't surprised there was no damage. Even though I was treating the death as suspicious, I'd formed the opinion that it *was* suicide. This was confirmed when I found a letter left by the man on his bed. It read: *Can't go on any longer. I'm sorry to the person who has to find me like this. Please don't let Mum see me in this state and tell her I love her.*

I left the letter there, as I didn't know what would need to be photographed by Scenes of Crime. I looked at the man's face again. Half of me felt gut-wrenching pity for a person who had obviously been unable to cope with life, and half of me felt irritated that he could do such a thing to his family. The body carried on slowly rotating. It didn't even enter my mind to get him down. Anyone could see that he was dead and, indeed, when the ambulance arrived they didn't get him down either. One of the ambulance crew held the dead man's wrist for about ten seconds and told me that he had been dead overnight. He was very matter-of-fact about the process. I knew I would have to get him down at some point, but I decided to wait for my shift sergeant to arrive.

I went outside again with the ambulance crew and watched as they drove off. Then I went back into my car and reluctantly looked for the dreaded Form 49. Just as I found it, my sergeant arrived and my ordeal of being alone with this situation was over.

'What have we got here, Mick?' he asked.

'It's a male hanging from the loft by electric cable, Sarge. Ambulance have been and gone. I've checked the house. There's no sign of foul play and I found a note from the deceased. It looks like suicide.'

'Good lad. Are you okay?'

'Fine, Sarge.'

We entered together and I pointed Sergeant Hopkins in the right direction. As we walked up the stairs, he pulled out a handkerchief and covered his nose and mouth with it. I was reassured that he, too, found the odour too much to bear. I would always carry a handkerchief with me at work after this particular incident. For now, though, I had to resort to burying my face in my jumper again.

Sergeant Hopkins looked closely at the man's face. 'Oh dear,' he muttered. 'Oh dear, oh dear. Come on, Mick, let's get him down.'

We both looked at the position of the body. There wasn't much room on the landing so getting him down was going to be awkward. Sergeant Hopkins climbed up the stepladder immediately next to the man's body and removed an impressive-looking folded utility knife from his pocket. 'Come on then, Mick. Grab him.'

'How do you mean, Sarge?'

'I'm gonna cut the flex and you catch him.'

I stood next to the hanging body. His waist was at the level of my head and the stench became almost too much to take. With straight, locked arms I took a firm hold of the man's belt around his trousers. Then I turned my face away.

'Go on then, Sarge. I'm ready.'

'Mick, I said grab him. It's dead weight. He'll flatten you like that. Really get hold of him.' As he said this, he gestured a bear hug with his arms. He wanted me to take hold of the man and catch him. My face would have to be touching him for this. I had to do it.

'Sarge ... Are you sure?'

'Just do it, lad. I know it's not nice. We've all had to do it.'

I knew he meant it. I took hold of the man's waist with a bear hug and braced myself ready for the fall. 'Go on then, Sarge. I've got him.'

So there I was, hugging a dead man with my sergeant standing next to me on the top step of the ladder with his Swiss army knife, about to cut the flex. Maybe one day I will be able to see an amusing side to this, but this man was someone's son, and someone's brother, and his last moments must have been desperate. I still look back on this with great sorrow. I tensed up, as I knew that catching the dead weight wouldn't be an easy task. 'Here goes, then.'

With these words, I felt the man's body weight plunge down onto me. I had no chance. The weight crashed down and the man's body came directly on top of me, forcing me to fall to the floor. The next thing I knew, I was flat on my back with the man's face directly above mine. All the trapped air slowly released from his lungs and out of his mouth. His eyes stared into mine and our noses touched. His inflated tongue brushed across my cheek. 'Shit!' I bellowed and I momentarily developed superhuman strength and shifted fourteen stones of dead weight from myself. Sergeant Hopkins looked down and despairingly shook his head. I stood up and shouted the same word again. I couldn't help it.

Once the body was down, we carefully placed the man flat and waited for the Scenes of Crime Officer (SOCO) to come and photograph the knot around his neck. This is necessary, because it's possible to tell from the way the knot is tied whether or not the deceased tied it. This obviously helps to determine whether the death is suicide or murder.

With this specific incident there were no suspicious circumstances. We later found out that the man had been on antide-pressants for around seven months, but he hadn't taken his tablets for the previous nine days. Clinical depression had killed him.

Such was the effect of the suicide on me that I needed to see my best friend, Tim, just to talk about it. I described to him what I'd seen that day. During the telling of the story, I kept referring to the deceased as the 'rich man hanging,' and that's how I'll always remember him.

Tim was a great help to me that evening just because he was a mate and he listened. I didn't know it then, but he and his wife Cath were to help me again in the future.

Chapter 3

Summer Madness

Within two years of becoming a police officer, I had established myself as a member of the PSU (Police Support Unit). Better known as riot police, the PSU are available for large-scale incidents both planned and unplanned, like high category football matches and riots, as well as carnivals and demonstrations and the like.

I enjoyed the training for the PSU as it was physically demanding and was based mainly on teamwork. From about my teens, I was always a keen sportsman and I have trained hard in the gym since before I can remember. It might seem odd, but it had been my ambition to be a contestant on the *Gladiators* TV programme and in 1998 I passed the physical fitness test for it. I managed to get down to the final hundred out of over sixteen thousand male applicants. Sport has always been a passion, and working long shifts in the police service hindered my training. I used to find this aspect of the job very frustrating.

The PSU training was done in the grounds of an old hospital and the derelict buildings were very useful for practising 'building entries' in riot situations. On training days, there would be maybe fifteen or twenty police officers who would role-play rioters. They would throw blocks of wood and petrol bombs at our line of shields in order to prevent us from advancing to a certain point given to us by the PSU commander. I remember that on one of our training days, I was in a line of eight officers all with full-length shields. We were on the front of three lines. One of the mock rioters threw a petrol bomb high in the air towards us. We were standing directly next to an old storeroom-type building. The petrol bomb landed on the roof, which unfortunately sloped directly down onto the officer at the end of the line. In a flash of flames, the whole roof lit with fire and as the petrol spilled down the slope, the officer was engulfed. His supposed flameproof overall was inadvertently put to the test. It failed miserably. He ran around in panic, screaming for help. The flames soared from his feet to his head. Three short blasts of the instructor's whistle sounded to indicate an immediate termination of the exercise. Three safety officers ran to the burning man, who by now looked like a stuntman as he walked, still ablaze, with his arms out in the crucifix position. One of the safety officers charged at him and rugby-tackled him to the ground. The other two used fire extinguishers on him and, within seconds, the flames were put out. We all lifted our helmet visors and watched with concern. To our relief, the officer got to his feet and removed his helmet. He shook his head, but was smiling. Due to the skill and speed of the safety officers, he'd escaped uninjured. One of them asked us to congregate at the car park so that he could debrief the incident. There was an unusual silence as we walked back. Occasionally, I would hear a shield crash to the ground, as an officer got too fatigued to keep it up. They weighed over twenty pounds.

For you to hear me say I loved these kind of things might make you question my sanity, but such incidents bring hundreds of police officers closer together. It's a feeling of kinship and we would always try to protect each other from harm. I loved that closeness. To me, a special part of being a police officer was the feeling of togetherness it produced. I was to learn how naive this view was later in my career.

To be called from normal duty onto a PSU team for the day, or sometimes longer, was something I enjoyed. It broke up the daily routine of being a patrol officer, which is nothing like the way it's portrayed on television. I found that a lot of what I did was mundane clerical work, not requiring the real skills of a police officer. However, the good days as a patrol officer were *very* good.

The summer of 1995 provided many PSU days for me to attend. The temperatures were record-breaking and there had been a prolonged drought in the UK, leaving water levels in many reservoirs at an all-time low. This was the year I gained experience of real riot situations.

The first riot I ever attended was in Bradford. At the time, I wasn't aware of the cause, but I later found out it was as a result of the arrest of two young men. Their arrests had sparked a violent reaction from the local community and it resulted in hundreds of people surrounding one of the local police stations.

I saw the news that morning before I went to work. I was due to start on a late shift at 2 p.m. Pictures on the television from the previous evening in Bradford showed police officers in full riot gear coming under fire from various missiles, ranging from house bricks to petrol bombs. Several cars were on fire and many of the shops had been looted. It didn't occur to me that, in just a few hours' time, I would be caught in the middle of it all myself.

I remember the day well. The temperature soared into the 90s. The prospect of working in full riot clothing, which comprised overalls, flameproof balaclava, shin and knee guards, arm protectors and, worst of all, body armour, was not a pleasant one. It was only when I arrived at work that I was told by my inspector that my collar number was listed to go to Bradford in a PSU serial. This would comprise six constables and a sergeant. Being crammed into a transit van with all those clothes on was going to be very uncomfortable in this heat. I didn't even contemplate the riot itself. I thought that if there had been trouble on the previous night then most of the violence would have subsided. How wrong I was.

The journey in the van from Dewsbury (where I was stationed) to Bradford was about twenty minutes. The disorder from the previous night became more and more evident the closer we got to Bradford. Bricks were still lying in the roads and most of the shop windows were broken. They displayed handwritten signs apologising to customers and saying it would be a while before they reopened. Occasionally, we drove past a burnt-out vehicle, or we'd see a large patch of black on the road from where one had been removed. The place seemed derelict, the streets told their own story: it was easy to visualise the previous night's disturbance.

I saw shopkeepers sweeping up outside their shops or boarding up their damaged windows. My colleagues walked the streets in groups of four. Exchanging waves with your colleagues in these circumstances seemed compulsory. I liked this as it strengthened the bond between us all.

'Right we're here, lads,' said our sergeant, who had the best seat in the van, in the front next to the driver. The rest of us were jammed in the middle compartment, fighting for space. We had arrived at the relevant police station in Bradford. 'I'll go in and see what we're doing for briefing. You lot stay 'ere.'

At least we could get out of the van for a few minutes and try to cool off. I stepped out and the scorching sun was immediately noticeable. I unzipped my overalls right down to my waist and sat on a grass verge. There were about thirty police vans lined up in the car park. I began to realise the scale of the incident.

Paul, one of my colleagues in my serial, came and sat with me. 'Hope it doesn't kick off in this heat,' he said as he lay back with his eyes tightly closed.

'Me too. Imagine running around in this with the shields.'

'We won't even get out of the van, Mick. The gaffers will be too bloody scared to upset folk by having us out of the vans. We don't want to look too aggressive now, do we?' Paul made no attempt to hide his sarcasm.

'What do you mean, mate?' I asked.

'Well, all they'll want now is for this to pass over without any more drama. They don't give a shit about locking up the villains. The gaffers don't need to worry about them in their world, do they? So long as we don't get criticised. Wankers.'

As we spoke, our sergeant ambled back from the station to our van.

'Right, lads…'

'And lasses, Sarge,' came a voice from inside the van. Helen, the only female officer in our serial, peered out of the side door and smiled at the sergeant.

'Sorry, Helen. Anyway, lads and lasses, listen in please. I've just been speaking to the chief super and he wants us to go to Neville Street and basically show a presence. We're under strict instructions not to get out of the van. I've been told to remind you that the press are buzzing around, so be aware, please.'

'Does he know how bloody hot it is in that van, Sarge?' Paul sounded angry.

'He's got pips and crowns, Paul. He doesn't need to think of things like that. Right, I suggest you all get a quick drink and we'll set off.'

As we walked across to the station, Paul continued making comments about what he thought was in store for us. I prepared myself for a long and uncomfortable shift.

Neville Street wasn't far from the station and when we arrived, there was a crowd of about two hundred youths in the street and approximately ten police vans, all with the windscreen protectors down. There were no officers to be seen out on foot. There was a dirty smell of burning rubber lingering in the air from the previous night. The crowd was chanting at us: 'Come on, pigs, pigs, pigs.'

Every so often, a brick would be launched from the middle of the crowd towards the vans; occasionally one would land on our roof. The noise each one made was deafening and menacing and every time it happened, our conversation was temporarily silenced. Every ten minutes or so, the senior officer at the station would ask to be updated on events. The crowd grew bigger and the number of missiles thrown increased.

'Are we sitting here like cannon fodder all day, or are we gonna start to lock these toe-rags up, Sarge?' asked Paul, with an ever-increasing sound of exasperation in his voice.

'I can only go by what I've been told to do, Paul, and that is that we sit tight until told otherwise.' From the sergeant's tone, I sensed he was intimidated by Paul, who had over twenty years' service.

'It's bloody ridiculous, this. Why have they got us all over here if they're not gonna use us?'

'Look, just wait and see what they want us to do. I'll let them know that it's kicking off a bit out there.'

By now, the frequency of bricks hitting us had increased and there was a loud bang at least every couple of minutes. The van was getting badly damaged. The chants got louder. I saw some graffiti on a shop front. It said, *Another Blakelock*. I assumed that this referred to PC Keith Blakelock, who was brutally murdered in Tottenham in disturbances during the 1980s. This was often reported in the media as *The Brixton Riots*. Whoever sprayed this was either planning to do something very serious to a police officer, or he was trying to frighten us. He had succeeded in the latter, for myself at least, but I didn't say anything.

As I thought about this, we were ordered to travel up Neville Street to a rendezvous point to meet with other units, as we were going to be deployed on foot with shields to try to disperse the mob.

'About bloody time,' said Paul, as he zipped up his overalls and pulled on his balaclava. 'Let's get these idiots locked up.'

We slowly drove up Neville Street only to be faced with about fifty of the crowd, blocking the road. To my horror, I saw a similar number of youths running towards the van from behind. We were trapped. Bricks and glass bottles rained down on the van, each one as frightening as the others had been. We all sat forward with our elbows on our knees and our heads down.

'I'm stuck here, Sarge,' explained the van driver, with panic in his voice.

'Urgent assistance, Neville Street,' bellowed the sergeant into the radio.

We were at the mercy of the rioters who had circled us. Bricks and bottles continued to smash into the van. There was nothing we could do as they closed in on us from all directions. They used scarves and bandanas to conceal their faces. Some had arms full of bricks, whilst others brandished long sticks and baseball bats. Once in a while, one or two of the rioters would pluck up the courage and come right up to us and strike the van with bats.

'Lock all the doors,' ordered the sergeant. This, I can assure you, had been done a long time before he'd said it.

The rioters were still chanting, but such was my fear at this point that I didn't hear what they were shouting. We were completely helpless; our fate lay in the hands of these youths. I hoped they would have at least a shred of decency about them and spare us from harm. My fear was amplified when I saw some of the crowd lighting papers stuffed in the necks of glass bottles. We were about to be petrol-bombed. They came closer. They started to rock the van. I peered out of the one-way glass and the anger and hatred in the eyes of these people was terrifying. I noticed that even Paul was beginning to look troubled. We had to shout at each other in order to communicate inside the van. It rocked more and more and then I saw a great flash of flames up the side. The youths temporarily dispersed from that side, but were back within seconds. I felt defenceless. Escaping was in the hands of the gods. I kept my head down and tied the chinstrap and pulled the visor down on my helmet. I thought it would only be a matter of time before the driver of our van would plough into the crowd. It was a decision I was glad I didn't have to make, as there would inevitably be casualties and consequences for the officer.

Three or four men at the rear of the van were trying to force the doors open with a crowbar. The look of determination in their eyes was alarming. Paul banged on the doors with his fist and this startled them. They retreated. The van carried on rocking and I was becoming increasingly concerned that it would tip over. I looked up at Paul. He was a hardy character but he was looking frightened, too.

More and more of the crowd came and banged on the van. They were like vultures at a carcass, every one fighting for his bit of space.

Eventually, a stalemate occurred. The crowd seemed to have reached the limit of how far they would go with the violence. We remained stationary. It was impossible for us to know whether assistance was on its way, or whether we'd have to get ourselves out of this unsavoury situation.

'Right, drive on and get us out of here,' said the sergeant to the driver. It was as if he had sensed my quandary.

'Okay, Sarge. I was gonna do it anyway.'

With this, he revved up the engine until it roared above the din of the crowd. The rioters at the front instinctively ran out of the way. Seeing the potential escape route, the driver accelerated into the gap. We were off and within seconds there was a welcome calm as we got far enough away to evade the bricks. I looked back at the hundred or so rioters. They were quite obviously furious about our escape and had now turned their anger onto a row of shops, smashing the windows with the bricks and looting the stock.

'That were a bit close, wasn't it?' said Paul.

'A little bit. Is everyone okay?' enquired the sergeant.

'We're alright, Sarge,' I said. I think I was trying to convince myself, as I knew that in a few minutes time we would be out on foot with the shields. The prospect worried me. I looked at everyone in the van. They all looked very alert, yet there was a stunned hush. Everybody made the final adjustments to themselves to make sure they were fully kitted up and ready to go out onto the streets. I pulled the straps on my shin guards tight, as I'd seen the size of the missiles they'd thrown at us. There would be no blasts on any instructor's whistle if one of us got injured today.

We arrived at the rendezvous point. For the first time in a while I felt safe again, as at least one hundred officers were lined up in full riot gear. We got out of the van and joined them. On the instructions of the commanding officer, we progressed down Neville Street in our respective lines. This was more like the training we had had at the derelict hospital. We were organised again and we were now dictating the pace.

Dispersing the crowds was very much easier and far less confrontational than I'd expected. Because we were now in large numbers, the crowd had lost their enthusiasm to try to overpower us and we spent the next two hours simply walking at them with our shields down. As we approached them, they would all run away. The occasional brick would come our way, but by this time we were well in control of the situation and by early evening the crowd had dispersed.

As things quietened down, we were called back to the station in turn, in order to have a meal and cool down. When it was our turn to go back, I was quite moved by the sight which greeted me when I arrived in the canteen. There were about fifty officers. Most of them had their overalls stripped to the waist and tied around their middle using the arms. They were all red-faced with their hair wet from sweat. There was a feeling of solidarity such as I'd never experienced before. Everyone seemed subdued by what had gone on that afternoon. I sat, gulped down a bottle of water and ate my meal.

Even though we spent two days at Bradford, there was little more trouble after that afternoon. The police are rarely caught out twice at the same incident and we maintained a heavy presence to keep the crowds at home. It worked. There were several arrests following the disturbances, but some of the offenders were later released without charge in order to prevent further trouble. I found that part of the job rather irritating.

When I arrived home that evening, the riots were on the news again. I soon switched channels when a community leader appeared, telling the public just how heavy-handed the police tactics had been in Bradford. He said how disgusting he found it that peaceful protesters were hounded from the streets by our police in what he described as a police state. I went to bed.

The widespread rioting in Bradford was not the end of large-scale disorder in West Yorkshire that year. Towards the end of the summer, there was similar violence in the Woodhouse area of Leeds. Two police officers had been called to a report of a female in distress by a parade of shops at the top of a cul-de-sac in a really notorious part of Woodhouse. As the officers drove their car up the street, it became apparent that the call was a hoax, as about thirty youths ran out throwing petrol bombs and bricks at them, blocking their exit in the process. The police response that night had been immediate and forceful, but the youths got the upper hand in the early stages as the group of thirty escalated to around four hundred. By now, I was used to the procedures. I looked at the list of officers to be sent to the area and there I was. It was all to start again, making the summer of 1995 one of the most memorable in my service.

Chapter 4

The Monkey Man

I used to find that after a very busy period, like that in the summer of 1995, things would go ominously quiet for a while. That's exactly what happened after the Bradford and Leeds riots that year.

As the leaves fell that autumn, I began to get restless, as I had been dealing with very mundane everyday matters since the riots. I requested a transfer to Millgarth Division, which was the city centre station of Leeds. I thought it would be a contrast to the smaller station I had worked at in Dewsbury Division since joining up. I had been there for well over two years and even though the people I worked with were fantastic, I felt I needed a change to maintain my high level of enthusiasm and to broaden my experience. I keenly anticipated the pull of city centre policing and all the variety that goes with it. My request was accepted, but I had to wait a few months before it would take place – around Christmas time of that year.

My acceptance to Millgarth Division seemed to spark off a busy period for my final few months at Dewsbury. One of the most common jobs for patrol officers to attend is the activation of intruder alarms in commercial premises. I would say that 80 per cent of activations are false alarms and of the other 20 per cent, the intruders were usually long gone by the time the police arrived. It's said that the average burglar will spend a maximum of two minutes inside a premises which he is burgling. If you imagine that the activated alarm sends a signal to the alarm company, who then telephone the police control room, who then radio to the officers on the ground, who then have to travel to the scene, it's not surprising the police attend such occurrences with complacency. With this in mind, the following incident surprised me.

I'd arrived at work one evening at about 9.40 p.m. for my night shift, which started at 10.00 p.m. I had my usual cup of tea and collected my personal radio and other equipment I needed. A message came over the radio. 'Any units free for a ten-fourteen at Co-op, Hill Top, Gomersal, reply with your call sign please.' (A 10-14 was the ten code for an intruder alarm.) With this, the people from the late shift grimaced as they were due to finish work at 10 o'clock.

'It's okay. I'll go. You get yourselves home,' I said. I thought that I'd have to sit at the premises for a while for the keyholder to arrive to re-set the alarm, which meant that if anyone from the late shift attended, then they'd almost certainly have to work late.

'No, Mick. You can't go on your own. It might be live,'

replied Brian, a member of the late shift. (A job is live if the premises have actually been burgled.)

'These jobs are never live, Brian. You may as well go,' I said.

'No way. Come on, Mick, let's go.'

I didn't know Brian very well, but he made it quite clear that my welfare was more important to him than him leaving work on time. I respected this. We rushed to the police car. To my annoyance, it was full of empty crisp packets and fizzy drink cans.

'What's all this rubbish, Brian?' I said in jest.

'I wasn't in this one, Mick. Don't know who it was.'

I started the engine, switched on the blue lamps and began the drive up to the Co-op. There was very little traffic on the roads due to the time and so making progress was easy. I had attended at the Co-op the night before when the alarm had been activated. It was a false alarm then and I didn't expect this to be any different. Nevertheless, I drove as quickly as I could in order to achieve the target response time.

Knowing the layout of any premises is fundamental in catching burglars because, if you give them a one second advantage, then they use it and evade capture. Because I had been to the Co-op the previous evening, I knew that the most likely point of entry would be a large steel shutter which was well concealed at the rear of the premises. I turned the car headlights off as I pulled onto the car park, so as not to alert anybody to our presence. I changed down into second gear and drove at speed round to the rear metal shutter. I couldn't believe what I saw as I turned the corner. Straight in front of us was a silver Ford Escort with its lights off. Both of the front doors were open. A three-by-three-feet square piece of the metal shutter had been removed by heavy duty cutting equipment and, at that very moment, a man poked his head through the hole from inside the Co-op. This job *was* live! Within a few seconds, two men darted out through the hole and ran off. I slammed on the brakes and we got out of the car and began to chase them.

There was a wall six feet high next to the parked Escort and both men scaled it effortlessly. I ran at the wall, and pulled myself over, also with relative ease. The men had split up. One of them was running back around to the front of the Co-op. I shouted at him, telling him that I wanted him to stop. I also informed the control room that I was chasing. He was just over five feet tall, but very stocky. He wore a black balaclava with two eyeholes. And he was quick.

He ran along the front of the Co-op and I sensed he wasn't local as he was heading back to where he had come from, which would make it more difficult for him to evade capture, compared to the maze of tiny streets he would have ended up in if he'd gone the other way.

He climbed up a banking which led back towards the car park where we'd disturbed them, then suddenly stopped dead in his tracks. I found this very peculiar, as I was only about twenty yards behind. I began to climb after him. He was standing directly above. He turned to face me and my head was at the level of his feet as I was still at the bottom of the banking. He unzipped his jacket and placed his hand inside it. My joy of almost catching him unexpectedly turned into fear, as I thought he was about to reveal a knife, or even a firearm. However, my instinct was to keep on climbing, as I felt extremely vulnerable beneath him.

I kept watching him. He frantically moved his hand inside his jacket as I tried to climb the banking. Maybe I could reach him and tackle him before he removed the object, whatever it was, I thought. But my optimism was premature. I planted my left boot onto a rock, but the earth beneath it crumbled and gave way just as I put my body weight onto it. I slipped back down the banking and ended up right back where I had started, with my head at the intruder's feet. This gave him valuable seconds. As I looked up again, I saw a crowbar coming straight down towards my head. I instinctively raised my right arm to protect myself. The crowbar struck my hand with considerable force. Strangely, though, it didn't hurt at that moment. I tried to pull myself up the banking once again before another blow landed. Fortunately, it didn't come. The effect of the first blow seemed to place springs in my feet, as I managed climb the banking in seconds. He dropped the crowbar and ran. At this point, I knew that I'd catch him because he ran onto open land and he had very little start on me this time. I put my head down, channelled all of my energy into my legs and sprinted towards him. The man stopped in his tracks again. I found this bewildering because I had almost caught up with him. He turned around and faced me square on. *What next?* I thought, with some trepidation.

'Okay, mate, you've got me.' He lifted his balaclava. I was shocked by what I saw. His face was covered in scars, nasty scars. He was hard-featured and his appearance intimidated me. He was gasping for breath.

'Get to the floor face down, now!' I bellowed. This may sound melodramatic, but when you're facing someone as unpredictable as this and you're frightened by what they've just done to you, you can't take any chances. I didn't know what he was going to do next. I was also extremely out of breath, which heightened my anxiety.

'Alright, mate. I won't kick off,' he replied.

'Get down!' I shouted.

'Fuck you,' he said. His compliance had altered back to aggression in a second. He was very volatile and therefore very dangerous; I was afraid for my safety.

I quickly took hold of him by his jacket sleeve. 'You're locked up,' I informed him.

The law requires that officers must inform suspects of the offence for which they have been arrested, followed by the verbal caution as soon as practicable. I didn't feel it was safe to caution him at this time, as I perceived that he still posed a threat to me. I was breathless, too. Even though I've always been very fit, I used to find that I became fatigued easily during a chase in the course of my duty, due to the surge of adrenaline which inevitably came with it. I used to get a burning sensation in the back of my throat and it was extremely uncomfortable following this particular chase.

The suspect bent his arms so that his elbows were at right angles and I felt him tense his whole body. From experience, I knew this meant he wasn't going to come quietly and that he was going to resist the arrest with some degree of force.

'Calm down, fella. It's over now,' I said, trying to diffuse the situation. He raised his elbows in an attempt to break free from my hold. It is impossible to use the radio in situations like this because it's dangerous to let go of someone so violent. I put my arms around him in a bear hug and tried to push him to the ground. He made a wide base with his feet and tensed up even more and he began to make a growling sound, a common feature with violent men. He was strong, much stronger than me, and I feared that the arrest was going to be far from easy.

'Get to the floor,' I demanded. He made no reply, and just

continued to struggle violently by throwing his arms around, using clenched fists.

'Brian!' I shouted. 'Brian. I'm in the car park. Can you hear me?'

It seems ironic that, with today's technology in communications, I had to resort to shouting, but fortunately it worked and just a few moments later Brian came charging around the corner. I was still holding the man in a bear hug, but his strength lifted me from the ground every five or six seconds. Just as Brian arrived, I managed to manoeuvre myself to the man's side and sweep my leg around his ankles and knock him off balance. I lost mine in the process and as I landed on the ground with the man, I felt a sharp pain in my right knee. Brian quickly joined us on the ground with his handcuffs out and ready. I pulled the man over onto his front, grabbed one of his arms and dragged it behind his back. It was difficult as he was still tensed up. Brian did the same with the other arm. The man's strength seemed to increase in proportion to his determination to avoid arrest. I knew that getting his hands close enough together in order to apply the handcuffs would be impossible even with the two of us, and so I knelt on him in order to make it possible for me to use my radio, the microphone of which had come unclipped from my shirt and was dangling around like a pendulum.

I eventually managed to call for more assistance. I could already hear sirens in the distance so I knew help was approaching. Within a couple of seconds of making the call, the man again demonstrated his unpredictability. His whole body went limp and the struggle seemed to end without bother. He lay face down on the ground. I didn't let go of him, though. I'd fallen for tricks like this in the past and I wasn't going to fall for this one. He remained completely motionless.

'Pass me the cuffs, mate,' I said to Brian.

'Here, Mick, what's up with him?'

'Don't know, mate, but let's find out when we've got him cuffed. He's tried to have me, has this one.'

To my amazement, the suspect remained still and lifeless even as I applied the handcuffs. He turned his head to the side. His face was pressed against the tarmac. He dribbled from the mouth and continued to breathe heavily. His eyes were closed. The once energetic and vicious man with seemingly killer instincts had now altered into a vulnerable, inert being who seemed utterly overwhelmed by the circumstances.

'Okay, mate. It's over,' he murmured. He opened his eyes slightly as he said it. They were heavy-looking and tired. This time, I knew the struggle *really* was over.

I asked Brian whether he'd seen the other suspect. He hadn't. Using my radio, I requested for a police dog to attend and also X-ray 99 (the helicopter) to assist us in the search for him. Brian and I helped the arrested man to his feet and placed him in the back of the car. I removed the balaclava and examined him more closely to see if I knew him. It wasn't uncommon to arrest the same person time and time again, but I didn't recognise him. He was white-faced and sweating profusely. It was a real effort for him to keep his eyes open and every so often he'd give in and allow them to close for a couple of seconds. When he opened them, his eyeballs rolled. After a matter of only a few seconds, he fell asleep, which worried me a little.

'Are you with us?' I asked him in a deliberately loud voice.

He gave no response. There was a very simple and very effective way of checking to see whether or not he was genuinely unconscious, or whether he was just acting to try to make us take him to hospital before taking him to the station. A lot of prisoners do this, as they feel they have a good chance of escaping from hospital, as the police are often put under pressure from doctors to release the handcuffs whilst the prisoner is being assessed. I pinched the lobe of his ear.

'Arrrggghhh. Fuck off,' he mumbled and I knew from this that he was probably fine.

Other officers arrived at the scene and a crowd of about twenty people had gathered to watch. This was also very common. I asked one of the officers if he'd transport my prisoner down to the cells. With little fuss, the man was put into the back of a van and driven away from the scene. Brian and I began to walk towards the suspects' vehicle, which remained with the doors open.

'You okay, Mick?' he asked.

'It's just my hand,' I replied. 'The bastard tried to whack me on the head with a bloody crowbar. He got my hand.' I looked at it for the first time and saw that there was blood dripping from a small cut along my little finger, which had swollen considerably.

The injury wasn't serious, and my interest in searching the vehicle intensified as we arrived at the silver Escort. I opened the boot and was amazed by what I saw. There was an array of equipment that was associated with burglaries, ranging from crowbars to cutting tools, several pairs of gloves and a couple more balaclavas, but most strikingly of all there were two monkey masks. These normally fun items, when seen in the boot of a violent burglar's car, soon take a sinister turn.

I checked the ignition, and it came as no surprise to me that it had been black-boxed (thieves damaging the ignition of a car in order to steal it). In fact, the car had been stolen from Manchester three days earlier. The most alarming items which I found were actually in the door wells: two seven-inch-bladed kitchen knives and a machete. These boys had meant business and it dawned on me that I'd been most fortunate that the man had been carrying only the crowbar. I knew his previous convictions would make interesting and lengthy reading. I'd find this out back at the station.

I took the vehicle into police possession and I requested a SOCO to attend in order to make a full examination. Finding fingerprints or matching fibres to the suspect's clothing would be useful evidence. I arranged for the keyholder of the premises to attend in order to secure it and re-set the alarm. With all this to do, it was well after one o'clock in the morning when I eventually arrived at the cell area to explain my reasons and grounds for the arrest to the custody sergeant. I was pleased to find out that 'the Monkey Man' was indeed a prolific burglar and was on bail for a similar offence. I did the necessary paperwork to hand the job over to CID, who would interview him the following morning.

When he eventually went to court, the Monkey Man pleaded guilty to four other burglaries and the assault on me. He received just a four-month prison sentence for the burglaries and a conditional discharge (a conviction without a punishment) for the assault. I received a written commendation from a senior officer for the arrest.

Chapter 5

Football Crazy

I made the transfer to Millgarth Division in December 1995, just weeks after the job at the Co-op. My first memory is one of bewilderment. I remember spending almost an hour in nose-to-tail traffic, as I made my first journey to the station, a complete contrast to Cleckheaton in the Dewsbury Division, where the journey took fifteen minutes at most. I wanted the change, though, and this was just a small price to pay. I yearned for the challenges of the hectic routine of city policing, something that up to this point I hadn't experienced.

When I arrived, I struggled into the station clasping onto a mountain of police uniform, which meant that I had to walk sideways so that I could see where I was going. I asked the office clerk to press the buzzer on the door to let me in. She seemed amused as I tripped over my long overcoat, which was hanging out of the pile of clothes I was carrying, and as I sprawled onto the floor, I looked up at her. She politely tried to hide her merriment.

It's okay, you can laugh,' I said as I scrambled to my feet. 'I would.'

'Are you PC Bunting?' she asked, rather red-faced.

'I am.' I brushed the front of my trousers down with my hands as I stood up. I walked over to the desk and held out my hand. 'Mick,' I said.

'Hello, Mick,' she replied, letting out a little giggle. 'I'm Christine. You need to take the lift to the third floor. Your sergeant is expecting you.'

Lift? This *was* a big place! Cleckheaton was a world away from here, its police station an old converted terraced house. My nerves and excitement amalgamated and I hurried to the third floor, where I found my unsuspecting sergeant tucking into a hearty English breakfast. I thought this might be my second mistake of the day, arriving just as he was on his meal break. He gave me instructions as to where to get my locker key and told me to get settled and he'd see me in ten minutes or so. He looked a little displeased by my arrival at this critical time in his day. I got on with the laborious task of making several visits from the car to my locker with heaps of police clothing. Christine looked amused each time I precariously walked past her. I think she anticipated another blunder. So did I.

Eventually, the job was done. I tidied myself up and went to my first Millgarth briefing. I felt a little nervous, but nothing out of the ordinary for someone starting a new job. I was introduced to the shift and began to find my way around the station. I was left off operational duties for the first hour so that I could get to know the building. I spent my time wisely and introduced myself to the various departments in the station. Every-body seemed welcoming and I felt at ease relatively quickly.

I was told that I'd have to spend the rest of the day driving around the division with my map of Leeds so that I could familiarise myself with the vastness of my new workplace. I already knew the city centre quite well, but I was amazed at just how hard it was to make progress through the busy traffic. I ventured to the outskirts, where I was faced with a different problem. The streets intertwined seemingly at random. I would spend long periods trying to get from one street to another, only to be beaten by the complexity of the layout. Just as I thought I'd cracked it, I'd be greeted by a set of bollards in the middle of the road. It seemed ironic that the bollards, put in place to prevent joy riders, were blocking my route in a marked police car.

I tried to respond to calls to which other units were being sent as a means of testing myself. Every so often, I'd need to pull into the side of the road, as I looked up the street which I would have had to attend. Usually the other units had arrived, sorted the job out and departed before I'd even got there.

I continued driving around and discovered two areas of Leeds which looked particularly problematic in terms of law and order. The first, Little London, was a small suburb com-prised mainly of high-rise flats. They were a depressing sight; just looking at them produced a feeling of inertia. They were listless. Even though they were spilling with inhabitants, to me they projected a sense of indolence, as people with seemingly little purpose tried to make the best of their lives. The greeting for visitors at the general entrance was usually a pile of dirty needles or a bag of used glue. I felt a sense of pity for the people in the flats who didn't match the image portrayed by the area. They were not the most salubrious of surroundings and the occasional burnt-out car in the car parks added to the uninviting vista. My first memories of Little London came as I was driving around trying to take it all in, when a brick thudded against the car door. I saw three children of about ten years old running away and gesticulating with their hands as they did so. I never dithered in Little London again.

The second area I noticed on my travels was Hyde Park. It was made up of row after row of old terraced houses. It did, however, display some similar characteristics to Little London. Every second street or so would have a burnt-out car and youths gathered in small groups. They'd cover their faces with bandanas and turn away from me as I drove past. This was their way of trying to get me to stop the car and challenge them. I may have been the new bobby on the patch, but I wasn't going to fall into that trap.

The calls kept coming in and I felt a little guilty as my colleagues raced from job to job. I listened as they were sent to a violent shoplifter at one of the city centre stores. I was familiar with its location and decided that I'd try to impress my new colleagues by getting there to help them. I knew they'd all be monitoring me in the early stages, and this would go some way to giving them the right impression of me as a hard worker.

I drove at speed through the city centre traffic. The sirens were near deafening as they reverberated from the buildings. I had never driven to a rush job in such heavy traffic. I had to concentrate like never before as pedestrians occasionally stepped out in front of the car, despite the volume of the sirens. Nevertheless, I arrived at the call and informed the control room. Another police car was already present and I ran into the store to back them up, as there had been no update over the radio.

Two sales assistants ran up to me. They looked shocked and just pointed to the other end of the store. 'Your friends are over there,' one of them said. 'Hurry up, he's a madman,' urged the other.

I made my way over as quickly as I could and saw my colleagues, a male and a female officer, rolling about on the floor desperately trying to restrain a man. He was thrashing around wildly and I saw two pairs of handcuffs strewn on the floor. He was trying to bite both officers, which prevented them from properly restraining him. I dashed over to help. It was almost impossible to do anything useful initially. Each time I tried to grab one of his hands, he'd pull away forcefully and quickly, knocking over display stands in the aisles as he did so. He began spitting and his attempts to bite were becoming more accurate as he took hold of my jumper sleeve. The other male officer rolled over on top of the man and I did the same almost straight away. With my extra body-weight on top of him, the struggle came to a hasty and peaceful conclusion. He was handcuffed and brought to his feet.

The male officer looked at me. 'Thanks,' he said. 'It's Mick isn't it?' he asked, shaking my hand.

'That's right.'

'I'm Matt,' he said.

The female officer approached me. 'I'm Sophie.'

'Nice to meet you, Sophie,' I said.

'We'll see you at the nick later. Thanks again,' Matt said.

They left with the prisoner, and I left with the contentment of knowing that the first impression I'd had made on my colleagues at Millgarth was a favourable one.

I spent the rest of the shift trying to repeat what I'd just done as the jobs came in, but all I actually managed to do was get lost several more times. I didn't mind too much, though, because when we paraded off duty that evening, Matt and Sophie invited me upstairs to the bar to have a drink with the shift. I met a few more members of the team and all seemed very friendly. Word had got round about me helping with the arrest of the shoplifter. I was the subject of several jokes, too; I'd been spotted a few times in the car at the side of the road with my head buried in my map and the hazard lights flashing. Apparently, police cars had whizzed past me with the blues and twos activated on a number of occasions. However, my honourable intentions had been noted and the founding of some wonderful friendships had begun. I went home feeling very pleased with my new job.

I had a lot to learn when I started at Millgarth. The day shifts were spent, in the main, collecting shoplifters who had been detained by security guards. Sometimes, there would be so many waiting to be collected that every officer in the division would be in the city centre, or in the Bridewell (the police custody suite). I remember one day I collected seven shoplifters from seven different locations in about twenty minutes. I had to call up on the radio to get extra pairs of handcuffs brought to me. After a while, such work loses its appeal, but it was a necessary part of the duties, and for this reason a special squad of officers was established to deal with the prisoners, once they'd arrived at the Bridewell. Interviewing, charging and photographing a prisoner can take hours, especially if house searches are involved, or there is a long wait for the solicitor. It was, therefore, impractical for patrol officers to get tied up with shoplifters. The 'shop squad', as it was called, was the busiest team of officers in the force. The more recent name for the team is the Retail Crime Unit.

The nature of the job changed again for the night shift in Leeds city centre, as partygoers from all over the North of England came to the pubs, bars and clubs. Inevitably, with illicit drugs and alcohol playing a large part in some people's nights, the shifts were riddled with incidents. Weekends were the worst. You could leave the police station at 10 p.m. and not get back in until 7 a.m. Whilst the nights passed quickly, because of the volume of calls, it meant you usually went home feeling exhausted and very hungry.

It was common to attend fight after fight. We would spend a large part of the shift in the Casualty Department of the hospital chasing witnesses and complainants to assaults. I remember one job in particular. We had been called to a public order incident at one of the more notorious venues in the city, Big Lil's on East Parade. Due to our heavy workload that night, by the time we arrived it was quiet and the club staff informed us that an ambulance had attended and taken several of the people involved to hospital. Naturally, we were obliged to follow up this lead and we duly made our way to the Casualty Department.

Whilst we were en route, we received a call from the hospital stating there was a fight in progress in the reception area and that one of the ambulance staff had been assaulted. We established that the people from the nightclub had turned on one of the ambulance crew, simply because there was a waiting time for treatment of about an hour. We arrested three of the trouble causers at the hospital, but it could have been more as the wait-ing area was filled with drunken thugs wanting to get involved. Several shouted and swore at us, whilst others spat blood at us from the wounds they'd sustained in their last fight. This was the kind of incident we had to deal with on a regular basis and we'd usually be criticised by various sections of society for our action (or lack of).

I would say that ten people should have been arrested from the incident at the hospital, but, because of personnel restric-tions, we weren't able to deal with it properly. One of the men I arrested was given a fine for causing an injury to someone's face. It had required nineteen stitches. In my years working as a policeman, I found that the only people who were affected by the punishments given by the courts were people who ostensi-bly had more to lose, like a motorist getting banned for speed-ing on his or her way to work, for example. To habitual offenders, court sentences were practically meaningless and had little effect on them. I've seen a man leave court with a bigger fine for speeding than another man's fine for a house burglary. I wish I could explain the wonders of the English judiciary to you, but like most police officers I'm usually left scratching my head.

Perhaps the most professionally challenging period of my police career was when I spent three months on the shop squad. The workload on this assignment was very high and officers would soon burn out from the constant pressure of having to deal with the endless flow of shoplifters. For this reason, each patrol officer has to take his or her turn on the unit. I never had aspirations to be a detective and so I found this three months harrowing. The paperwork involved for each shoplifter could take up to four hours; I can leave you to guess how I felt when I saw six or seven prisoners on the board for my attention. I could quite easily be dealing with shoplifters until one or two in the morning. In the main, the average offender was aged between sixteen and twenty-five and often they stole to feed their drug addiction.

Of course, there were exceptions. The strangest job I encountered whilst I was on the squad was when I arrested a woman in her mid-fifties at House of Fraser in the city. She was quiet and very well-spoken and looked immaculate. She had a ring on her finger with a gem the size of my thumbnail. It must have been worth thousands. Her perfume was recognisably one of the highest quality. When I searched through the property she was carrying with her, I found she had several gold credit cards and an equal number of debit cards and cheque-books, all of which were legitimate. There was no doubt she had considerable spending power, yet here I was arresting her for the theft of a £20 cutlery set. I lodged her in a cell before going to her house to perform a search in accordance with PACE (Police and Criminal Evidence Act).

I was amazed by what I found. It was not the usual journey to Hyde Park or Little London, but to one of the more affluent areas of Leeds – Alwoodley, not an area where you would usually suspect its inhabitants of being shoplifters. Upon my arrival, I informed the lady's husband what had happened. He just looked at me with a sorry expression and said, 'Oh no, not again.' I suspected that she had an ongoing problem.

Searching the house was no easy task. In the basement, there was a large gymnasium and a swimming pool, beautifully lit with underwater lights which made the water glow green. I found nothing of any note until I got to one of the spare rooms upstairs. I opened the door and it was like a department store warehouse, full of brand new goods, still in their original wrappers. There were about twenty sets of cutlery and the woman obviously had a fetish for soap, as I found about three hundred bars, ranging from store own-brands to the best quality bars costing over £20 each. There were no receipts to be found anywhere. The husband looked mortified. I believed him when he told me that he didn't know those things were there, as the house was so large and the room felt cold, as if it wasn't used for living in. I called for a van and then began the massive task of seizing and logging all of the suspected stolen items. It took me three hours just to list them on a property record sheet.

I returned to the Bridewell, to a rather angry-looking custody sergeant who wanted to know where I had been. I informed him of the situation and so he called the lady's solicitor, despite the fact that she had stated that she didn't wish him to be present.

I conducted the interview with her. It took over two hours, as I had to question her about every item. In her quiet manner, she admitted to stealing them all. What I found most surprising was the fact she remembered the date and location of the theft of everything. She was remorseless, but I don't think she knew what she'd been doing, I think it was more an addiction. It was decided that the best way of dealing with the woman was by means of a help group and her condition of bail was to attend weekly meetings to rid her of her habitual stealing. She agreed to this and the decision was eventually taken not to prosecute her. As far as I know, she never offended again. It took me over two months to return all the stolen property to the appropriate stores, some of which weren't aware they'd even had goods stolen from them.

Whilst on the same squad, I once did a house search in Beeston, a suburb of South Leeds, following the arrest of a habitual shoplifter. The house was a two bedroom terraced dwelling and the first thing I noticed was flies buzzing around the bare light bulb, which precariously hung from the ceiling. There were piles of soiled clothing on the floor and the only remaining carpet spaces were covered with cat excrement. There were remains of food on a plate on the sofa, but this had formed a layer of mould and looked virtually unrecognisable. There were several used needles in the bedroom and I found a spoon with a burn mark on it in the bed.

The most repulsive sight was the bathroom. The water in the toilet filled the pan to the top and it was stained black. There were carrier bags tied up on the floor, containing human excrement. There were faeces floating in the bath, too. More distressing was the presence of a cot on the landing right outside the bathroom. The stench was too much and I did the best search possible under the circumstances, before going back to interview the eighteen-year-old mother of two. She was charged with the offence of theft from shops: she'd stolen toiletries and nappies.

Dealing with people like this saddened me. This woman had no chance of breaking her cycle of crime and I felt no satisfaction from charging her, as I knew that her crime was not driven by malice, but by an instinct to survive. I pitied her greatly and found myself making her several cups of tea during her time in custody. Just three days before her court appearance, she was found dead in her house. She had drawn a headstone on her bedroom wall and written the letters *RIP* on it. She had then lain next to it and taken an overdose of heroin. Her life had become too much. Her children had been with the body for two days before it was discovered. The eldest had eaten bits of flesh from her arms just to stay alive. This was another part of the job that I found difficult to deal with.

As you'd expect, I was glad when those three months were completed. I was pleased to be back with my shift patrolling the streets of Leeds city centre. Almost as soon as I'd finished my time in the shop squad, I made an arrest that attracted national media attention.

One night in January 1997, I was on another night duty. It was Saturday and, as always, we were anticipating a busy night. I didn't expect, however, to arrest this particular person. It was around midnight and I was driving the police van past the Majestyk nightclub in the centre of the city. I was with my colleague, PC Dave Braddock. There was a long queue of people outside the club, shivering in the freezing temperatures. My attention was then drawn to the other side of the road, to a group of men. They were lively, excitable and loud, but seemingly nothing other than in good spirits on a night out.

Then, without reason, one of the men shouted across towards us. His words were scathing of the police in general and his language was expletive. I was surprised by the blatant nature of the comments. He was a tall, thin man, well dressed and daubed in chunky gold jewellery. He kept on walking towards us and stood directly in front of the car. He looked in at us and shouted once again, 'You fucking pigs.' It was at this point that I recognised him.

The rest of his gang stood nearby. They, too, were smartly dressed and high quality clothing brand names were abundant. I recognised some of them as well. Dave and I looked at each other in amazement. It also seemed apparent to him who these men were. I got out of the car and approached the man, who by now was shouting more abuse at me. His face exuded arrogance as I approached. By this time, he was leaning against the police car. Most people in the queue had realised who he was as well, causing great interest in what was happening. I called for another unit to be nearby just in case the onlookers got involved, for which there was a potential. The man raised a palm and pushed past, swearing at me as he did so. I warned him that he'd be arrested if he carried on. My comments were met with yet more swearing.

I couldn't exercise my discretion any more. Action had to be taken. I took hold of his arm and informed him I was arresting him for disorderly conduct and assaulting police. I'd just arrested the Leeds United and ex-England midfielder, Carlton Palmer. He struggled momentarily and several other members of the Leeds United team approached, trying to persuade me to let him go. I recall Rod Wallace approaching me, trying to enter into dialogue, asking for me to let Palmer go. I asked him to stand aside as acceding to his request was not an option. He joined Brian Deane, who had kept out of the way for the duration of the incident. I requested a van, which arrived almost instantly. Palmer was placed into it and we tried to disperse the crowd, which was by now about two or three hundred strong. I took Palmer to the Bridewell. His conduct, if anything, actually worsened. He banged around in the back of the van and his abusive language was appalling. He seemed out of control.

I presented him to the custody sergeant and explained the circumstances leading to his arrest. His detention was authorised and I began the routine task of searching him amid the onslaught of more verbal abuse. His wallet contained several hundred pounds in cash and as we counted it out to document it, he said disdainfully, in his Midlands accent, 'I earn more than you lot put together.' He was probably right. He continued with the affront and was eventually placed in his cell. I think the realisation of what he had done hit him when I closed the door, as he went very quiet.

I was with to the custody sergeant discussing the next course of action, when I was approached by a colleague who had attended the scene at the nightclub just prior to me leaving with Palmer. The officer told me that a young lady had approached her and alleged that Carlton Palmer had indecently assaulted her in a bar, just minutes before I'd arrested him. It was only by chance that she had then seen me arresting him for the entirely separate matter. The complainant was happy to give a statement and so I went down to Palmer's cell and informed him that he was also under arrest on suspicion of indecent assault. He was subsequently interviewed and charged with both offences.

Being the high profile player that he was at the time, there was substantial media coverage of his arrest. And his court appearances were always in the paper and local news bulletins. I remember getting ready for work on the morning of his trial, Monday 11th August 1997. I anticipated that the media would be waiting outside the court building and so I made a concerted effort to make my uniform as smart as possible. Wearing your tunic at court was still a requirement, so I spent the morning brushing it down and pressing the sleeves. When I arrived at Millgarth, which is about a ten-minute walk from the court, I was told by the duty inspector that the media had rung the station asking if they could speak to me. I was told to make no comment whatsoever. There were the usual jokes flying around the station as I polished my boots in the report room. I was unaffected. If anyone else had acted in the way that Carlton Palmer had done, then they, too, would have been arrested. This was just another Saturday night arrest and the fact that Palmer was famous did not alter my attitude in any way.

As I left for court, colleagues jokingly told me not to take too long as Leeds had a game in a few days and Palmer was selected. Being an avid Leeds fan myself, I was keen to get this over, too. I left the station with my colleague, Dave, and we made our way over to the court on foot. As I walked along the Headrow (the main road leading to the court), I was surprised by what I saw. Not only were there newspaper photographers but television cameras as well, all camped outside. They stood around drinking cups of tea and coffee, casually chatting to each other.

As Dave and I walked through the swarm of people, there were a lot of whispers. We entered the building. As far as I was aware, not a single picture had been taken. I immediately went to the police room and prepared to give my evidence. I made my way over to the courtroom where the case was due to be heard and sat outside and waited. Other defendants and their associates who were waiting for their appearance, were clearly not happy about having two police officers sitting nearby. One of them deliberately dropped some litter in front of us. His friend sarcastically told him to pick it up, as it was an offence to do such a thing. They were wasting their efforts, as I remained focused on our own forthcoming trial.

Then the moment arrived. Carlton Palmer and his solicitor were here. Palmer, once again, had spared no effort or expense in his appearance. He wore a top quality suit and an abundance of expensive jewellery was openly on show again. He didn't acknowledge Dave or me. His solicitor was ceremonial in his expression and walked around briskly and confidently, carrying an abundance of paperwork. I felt a little intimidated, but I knew the truth of the situation and that was all that mattered. Palmer looked even taller than he had on the night of the incident. Everyone else in the court watched him in wonderment, perhaps curious as to why such a high profile figure was there. He and his solicitor were called to enter the courtroom and so I braced myself, ready for my call. It came about ten minutes later as the usher came and collected me.

As I entered, a number of the people sitting in the waiting area began chanting, 'Leeds', as a gesture of support for Palmer. I made no reaction and as I walked into the court, the magistrate ordered the usher to maintain order in the building. I took the stand and was sworn in. The public gallery was packed with people from the media, frantically scribbling notes on their pads. They knew who I was now and I realised that they'd probably photograph me as I left the court.

The proceedings got underway and I was scrutinised in minute detail about the events of the night in question. Throughout the whole two hours I was questioned, Palmer just sat with his solicitor, who would occasionally stand up and walk around a little, sometimes coming right up to the stand where I was giving evidence. It was stressful, but I was quite pleased that *he* seemed rather harassed by the time I stood down. A large part of his evidence against me was that I had failed to sign an important legal document when Palmer had been arrested. He had spent over twenty minutes interrogating me over it, only to find at the end that he had the wrong document with him. When the matter was checked out, it was established that I *had* signed the form. This was a very satisfying moment, as he'd tried to make me out to be incompetent.

At just after midday, the magistrate ordered a one hour lunch adjournment and so Dave and I went back to the police room in order to collect our helmets and make the short walk back to Millgarth for lunch. An army of press besieged us as we left the building. The flash photography was overwhelming and as we walked up the road, two television cameras followed us, filming. I was asked to make a comment on the trial, but I ignored the question.

We eventually arrived at the station. We got well out of the way of the cameras and looked at each other in amazement at the experience of being the subjects of such clamouring press interest. We listened to local radio whilst eating lunch and, sure enough, we were both mentioned. To my surprise, we were given a favourable representation by the reporter. My appetite was curbed but I tried to eat a sandwich. Dave was less bothered as he tucked into his steak and ale pie. Jibes were abundant as colleagues came and sat at the table with us, ironically asking for autographs. To be honest, Dave and I enjoyed all the attention we were getting as it broke up the monotony of our jobs.

As soon as we'd finished, we made our way back to the court and, once again, the cameras were on us. For the very short time that we had this attention, I found it all quite exciting, but

I can now understand why the rich and famous get frustrated with it. It was a relief to get to the court building and escape from the mayhem.

The trial didn't last much longer. Dave gave evidence for about an hour and soon after that, the magistrate found Carlton Palmer guilty of disorderly conduct, despite his consistent denial of any wrongdoing. He was fined something in the region of £500, which to him was less than half a day's wage.

'That'll teach him,' Dave said mordantly as we left the court. Palmer was mobbed by autograph-hunting fans as he stepped out into the torrent of cameras. This time they ignored Dave and me.

That evening, I was on the local and national news programmes and Carlton Palmer received some very negative publicity as details of his previous convictions were also broadcast.

The following day, Dave and I appeared in several of the national newspapers. The *Daily Star* made the following comment: *Soccer hero Carlton Palmer gave Police a verbal kicking after a boozy night out. He used the F-word repeatedly and boasted about his big earnings, proving nothing except that convicted groper Palmer is a disgrace to the sport that has made him rich.*

Palmer also received a fine for his conviction of indecent assault and I had stumbled into my five minutes of fame, just for doing my duty.

Chapter 6

Carried by Six or Tried by Twelve?

I remember the night of Sunday, 24th August 1997, as if it were yesterday. It's hardly surprising, considering the devastating effects that it would have on my life. Things would never be the same again.

Writing this chapter triggers unpleasant memories of an evening when I genuinely thought that I was going to die. This is compounded with frustration, as I recall the adverse consequences another man's actions have had on me.

I had arrived at work just before 10 p.m. as usual. I was surprised there were only four other officers in the room when I paraded for duty. The sergeant gave us the briefing, and allocated us to our partner and vehicle, followed by a rundown on the day's crimes and incidents. He was apologetic at the end, as the staffing levels were below the requirement. There was an ongoing incident in another division of the force and this was draining resources. There was nothing further of any significance to note.

As he got up to leave the room, I raised my hand. 'Excuse me, Sarge.'

'Yes, Mick?'

'I'm a little concerned that we are turning out just five for nights. There's a safety issue here, isn't there?'

He looked at me and seemed surprised, even annoyed. I hadn't intended to provoke him; I was just concerned that there were too few officers for the demands of a busy city centre night shift.

'It's because we have a load on a respond at Chapletown,' he replied, making it clear the matter was not up for discussion.

I decided not to pursue it. I now wish I had. I gathered my equipment and walked to the report room in order to attend to any paperwork that had accumulated since the previous shift. Fortunately, there wasn't much and so within half an hour, I was out on mobile patrol with PC Amanda Williams, my partner for this particular tour of duty. Amanda had about the same level of service as me, but she'd spent all of her time at Millgarth Division and I sensed she wanted a move, probably to go on to the Traffic Department. I thought she was a very competent officer and I enjoyed working with her.

I made a preliminary drive around the city centre in order to see how busy things were. It was extremely quiet; Sundays usually were. Our first call of the night was to a burglary in the Hyde Park area. It was the usual story: the burglars had kicked in the front door, ransacked the place and then taken anything of value they could carry, like jewellery, cash and electrical equipment. The occupants were away on holiday and so we secured the premises as best we could. After about an hour or so at the scene, we resumed and set off to pick up an officer who had been taking statements all evening from a nearby address. He required transport to the station so that he could team up with his partner for the night. The radio was quiet and so we made the journey to collect him uninterrupted. He clambered into the back of the car and we set off back to Millgarth.

It was after 11.30 p.m. and the city was silent. Quiet streets are a pleasing sight to a police officer, but there is always something happening, whether we know about it or not. It's tempting fate to be thankful for any calm. A classic example of this was when I worked at Cleckheaton. A colleague passed comment on how long it had been since the town had fallen victim to its last armed robbery. Within thirty minutes of him saying this, there was a live job at one of the banks in town, in which a firearm was discharged. Fortunately no one was killed, but it went to show that complacency is the enemy of any officer.

As I pondered on how quiet it was on this particular Leeds night, the night of Sunday, 24th August 1997, the inevitable happened: a call graded 'immediate response' was passed over the radio with a report of a disturbance at 268 Harold Terrace in Burley.

It would take us only a couple of minutes to get to this location and so, without delay, I turned the car around in the middle of the road, illuminated the blue lamps and began to drive at speed to the address.

We informed the control room that we were attending and, whilst en route, it was established that the address had markers for assaults on police.

I could see Paul, the officer we'd picked up to take back to Millgarth, through the rear-view mirror. He was pulling on his body armour. Amanda had gone from a relatively relaxed posture to one of upright rigidity. It's very difficult to convey the feelings a police officer experiences whilst travelling to an incident which is known to be potentially violent. Fortunately, as the driver of the vehicle, my attention was focused on driving safely and so I didn't have time for nerves to accumulate. Another message came through asking us to expedite, as another call had come in suggesting that things were getting out of hand.

I drove at speed along the road running off Harold Terrace. I noticed that Amanda was now looking apprehensive. We were only seconds away from an incident that was to have a calamitous influence on my life. However, as I drove, it was still just another domestic.

The area is a relatively downbeat part of Leeds with a high crime rate. The terraced houses seemed endless and the streets merged with thoughtless architecture. Houses had graffiti daubed all over them and dustbins were strewn about. Washing hung on lines attached from house to house across the road. It wasn't uncommon to see children as young as five and six walking the streets alone at this time of night. It was a depressing sight and it was little wonder that tensions ran high in the area from time to time. This was only a matter of a couple of miles from where the Woodhouse riots had taken place in 1995.

I turned onto Harold Terrace. Almost immediately, two men ran out of a house. They sprinted down the road, passed us and were away from the scene. They were dishevelled and they appeared aggressive, both in their general demeanour and in their facial expressions. One of them was naked from the waist up. These were clearly the two men that the call had related to. I stopped the vehicle as quickly as I could and without hesitation began the chase on foot, along with Amanda and Paul. I shouted at the men, telling them to stop. They were about thirty yards or so in front of us, but I was confident we would catch them, especially as at this time of night it was likely they would be heavily in drink.

The man without the shirt looked round. He grimaced and tried to increase the pace. The other man started to fatigue, and I knew that I was only seconds away from catching him. The gap between us shortened with every stride. I mumbled into my radio as I tried to maintain the speed. The men got to the bottom of the road and disappeared around the corner. I kept running, as did Amanda. Paul was tiring due to his body armour, which I think was restricting his breathing. Mine was on the back seat of the car, as I found prolonged periods of use very uncomfortable. You can manage to run for only a couple of minutes at speed whilst wearing such an article. I was wearing just my normal shirt, and therefore I was ahead of my colleagues.

One of the men had stopped almost immediately around the corner, whilst the second man (with no shirt) stood about twenty yards further up the road. I stopped and told the first man to face the wall, which he was standing next to. He complied immediately, raising his hands as a gesture of surrender. This sudden change in demeanour heightened my suspicion, and so I told him to remain exactly where he was. Paul and Amanda ran further up the road to where the other man had stopped.

I approached the man I had caught. He was taller than me. He was breathless and I could smell alcohol on his breath despite the distance between us. 'I haven't fucking done owt,' he slurred. He was very drunk.

'Keep your language down, please,' I replied.

'I haven't fucking done owt,' he garbled again as he turned to face me.

'Turn round and face the wall,' I demanded. He stumbled back into position. 'If you swear again, then you're under arrest under the Public Order Act, is that clear?'

'Sorry,' he said sarcastically.

'Why have you run away from us, what's happened up there?' I asked.

'I get nervous when I see coppers. We haven't done owt.' His tone was a little less threatening this time. I took a step forward so that I was standing closer to him. The smell of stale alcohol and body odour made a repugnant combination and so I turned my head in order to breathe cleaner air.

'What's going on?' he asked in desperation.

'We just need to make sure that everything's okay at the house where you just legged it from. If it is, then there's no problem.'

I'd decided there were no grounds for an arrest at this time, but I wasn't willing to let him walk away until the occupants of the house had been spoken to. This was a fine line, but fortunately he was happy to accompany me back to the house. We walked back up Harold Terrace. Paul and Amanda followed with the other man. Both men remained agitated, but were otherwise reasonably compliant. There seemed nothing out of the ordinary about this job. Another police car arrived. A number of local residents came onto the street in order to see why there were two police cars seemingly abandoned.

As we got to the house, the shirtless man's demeanour changed. He burst past me and ran towards the house. 'I'll fucking kill you!' he bawled.

Amanda and Paul raced after him as he entered. I stayed

outside with the other man just by the front door. He appeared to be quite calm about the whole thing. The shouting continued from inside the house for a few minutes and so I decided that I would stand at the door to make sure my colleagues had safely effected the arrest. A back-up unit had arrived and there was a third officer in the house by this time and the situation seemed to be under control.

The female occupant inside the house looked frightened and was crying. She held her hands into her chest and she was shaking. The male who had entered the house began to threaten her again, despite the fact that he was lying in a prone position, being in the final stages of his arrest. I remained standing at the doorway as my presence wasn't needed inside. Paul and Amanda lifted the arrested man to his feet and began to walk him towards the door and so I stepped back outside.

I noticed that the other man was still waiting. The crowd had grown and adverse comments were being made towards us. This was beginning to have the potential of becoming a larger public order situation. We knew that the best tactic would be to get the arrested man away from the scene as soon as possible, in order to diffuse the excitement amongst the onlookers.

As Paul and Amanda led him out, the other man started getting involved. 'Let my fucking mate go, you bastards!' he bellowed. He tried to barge past me but I made a barrier between the arrested man and him.

I raised my right hand with the palm showing, just as I had been trained to do. 'Get back!' I shouted. I told him that he would be arrested if his conduct continued in the same manner.

This time, my instructions were met with contempt. His face filled with fury and his eyes raged. He looked straight through me and tried to get past again. He walked into my raised hand.

Once again, I told him to get back. I had decided to arrest him but wanted to wait until the other officers were able to assist me. I turned to the left in order to check that the arrested man had been placed into the car. The crowd was getting increasingly agitated. Suddenly, and without warning, I felt a heavy thud on my chin which caused me to black out for a split second. The blow was accompanied by a ringing sound in my ears. I stumbled and widened my base so as not to fall to the ground. My awareness of things around me dissipated in an instant. As I tried to regain my focus, all I could see was the man in front of me. He landed the perfect punch on my chin and I was shaken enough not to be able to respond.

Within two seconds of the first blow, he punched me for the second time: on the chin again. He certainly knew where to hit. This time, I saw him do it but was unable to do anything, because of the disorienting effects of the first punch. I felt a crack in my jaw and I got a salty taste in my mouth. I nearly lost my footing and began to fall, so I widened my stance further in order to remain standing. I felt a crunching sensation in my mouth which made me instinctively spit. Bits of a tooth flew onto the ground. Before I could open my eyes, I felt the man's hand grasp my collar and he pulled me down so that I was bent at right angles at the waist, facing the ground. I tried to step back but his grip was too strong. His other fist struck me repeatedly in my face and head. Once again, everything went black and the ringing accompanied each blow.

It's difficult to describe what the situation felt like, but I didn't feel like a policeman. He was in control of events and I was in his hands. I had never experienced this before and I was frightened, but it didn't feel real. I had been assaulted previously, but not like this. The attack was relentless and the man was making a real effort to hurt me. I still couldn't loosen his grip on my shirt and as I tried desperately to stay on my feet, he hit me again.

This time I was lucky, as the blow landed to the top of my head and my skull took the brunt of the force. Panic surged through me and, for the first time in my life, I thought I was going to be seriously hurt. I didn't have the strength to get away from him because of his enhanced power, aided by the drink that he'd consumed. I couldn't get a strike on him because he had me bent over and I was, by now, unable to co-ordinate anything I was doing.

The blows still kept on coming, all to my head and face. Each time he swung to punch me, he made a growling sound. Everything around me seemed to disappear, as my attention focused solely on him and myself. I was still facing the ground and as I opened my eyes, I saw there were splashes of blood on the pavement: my blood. The salty taste in my mouth had got stronger. I needed to stop this man, but I couldn't. His arm that was holding onto my shirt prevented me from defending myself from the blows. I knew that it was only a matter of time before I completely lost consciousness.

The next few moments are still a blur, I suppose because my assailant kept on hitting me, but I remember seeing a pair of police trousers standing next to him. I was still pulled over at the waist. A police baton struck him repeatedly on his legs but it bounced off like a tennis ball from a racquet. The punches continued and the strikes from the baton seemed to increase the force of them as he became angrier.

Next, there was a stinging sensation in my eyes and my throat began to tighten. My eyes streamed with tears and my face began to hurt. One of my colleagues had tried to restrain the man with CS spray but had inadvertently sprayed me with it. The man's grip on me tightened again and this turned out to be my saviour, as every button ripped off my shirt in turn, giving me some slack with which to pull back. Exhausted, disoriented and injured, I stepped back with the limited strength I had left. The man went down onto one knee and one foot, half kneeling directly in front of me. I shook my head in order to get a clear view of him, but the tears in my eyes blurred my vision. He was making the growling sound again and he raised a clenched fist. I thought he was about to launch into another attack. I was backed onto a wall of the row of terraced houses and had no escape. I had less than a second to make my decision. I had no idea where the attack would end.

I tried to grab my baton, but it was no longer by my side, having swivelled into the small of my back during the attack. Aware that the man hadn't been grounded by the use of CS spray or baton strikes, I kicked out at him in order to knock him off balance. He fell to the ground. Relieved that I had a few more seconds in which to think, I shook my head and tried to clear my eyes once again. The burning feeling was excruciating and I still couldn't see properly, but to my relief I saw two officers attempting to restrain him. He was still resisting, but after a few moments they had managed to apply the handcuffs. I rubbed my eyes and a sharp pain developed in my broken tooth. My shirt had been ripped from my back. I noticed lots of police cars. Someone must have put out an assistance call.

My head and face were extremely painful and I was shaking. People came up to me and started prodding me. 'We saw you fucking kick him.' I was too shocked to answer. I just wanted to get away. 'We've got your fucking number,' they continued.

I found their verbal onslaught utterly callous, as I wandered around dazed and dripping with blood. As I walked away, another officer approached me. 'Are you okay, Mick?' he asked.

'I don't know,' I replied, as I prodded my tooth.

'Let's take a look,' he said, as he peered into my gaping mouth. 'It's broken.'

'The bastard,' I said, rather more loudly than perhaps I should have done.

I got into a police car, desperate to get away from the scene and the abuse from onlookers. I don't suppose I can hold that against them, though, because unless you yourself have been attacked in such a manner, then it's difficult to appreciate the effects of such an occurrence. They didn't see me as an innocent person who had just been injured in an unprovoked attack; they saw me only as a policeman and that was why I wanted to get away.

Little did he know it, and he probably still doesn't, but what my assailant did to me that night was to cost me my job, my freedom and my health.

I went to the toilet and looked at my face in the mirror. My forehead and my left cheek were red and my left eye was beginning to swell. My tooth was badly damaged. I had really bad vision as well, but I put that down to the CS gas. I removed my torn shirt and put on a clean one, then sat down and gathered my thoughts, trying to come to terms with what had happened to me. My attacker's indiscriminate and extreme violence was something I'd never experienced before. Any police officer is conscious that they may be assaulted in the course of their duties, but this was more than that.

The doctor eventually examined me and I went home feeling rather poorly and deeply upset and traumatised. The man was charged with assaulting a police officer. He was released on bail the following morning and whilst this annoyed me, it came as no surprise. Assaulting a police officer is no longer viewed with the weightiness that it used to be. I just hoped that the magistrates would see this for what it was and punish him accordingly. Time would tell.

I spent the next five weeks off work, recovering from my head injuries. After visiting my own doctor, I was referred to an eye specialist at Dewsbury District Hospital following partial loss of vision in my left eye. The blurred vision was due to an injury and not the CS gas as I'd first thought. I also consulted my dentist. It was a slow recovery and I suffered with frequent migraines, but I was determined to get back to work at the earliest opportunity; I loved my job despite what had happened. I spent most of the five weeks at home and found the time painfully boring. I'd been advised by my doctor to get plenty of rest in order to speed up the recovery from the concussion I'd suffered.

Soon after the incident, a senior officer had informed me that when I was fit to return to work, I would be starting in another division of the force. I puzzled over this, as it was unusual to transfer an officer without giving any explanation as to why. I was very happy at Millgarth and I had a lot of friends there. I didn't want to leave.

My return to work was daunting. I had received one phone call from a senior officer during my absence. She told me that I'd been allocated to a community-policing unit in Rothwell and that I should report there. The call was brief and mechanical. No one had enquired about my welfare, and I became suspicious. I wondered why I hadn't been offered any support following the assault. This was the first time I knew something was wrong. Nevertheless, I made the journey to Rothwell Police Station exactly five weeks after the incident.

My new colleagues greeted me with scepticism and caution. Rothwell is comparatively small and therefore a complete contrast to Millgarth. There were just four constables and a sergeant on this community team and the role was far different from that of a patrol officer. Community policing is far less reactive and more proactive. Therefore the pace was slower and the days were more structured and planned. When I arrived on the team, they were in the middle of a one-week operation observing a known criminal in the anticipation of a big job coming off at a local post office. My colleagues' reservations were soon dispelled as I got to know them better. They became as mystified as myself as to the reasons for my transfer. We would become good friends.

The weeks and months passed and my assailant's court appearance drew nearer. I hoped that once he had attended, then I would be allowed back to Millgarth. The community job had come too early in my career and I was still keen to continue being a front-line police officer.

When his first appearance at court was adjourned, my patience diminished and I began to find the daily grind of doing a job that I had been forced to do against my will increasingly stressful. On top of this, my grandad had become extremely ill with cancer and I had the added misery of seeing him suffer terribly. The worry must have been twice as bad for my dad, who now had his son and his father to fret about. My dad visited Grandad daily as his health deteriorated over the months. I considered meeting the Assistant Chief Constable to discuss my position. I desperately wanted to be with my friends at Millgarth. I missed them and I missed the work in the city centre. The stress of the work situation and seeing my grandad so poorly was taking a toll on me.

A dramatic turn of events unfolded in the following days. It was a very quiet day at work and we had no planned jobs and so we were spending the day in the office collecting intelligence on our next target. The phone rang and I answered it.

'Hello, PC Bunting?' asked the solemn-sounding voice.

'Speaking,' I replied.

'This is Inspector Parker from Discipline and Complaints,' he continued.

'How can I help you, sir?'

'We need to see you urgently,' he said. 'Can you come to Brotherton House straight away?'

'I'll ask my boss,' I replied, feeling rather anxious about the brief and formal conversation. There was something wrong, I could tell.

I made the short journey into Leeds. I arrived to a stiff, cold reception. Inspector Parker looked at me with a dour expression. His words were almost all monosyllabic and his sentences were concise. It was clear he didn't want to enter into a conversation and it was even clearer that my suspicions that this was serious were right.

He asked me to sit in a waiting room. I sat there for over twenty minutes, alone, hearing a low conversational buzz from the room next door. Discipline and Complaints officers, because of the nature of their job, automatically intimidate many police officers. I'd always appreciated the need to be accountable, so I'd not had a problem with them until this point in my career. However, the whole atmosphere of this place was enough to unnerve a saint.

Eventually, I couldn't stand it any more and I knocked on the door of the office. Inspector Parker coyly opened it just a few inches. 'Sir, what's going on?' I asked, forcefully aggrieved by the unwarranted, oppressive treatment I was receiving.

'Come in, PC Bunting,' he said.

The room was full of officers from the department. They all sat working at their individual desks. It was disturbingly quiet and it felt as though everyone was looking at me.

Inspector Parker asked me to sit down by his desk. 'I'm afraid I have rather disappointing news for you, PC Bunting.'

'What's that, sir?'

'We have received a complaint from a member of the public with regard to your conduct,' he said.

'What about?' I asked instantly.

'Before we go any further, I must tell you that you do not have to say anything but it may harm your defence if you do not mention when questioned something which you later rely on in court. Anything you do say may be given in evidence.'

'Are you gonna tell me what this is about, or what?' I

demanded. I had been in the building for almost forty minutes by this point. I had been made to wait, I had been ignored and now I was the subject of a caution.

'You are currently under investigation on suspicion of assault,' he continued.

'Assault?' I asked, mystified.

'Yes, on John Patterson on Sunday, 24th August 1997.' It seemed that my assailant who had caused me so much suffering had now lodged a complaint of assault against me. I couldn't believe his audacity, and even more dumbfounding was the fact that the Discipline and Complaints Department were putting resources into investigating it. I felt utterly betrayed.

'You've got to be kidding. What did I do? I thought he was going to kill me!'

'You'll get your say when we interview you in due course,' he replied.

'When will that be? This has been going on long enough as it is. I just want to go back to Millgarth.'

'We'll have some enquiries to do first, then we'll speak properly about it.'

He rummaged around in his briefcase and produced a Regulation 7 notice, the official document to be served on me to show the exact nature of the allegation made. They are usually quite vague and this one just alleged that, on the night in question, I had assaulted the man who had attacked me. I signed the form, acknowledging that the matter had been brought to my attention. Inspector Parker told me he would be in touch and I left the office. I went to the toilets, swilled my face with cold water and left Brotherton House in total bewilderment.

The traffic was heavy and so my journey back took longer than it normally would have. This gave me time to consider what I would do about my situation. Even though I knew I hadn't done anything wrong, it was beginning to feel as if I had. Given the fact that my assailant had apologised for the assault when he'd been interviewed, it made what was happening seem utterly bizarre. I began to suspect something rather sinister about the whole thing.

I arrived at Rothwell and Sergeant Burrows was waiting for me. He frowned and pointed upstairs to his office. I followed him up the stairs and he closed the door behind me.

'I take it you know, then?' I said.

'Yes, I do and I just want you to know that you have my full support, Mick. I don't know what went on that night and I don't want to, but what I do know is that you are a bloody good bobby and you are doing a good job for me here.'

'Cheers, Sarge. I've done fuck all wrong. He was a bloody animal. What do they expect us to do?'

'I've called the Federation and they want to see you tomorrow so that they can discuss getting you a solicitor. I think it's best that you have one, but it's up to you.'

'I'll be having one. They treated me like the bloody mafia down there. Who do they think they are? I was still in nappies when they were last on the streets.'

Sergeant Burrows seemed to be rather more open-minded. After all, he had done twenty years on the streets, so he knew that dealing with violent men was often extremely difficult, and simply shouting, 'Get back!', and waving a piece of plastic was usually completely ineffective. Unfortunately, the officers conducting the investigation were not in the front line and probably had little understanding of the dangers faced by police officers on the streets.

We chatted for half an hour or so and I told him exactly

what had happened when I had made the arrest. Sergeant Burrows told me to try not to worry, as he believed the investigation was just another example of the timorous behaviour of a police force that was becoming ever more subservient to pressures imposed by the vocal minority.

Sergeant Burrows could see I was upset and told me to go home for the rest of the day. I knew that sitting at home thinking about the day's events would be harmful, but I wasn't fit to complete my day's work with my mind in the state that it was. I drove home thinking, for the first time ever, that being a policeman was perhaps not the job for me.

I returned to work the following day, though I must admit that I didn't feel up to it. However, I realised that wrong conclusions would be drawn if I didn't go in. I had nothing to hide and I had done nothing wrong. I hoped my early return to work would go some way to showing this. By this time, news of the incident had circulated the force and I was receiving a lot of support from my peers. They all appreciated the difficulties in trying to restrain a violent man. I would just have to ride this one out. I had no control over my fate, but I was not unduly worried. Besides, the feeling of betrayal left little room for any other emotions.

The days and weeks passed. I heard nothing more about the investigation. I would frequently anticipate being summoned for interview each time I went to work, but there was nothing. Once again, the weeks turned to months. I became more and more unhappy with my new role at Rothwell and I felt increasingly uncomfortable as each day passed with the investigation still hanging over me.

My family noticed the change in me and this signalled the start in the deterioration of my mother's health. Each time I visited my parents, I could see the anguish in her face as she asked me whether the matter had been sorted out. There seemed to be no end to the suffering and Dad had the hard work of calming Mum down. This inevitably took its toll on him and, month by month, her condition got worse. When I couldn't bear to see their pain any longer, I decided to call the Discipline and Complaints Department. With very little dialogue, I was told I would be interviewed when the investigation had been completed. I didn't give the officer the pleasure of knowing the devastating effects the matter was having on me and, more importantly, my parents.

As the stress of the situation compounded, my ability to remain focused on my job diminished proportionately. Eventually, I couldn't take any more and I went to see an assistant chief constable in the Police HQ at Wakefield, in order to try to find out exactly what was happening and to try to re-establish a direction in my career.

I went to the meeting with naive optimism, hoping that the treatment I had received from the Discipline and Complaints Department was an exception and that they had been this way simply to maintain professional distance. My hopes were terminated mercilessly. The officer sat in an expensive-looking upholstered chair. One thing was for sure, my pleas for help fell on deaf ears and, by the end of the meeting, I had gained nothing except a huge amount of annoyance. Plus, I was being transferred to yet another station against my will. My career and my world were collapsing around me and I left the office feeling devastated. As my tongue brushed over my damaged tooth, I was reminded of the incident once again. My bewilderment and irritation continued.

It was at this point, in January 1998, that Grandad's battle against cancer was lost. He died relatively peacefully in his sleep following his unremitting illness, which had rendered him completely dependent for the past twelve months or so. I didn't think it was possible to feel unhappier than I did at that time. I'd become very close to Grandad and losing him seemed cruel. I couldn't even begin to imagine how Dad was feeling.

A couple of days after the meeting, I started on my new shift at Holbeck Police Station. I didn't know anybody there and my usually ebullient personality was suppressed by yet another new start. Nights were becoming longer and I was finding it very difficult to sleep. I began to worry more and more about my pending investigation, not because of what I'd done, but because of the way it was being handled.

I spent hours at my mum and dad's, going over the incident with them. With tensions running high, these discussions would often lead to lengthy and heated exchanges, leaving me riddled with guilt as I drove home. I needed someone to lean on and the only people I had at this time were my parents, but little did I appreciate the true extent of the effects my situation was having on them. I was hardly in the right mind for my new job at Holbeck, but I was determined not to be beaten by the system that I'd grown to loathe.

The shift at Holbeck was predominantly made up of young officers in their twenties and thirties, and I was made to feel welcome. Despite not wanting the move, I was back doing what I loved and I soon got to know everybody on the team. I began to enjoy my work again, though the investigation was never far from my mind. Still the months passed, yet I heard nothing. It was now almost a year since the incident and I still hadn't been interviewed about it.

I tried to carry on as normal, but this was impossible. My sleepless nights continued and my interest in my new job eventually dwindled. It got to the stage where I was just turning up for work like a robot, motivated only by personal pride and the desire still to show my innocence. However, I received three commendations for good work whilst at Holbeck. Once again, I toyed with the idea of having some time off work to try to recover from the enormous stress that I was under, but I didn't want to give any ammunition to the rumour squad. And so I carried on working. Sometimes I would sit through a whole briefing in a daze, hardly hearing a word that had been said. At times, my colleagues had to tell me I was being called up on the radio, as I didn't notice. I was in a mess. I was in desperate need of some good news.

As I pulled into the car park one evening, I saw one of my friends who worked in the CID. He flagged me down as I tried to steer past him in order to park my car. Rather bemused, I lowered the window.

'Bet you're happy, aren't you, mate?' he said with a smile.

'Why's that?' I asked.

'He got done this morning. He's pleaded guilty to assaulting you,' he said.

'Oh, brilliant!' I shouted. 'What did he get?'

'Don't know, to be honest, but at least he got done.'

I parked my car and ran into the station, desperate to find out more. Before getting changed, I went to the report room in order to look in my tray and check for paperwork. There was nothing, but I was almost immediately swarmed upon by people shaking my hand and congratulating me on his conviction. However, my jubilation was cut short when I found out the punishment administered to him by the court. He had been given a community service order and a fine. I was exasperated by the lack of compassion shown to me by the magistrates who had imposed the sentence. It would have been a different story if he'd knocked one of *their* teeth out. Nevertheless, I tried not to let this rather familiar leniency spoil the news of his conviction. I rang my mum and dad straight away. They were delighted by the news, if a little bemused by the sentence.

I knew then that it would only be a short time to my own interview. Sure enough, an appointment was made for me to attend at Brotherton House in June 1998, just a couple of weeks away. This time, I would be going with my solicitor and I was determined not to feel intimidated by the officers again.

I spent another few uneventful weeks at Holbeck before the day arrived. It was a warm and sunny day in June. Ten months had passed since the incident, and here I was on my way to an interview where I would be expected to remember the events of a short incident in minute detail, and after being concussed. I spent the whole of the journey running the incident through my mind repeatedly, so that my answers would be as accurate as they possibly could be. My solicitor, Mr Bell, met me at the entrance door. We shook hands. He was a smart man, rather eccentric in his dress sense, too, as a flowery handkerchief precariously hung from his breast pocket. He sneezed theatrically as the symptoms of his hayfever took hold. We entered the building and sat in a room together. He opened his briefcase, removed a big pile of paperwork and hastily sipped a glass of water. After a brief chat we were ready for the interview.

It was held in a standard interview room, the sort in which I had interviewed hundreds of suspects myself. It contained four chairs, a table and a fixed tape recording machine. It was disturbing to know that this time I was the suspect. Two officers entered the room. They each carried a file and neither spoke, either to me or to each other. They had aggressive expressions. In turn, they stared into my eyes. They couldn't have been more imperious if they'd tried. I suppose that they had been trained to be like this, but it was over-the-top, unnecessary and felt incredibly overbearing.

The interview was a long and tiresome affair. The officers kept reiterating the prosecution case to me, stating that on the night in question I had lost my temper and used gratuitous violence on my assailant as a punitive measure for the assault he had committed on me. I answered the questions truthfully and consistently, stating that I had kicked him as a means of defending myself from a perceived further imminent attack. I made the point that it is very easy to be critical with hindsight, but it had been a fast-moving incident: I was injured, frightened, fatigued and my senses were numbed; I had a split second in which to decide what to do. If I had made a mistake, then it had been an honest one, simply because I was in fear for my safety. My actions – which had lasted maybe one or two seconds – were being scrutinised for hours by two men who hadn't been present at the scene. They seemed to treat me with contempt for the duration of the interview.

It was finally ended. I was informed that the case against me would be forwarded to the Crown Prosecution Service (CPS)

and a decision would be made as to whether I would be prose-
cuted on a charge of assault. The implications of such a charge
were too much for me to even consider, but I was confident of
the right outcome, particularly in light of my assailant's conviction for assault against me.

On Friday, 8th August 1998, almost a year from the night that
I had been attacked, I was on a special duty with six other officers from Holbeck. It was the day the England cricket team
were playing South Africa at Headingley and I was involved in
the crowd control duties on the terraces. It was a hot day and
we had to take occasional breaks from the sun in order to take
refreshments, as we roasted in our uncompromising uniforms.
The crowd was in its usual high spirits and the beer was flow-
ing in the stand. The usual banter between fans and the police
was in abundance, but it was all harmless fun, unlike the con-
frontations I'd experienced at some football matches.

Part way through the tour of duty, I received a radio message
to go and see the chief inspector in charge of policing the
match. To be called from your designated spot during crowd
control is highly unusual and as I made the short walk through
the terraces to the control room, I just knew that something
was wrong. Amidst a couple more jibes from good-humoured
fans, I arrived at the control room. The chief inspector handed
me a mobile phone. I noticed that a number had already been
dialled on the display and he told me to go outside and call it,
as the chief inspector from Holbeck wanted to speak to me. I
had gone through a rigorous selection procedure to join the
West Yorkshire Police FSU (Firearms Support Unit), and I

knew that the results were due out soon. I hoped this was the reason for the call.

I walked out to the edge of the terrace, removed my earpiece and held the phone to my ear with my index finger in the other. I could just about hear the phone ringing. I was impatient for him to answer.

'Hello, Chief Inspector Goodall,' came the stern reply.

'Hello, sir. It's PC Bunting. I've been told to call you.'

'Ah yes, PC Bunting.' He hesitated. I thought the line had disconnected.

'Hello,' I said, 'are you there?'

'Yes, I'm here. It's about your case that's been reviewed by the CPS.'

'Yes,' I replied, surprised at the topic of conversation.

'You have been summoned to court on suspicion of assault,' he said casually.

'*What*?' The words reverberated in my mind and my body went weak. Everything around me seemed to disappear. My mouth went dry instantly. My worst fear had come true. I immediately felt sick.

'You need to come straight back to Holbeck now. You can no longer be allowed contact with the public in the course of your duties.'

I walked back into the control room and handed the phone to the chief inspector.

'I can't believe what he's just done,' I said in disgust. He looked bewildered. 'He's just told me that I'm being charged with assault and I have to go straight back to Holbeck.' He shook his head. He also seemed disgusted at the way I'd been informed.

He arranged for my transport back to Holbeck and when I

arrived back at the station, approximately half an hour after the news had been broken to me, I discovered that Chief Inspector Goodall had gone home. It would be a struggle for me to call this man 'sir' ever again.

The media were bound to follow my court appearances closely, and once again my thoughts turned to my parents. The previous year had been tough, but there was no doubt that the toughest times were yet to come, as I faced a criminal charge of assault occasioning actual bodily harm, the maximum sentence for which was five years' imprisonment. Ironically, on this same day, I also found out that my application onto the basic firearms course had been successful. But finding an officer with the courage to allow me to attend it with the pending charge hanging over me would be impossible, and so I resigned myself to not being allowed to go. Instead of celebrating my success, I spent the night contemplating going to prison, which was now becoming a serious possibility.

Chapter 7

'Not Guilty'

The thought of an impending court appearance is enough to unsettle any respectable person. The effects on a police officer are possibly greater and the news that I'd been charged with this offence was a devastating blow. Being sent to prison is every policeman's worst nightmare and I swore I'd kill myself before it ever happened to me. Perhaps naively, I was still confident our judiciary was the best in the world and that ultimately I had nothing to worry about.

The trauma the news of my charge brought deepened the stress which I had been suffering and I was unable to return to work for quite some time. I felt less guilty about being off this time, though. The long nights I had been experiencing blended into long days, too, and my purpose felt as if it had completely gone. Some days I was so depressed that I couldn't even get dressed or washed. The prospects of prison, although distant from my mind for most of the time, terrified me when I allowed myself to think about them.

I made regular visits to my doctor. He was very sympathetic and did everything he could to help, but was powerless to remove the cause of my illness. I received very little official contact from work. The months passed by. To say that I felt abandoned by the force is an understatement and the only things keeping my sanity were the regular visits from my peers and friends, who never wavered in their support for me. At this time in my life I had nothing to offer them, yet they still cared about me. They were, and still are, true friends.

Ironically, about two weeks after I had been charged, something quite bizarre happened. I was drinking a cup of tea when I was startled by the rattle of my letterbox as the postman forcefully pushed my mail through. One of the letters looked official, which unnerved me. I opened it warily and noticed what looked like a cheque as I tore through the envelope. I wasn't expecting any money, I didn't think anybody owed me any, so I couldn't believe it when I saw a cheque for £1,000, made out to me. I had been awarded compensation from the Criminal Injuries Compensation Authority for my injuries sustained during the assault. I put it on the coffee table with the politely worded letter that accompanied it. It was all becoming too weird.

When I woke up on the morning of my first court appearance (the preliminary hearing on 29th September 1998), I knew that I wouldn't be in the dock for too long, but I was still a little nervous all the same. I hadn't slept well that night and so I got up and had a shower at about 5 a.m. I had a strong feeling of relief; this day was surely the beginning of the end of this horrible saga. Even though the matter wouldn't be finalised at the first hearing, I knew that a bail date would be fixed and then I'd know more of where I stood in terms of timescale. This was important to me following the long and agonising thirteen months of my life since the incident had occurred.

I tried to eat breakfast, but I couldn't. I felt nauseous and my stomach churned with trepidation. I sat and waited for my dad to pick me up. He would be arriving at about eight o'clock, as I had to be at court for 9.30, and even though Wakefield wasn't far, he had always been a believer in being prepared and accounting for every eventuality.

I went upstairs to get dressed. My hands shook violently as I tried to do up the knot on my tie. I looked in the mirror and saw that I was pale and tense. My father arrived ten minutes early. He, too, looked apprehensive but he spoke with words of encouragement and determination, just what I needed. He told me that no matter what happened to me, I had both his and Mum's support. He expressed once again his contempt for the people who had put me in this position. I felt his sense of betrayal by the organisation for which he had performed with commitment and enthusiasm for all those years. This made me feel guilty, as the early years of his retirement were being spoiled by what was happening to me and I felt as though I had let him down.

We didn't say much to each other on the way to Wakefield. I was charging myself up for the most unpleasant event of my life and Dad left me to it. We arrived at court early. The doors were locked. There was another defendant waiting outside. He was dressed in dirty trainers and an old tracksuit and he also wore a baseball cap. He paced around impatiently, spitting on the floor every so often as he did so. I just stood there with my father. When I saw the man's contempt for the position he was in, I realised that my policeman's mentality would never desert me. His arrogance was appalling and there was no way on earth I deserved to be likened to someone like him. A number of similar looking individuals arrived. I still find it hard to accept that I was on a list of defendants with them.

After ten minutes or so, an ageing security guard opened the doors. Without hesitation, Dad and I went into the old building. The others just stayed outside. Smoking seemed far more important to them than their impending court cases.

We sat and waited in the court reception area. Mr Bell was a little late, but he arrived well before I was due in court. We found a private room and he explained what was going to happen. He informed me he had seen a number of reporters congregating outside the courtroom that I was listed to attend. He had also seen my assailant, which concerned me as I would be asked my full postal address in court and this would give him information I didn't want him to have. I didn't want him and his entourage knowing where I lived for fear of my home being attacked. I wasn't keen on the media having it, either. Mr Bell told me that he would address this matter with the clerk before open court commenced and he'd instruct me accordingly before I took to the dock. We tended to a few other administrative matters, then made our way to the courtroom.

I had never been to Wakefield Magistrates Court in the course of my duties, but it was just like all the others I'd attended. The bench was set higher than the rest of the seats. The stained woodwork looked brilliant, with an impressive polished finish. Law books were scattered randomly and there was a big pile of files, presumably for this particular courtroom's day's cases. I was free to walk around at first. I saw my name on the top file. It unnerved me as I read the words *Regina vs Bunting*. It was a strange irony; there I was as one of the Queen's servants, now being taken to one of Her Majesty's courts.

I eventually went and sat down with my dad at the back of the court. He sat poised with a serious and slightly disbelieving look on his face. The courtroom slowly began to fill up as, one by one, various solicitors and court officials entered. Each extra person in the room added to the oppressive atmosphere for me. As was the norm, I heard whispers between the various solicitors. I tried desperately to hear what was being said about my case. At one point I heard the prosecuting solicitor say, 'There but for the grace of God go I.' I discovered later that he had once been a police officer.

I barely had time to dwell on this, however, as my assailant entered the court, with a smirk on his face. He looked as though he had just got out of bed, but I thought that would probably go in my favour. I hadn't seen him since the night of the incident and I turned my head so as to look away from him and I didn't look at him again. I was then called to take the stand in the box.

'All rise,' called the court usher as the magistrates entered. They were two respectable-looking men in their sixties and a lady who looked equally refined, of about the same age. I don't wish to sound disrespectful, but what did these people know about life on the streets of suburban Leeds, the kind of scene which a police officer has to deal with? The answer, realistically speaking, has to be *very little*.

The proceedings got underway.

'Are you Michael Edward Bunting?' asked the female magistrate sitting in the middle chair.

'Yes, Your Worships,' I said.

'And what is your current address, please?' she asked. I made eyes towards my solicitor but was unable to attract his attention.

'Your Worship, I am aware that there are members of the media in the room and the complainant who is a known offender is also present. As a serving police officer, could I have leave to write my address and pass it to you, please?'

I said this as respectfully as I could so as not to appear to be rude or pushy. It was obviously unanticipated. The magistrates had a look of shock and slight panic on their faces. They didn't seem to know the answer to my question. They looked down at the clerk, who was already flicking through a law book which appeared almost too heavy for him to pick up. My solicitor stood up and politely reaffirmed to the bench what I had said.

After about ten minutes' delay, the clerk stood up and looked across at me. He held the book open in front of him. 'PC Bunting, do you know what Section Twelve of the Contempt of Court Act states in relation to a defendant failing to give correct personal details to a court official?' he said, rather highhandedly. He probably knew that I wouldn't know. He worked in the court every day and it had taken *him* over ten minutes to find the answer. Anyway, I had no intention of not furnishing these details to the court, I just wanted to do it discreetly, but I knew that it was not in my interests to assert my point.

'I am not aware of the full contents of this section,' I said.

'It states that a defendant is in contempt if he or she fails to deliver to the open court his or her correct personal details. If you fail to give these details to the magistrates, then you will be dealt with accordingly under this act. Being a police officer affords you no protection.' His lack of empathy was pitiful. I looked at Mr Bell but he was unable to help. And so I gave my full address to the court. My assailant and the media now knew where I lived.

The magistrate turned to me once again. 'PC Bunting, you are charged with the following offence. That you did between the twenty-third and twenty-seventh of August 1997 assault John Patterson, thereby causing him actual bodily harm. Do you plead guilty or not guilty?'

I was puzzled why the charge wasn't more specific about the date in question. 'Not guilty, Your Worships.'

Mr Bell then made a submission that my case be committed to Crown Court for trial. The magistrates granted this and I was given unconditional bail until my next court appearance. I stood down from the box and walked straight across to Mr Bell. He apologised for the fact that I had been forced to give my address to the open court. He said that it was a matter of discretion for the clerk, but this particular one did not seem to have any. My more immediate problem was the members of the press, who were waiting outside the court building with their cameras at the ready. My solicitor told me that he would leave through the main entrance with my father, which gave me the opportunity to leave through the back door, unnoticed.

We arranged our next consultation and said our goodbyes and I arranged to meet Dad back at the car. I opened the back door and was immediately confronted by a lookout who quickly waved to one of his colleagues, who sprinted round with his camera swinging around his neck. I walked out and deliberately raised my head. I had nothing to hide and this was the best way of showing it. I walked with a complete loss of direction as the surprise of having my picture taken overrode any other thoughts in my mind. The photographer took shot after shot of me. He followed me all the way up Westgate, clicking away as he did so. Onlookers appeared bewildered. The fact that the man did not speak to me was surreal. When he had taken enough pictures, he stopped walking and pressed another button on his camera and I heard the film winding back. He nodded at me. He clearly didn't care about my feelings and the effect having my picture in the papers would have on my family. I found his conduct offensive. He walked off without saying a word, whilst the puzzled bystanders tried to work out what was going on. Once he had gone, I began to run. I just wanted to get to the car and go home. He was doing his job, but the consequences of it for me seemed rather unfair.

My dad was waiting in the car and I told him what had happened. But now my main concern was my house. I called my shift inspector and explained that my address had been disclosed to my assailant and to the media. He was as appalled as me. He assured me he would try to sort something out to help protect my home. He called me back and, later that day, a Home Office alarm was fitted into my house. (This is a silent alarm temporarily fitted into premises, which alerts the police control room immediately to any unauthorised entry.) Again, the hypocrisy was astounding, as the police tried to protect me from a situation which they themselves had caused.

Next morning, I rushed to the newsagent's in order to see what had been written about me in the local newspaper. Several of my friends had already telephoned me to warn me that they had heard the story on news bulletins on the radio. They also told me that my address had been broadcast. I felt as if the whole world was against me.

I entered the newsagent's and grabbed the paper. The article about me was on the front page, and I quickly scanned it to see if they had disclosed my address. Once again, I filled with irritation as I saw my street named in the article. I paid for the paper and left with it tucked under my arm. Despite promises from the journalists to Mr Bell that they wouldn't print it, it was there.

I spent the next few weeks in regular contact with my solicitor. He sent me various reports and witness statements which he needed my input on, so that he could form the best possible defence case. The most encouraging reports came in the form of the medical evidence from one of the force doctors. It had been established that my assailant had not sustained any injuries on the night of 24th August 1997. I thought this was enough in itself to cast the necessary doubt to secure my acquittal, given the fact that I had been charged with assault occasioning actual bodily harm, where injuries must be present in order to secure a conviction. It was becoming increasingly clear that the case against me was a tenuous one.

Time passed by and I spent each day meticulously reading the case notes. The whole affair was becoming my life and I soon began to realise that I needed another interest to occupy my mind, to prevent the negative effects of it all taking me over. I wanted to show West Yorkshire Police that I hadn't given up on the job I loved so much and even though I wasn't fit for any kind of police duties at this particular time, I decided to begin studying for my sergeant's examination. The previous year had seen only a 20 per cent success rate. I knew that, with the time I had at home, I could do a lot of studying. The exam was due the following March. Even though I anticipated that my trial would be finished by then, at least I would be able to show that I still cared, despite what had happened to me.

I spent four hours a day revising from law books and another four hours per day reading the notes on my trial. To give you an idea of how much paperwork there was in my case: piled up on the floor, the top of the papers would reach my waist. The whole thing was costing hundreds of thousands of pounds.

My next court appearance was as brief as the first. It came on 21st October 1998. It was simply a plea hearing, where I formally pleaded not guilty to the offence alleged. The matter could then be listed for the Crown Court. I had hoped that the trial would have been finished for Christmas, but Mr Bell told me that, due to the current waiting list of cases, it would almost certainly be after. More weeks went by and I had heard nothing. I had not even received a trial date, so the week before Christmas I contacted Mr Bell. He told me that he would chase the matter up after the festive period. It was about this time when I received a letter from the Chief Constable stating that I was due to be put on half pay at the end of January because I had been on sick leave for six months. How would I pay my mortgage? The pressure mounted.

Just like the previous one, that particular Christmas was ruined as my future hung in the balance. Christmas Day at Mum's was a rather subdued affair. It was also the first Christmas without Grandad, who had always spent the day with us.

The only little bit of joy that year had been the birth of my nephew, my sister and her husband's first child. Everything else seemed to have gone wrong and Christmas passed virtually unnoticed as we all hoped that things would be better for the family the following year. Once again, I was consumed with guilt, as Mum and Dad should have been allowed to enjoy their first Christmas with their grandchild. I was determined to make things up to them in the future and I hoped I'd have a trial date early in the New Year.

It didn't get off to a good start, though. My grandpa (my mum's father) became terminally ill with cancer. He lived 130 miles away from Leeds and my mum made regular trips to Northampton in order to care for him and my nan. She found herself torn between caring for them and being at home to help me. This was an added pressure in Mum's life, and she made the heartbreaking decision not to tell either Nan or Grandpa what was happening to me. It looked unlikely that Grandpa would be alive to see the end result, as his deterioration accelerated.

Her decision proved to be correct when, in January, I finally received details of my trial. It was to be held at Leeds Crown Court starting on 26th July 1999, almost two years from the date when the incident had occurred. It was unlikely that Grandpa would live this long, so we all decided to maintain the pretence for, Nan's sake as well.

The court date came as a psychological blow. I feared the long-term effects of not working as I waited for my trial. Like most people, I had my bills to pay, too, so I needed to return to work. I rang my inspector and we agreed that I could do some administrative duties for him at Holbeck Police Station. I didn't really feel up to it, but felt I had no choice.

My first morning back at work was harrowing. I had got my uniform out of the wardrobe the night before and just seeing it triggered tremendous anxiety. I couldn't imagine putting it on. I felt I was on the other side now. I was, after all, on bail on suspicion of assault. Although I didn't feel like a criminal, I didn't feel like a policeman any more, either. It was a horrible, lonely feeling.

The alarm clock went off at about seven, but as usual I was wide awake anyway. I had spent the last hour staring at my police shirt as it hung next to my bed. I really didn't think I could put it on. I felt sick. Why had the job treated me like this? I languidly clambered out of bed and into the shower. My hands shook and I couldn't seem to get warm even though the water was piping hot. The DJ on the radio was jovial and happy. I dried myself off and took my shirt from its hanger.

I pulled it on without thinking about it, turning away as I walked past the mirror. I didn't want to see myself as a policeman. This feeling went against all my instincts of being happy in the job that I had wanted to do all of my life; a job that was in my blood, passed down from Dad. This would all have been far easier for me to accept if I had known, deep in my heart, that I was guilty of the assault alleged. There wouldn't have been the constant battle in my mind and the overwhelming feeling of disloyalty. I think that if I'd received some kind of support from the higher-ranking officers in the force, then my mental state wouldn't have suffered in the way that it did. Good wishes from members of the public flooded in to me and that helped; it was this response from people that kept me going, as even complete strangers, who became aware of my situation, wished me well and expressed their disgust at the way my employer and the law were treating me.

As I entered the station, I deliberately kept my head down as I walked by the report room where friends and colleagues would be. Entering into a conversation in my normal working environment wasn't an appealing option and despite their best intentions, my friends couldn't appreciate what I'd been through over the past eighteen months, or how I was feeling.

I arrived at the office where I was due to work. Fortunately, it was at the other end of the building and much quieter than the operational end. Inspector Crabb, an intelligence officer, waited for me and greeted me warmly. He explained the exact nature of my role and, even though administrative duties were not my favourite, I was determined to pay back his goodwill with hard work. He left me alone in the office to rearrange over a thousand photographs of local villains into alphabetical order, and I felt I was now heading in the right direction.

I had been in the office a couple of hours and was feeling relatively relaxed. I needed to be out of the way of other people. Then something happened which I find hard to describe even now. I was sitting at my desk when a traffic warden popped his head around the door asking the whereabouts of Inspector Crabb. As he did so, his personal radio began to make a bleeping sound and a message was passed from the control room to officers on the ground. I don't know why, but my reaction to this was disturbing. I felt oppressed and the volume of the radio transmission seemed deafening. Everything else around me paled into insignificance and all I could focus on was the radio transmission. The beeps between the sentences seemed to get louder and louder. I think the traffic warden was still talking to me but I couldn't hear him. I just stared at his radio. I couldn't bear the sound as it reminded me of the job I should have been doing, so I closed my eyes and tried to block out the noise by humming to myself.

'Mick ... Mick ... are you okay?'

'No, I'm not,' I replied, as I brushed past him in an attempt to get out of the office away from the crushing sound of the radio. I ran to the toilets and there I remained until I'd calmed down. It took over half an hour as the noise of the beeps kept reverberating through my mind.

Eventually, I went back to the office where Inspector Crabb was waiting. He looked at me. 'Are you okay, Mick? You don't look so cracking.'

'Sorry about that, boss, I'll be okay.' Who was I trying convince?

'You shouldn't be here, lad,' he said, concerned.

'I'll be okay,' I replied.

'No, you won't. I'm taking you home straight away.'

I knew it was the only realistic solution: even the most straightforward of duties had proved to be too much for me. I knew at this point that even with the thoughts of my looming half pay, there was no way I was fit to work again until after the trial. My financial worries seemed less significant following the panic attack and I was glad that Inspector Crabb had seen it for himself. Putting me on half pay made economic sense and it seemed to me that this was the main criteria for his decision.

I arrived home, put my shirt in the washing basket and went

straight to bed feeling just about as low as I had ever done. I was beginning to distance myself emotionally from my house as it was becoming a real possibility that I was going to lose it. I was eating less and less and the stress was now taking hold of every part of my life.

Inspector Crabb made frequent visits to my home over the months leading up to my trial. He encouraged me to continue with my studies for the sergeant's examination and even though I was beginning to lose the desire to do anything connected with police work, I did it as a gesture of reciprocation to a man who was giving me much needed help and support.

In March 1999 I took the police promotion examination. I was reasonably happy with my performance, given the circumstances. To be honest, I wasn't too bothered about the outcome, but I had spent many hours revising and it would have been nice to be successful. The national pass rate that year was again under 20 per cent and so I was naturally pleased to find out I was in that minority. My celebrations were tempered, however, by grim thoughts of what the future held.

There was little to fill my days from then on and each merged into the next with uneventful boredom. I would rarely get dressed before lunchtime, as I wallowed in negative thoughts about the future. I visited my grandpa in Northampton as his condition had worsened considerably. On 23rd April 1999, his suffering ended when his fight against cancer was lost. We attended his funeral, just three months before the start of my trial. We had decided not to tell Nan about my situation and she remained completely unaware that I was facing a prosecution at court. I found her questions about how I was doing at work hard to deal with.

Just after the funeral, I received a letter from the chief inspector who had broken the news to me at the cricket match. The letter was in connection with the period of time I had been on sick leave. It was a pathetic attempt at trying to show that the force cared. It was a standard printed letter with my details handwritten in the blank spaces. The letter offered me the chance to go to the Force Occupational Health Unit in order to discuss my position with the personnel doctor. Little did they know or care that this letter had arrived over eighteen months too late. Nevertheless, I saw the doctor and he tried to help. It was clear from the consultation, however, that until the cause was removed, my symptoms would remain. Once again, I went home having achieved nothing to help my situation.

Spring arrived, days became longer and the weather improved from the miserable cold and wet we had been experiencing. The environmental radiance which nature produced in the form of beautiful flowers and singing birds began to mean more to me, as I had little else to focus on. Seeing wonderful sunsets making elegant patterns in the broken clouds came as a welcome break from my turmoil.

The consultations with Mr Bell continued and we meticulously prepared my case against the charge I faced. It was at this point that I met my barrister, Mr Stewart, for the first time. My immediate impressions of him, I have to say, were not favourable. On our very first meeting, he told me I would almost certainly face a lengthy prison sentence if convicted, but entering a plea of guilty from the outset would go a long way to prevent this from happening. The course of justice didn't seem important to him. I soon dispelled any thoughts in him of a guilty plea, telling him I was prepared to go to prison rather than plead guilty to an offence I hadn't committed.

We would discuss different points of my defence case on each visit and I felt reasonably optimistic as time went by. Spring gave way to summer. The final preparations were made and my defence case was ready. My best friend, Tim, and his wife, Cath, flew over from their home in the Isle of Man. They had taken time off work just to be present at the trial. They even planned a celebration party for me when my inevitable acquittal arrived. After two years, the waiting was finally over.

Chapter 8

Trial and Sentence

My dad came to pick me up early on the morning of 26th July 1999. Tim and Cath were already in the car. 'Well, this is it for real,' I said jovially as I got in. In his usual unruffled manner, my dad just remained quiet. Tim and Cath looked immaculate and a little nervous, too. The imminent end of the long wait generated a feeling of ease in me.

It was a glorious sunny morning and Leeds Crown Court was busy when we arrived. There was a long queue as the security guards searched everybody as they went in. Ironically, I used my warrant card to avoid being searched. I guess it was not apparent to them that I was, in fact, a defendant. We made our way to courtroom 12, listed as *Regina versus Bunting*. The judge in my case had been changed at very short notice, which I found odd. I was later informed that it was because he was overrunning.

Mr Bell and Mr Stewart arrived shortly afterwards and I told them about my concerns. They seemed equally perplexed but said that they were powerless to do anything. As was the norm, the outstanding administrative matters were attended to. With a firm handshake from them both, we entered the court-room and I was taken into custody and locked in the dock with a Group 4 security officer, who couldn't have prevented my escape if I had so chosen, even on one of her better days. She was quite old and looked unfit, but she was very pleasant to me and I think she realised I wasn't a risk. She commented about how sick she was to hear of the position I was in, then busied herself with her crossword puzzle book. The judge entered and the legal deliberations began before the jury was sworn in.

The morning was taken up with legal argument. Mr Stewart pleaded that the evidence was such that there was no case to answer and therefore the trial should not proceed. He argued that because I had been charged with assault occasioning actual bodily harm, the prosecution was obliged to prove that I had caused such a degree of injury to my assailant, as came within the legally defined parameters of the offence. He went on to say that my assailant had sustained no such injury and therefore the only course of action should be that no evidence was to be offered by the prosecution. Furthermore, he said, the offence of assault occasioning actual bodily harm could not be reduced by the court to one of common assault (i.e. assault without injury) because the law didn't allow it. He further argued that I could not be charged with common assault because that particular offence is *statute barred* after six months. That is to say that if action is not taken to charge or summons an alleged offender within six months of such an offence coming to light, no action may be taken. In any case, said Mr Stewart, the offence of common assault could only be tried at Magistrates Court, not at Crown Court, and the prosecution had told him they would not seek to pursue any offence other than that for which I was appearing.

However, the judge said he could impose a common assault charge at any point during the trial and that it could be tried by his court alongside the more serious offence of AOABH (assault occasioning actual bodily harm). He said that he would exercise his prerogative in this regard at any stage, if he thought it necessary, despite the fact that the prosecution barrister had already made it clear that it was not his intention to pursue such an offence. In all my time as a police officer, I had never experienced anything like this. It was clear to me that it was going to continue, whatever.

The trial was adjourned and I spoke with Mr Stewart. 'I'm afraid the judge doesn't seem to like me. We are going to be swimming against the tide on this one,' he told me.

At this stage, for the first time, I had a sinking feeling that things were going to go horribly wrong for me, despite the overwhelming evidence in my favour. And the trial hadn't even begun.

Eventually, it got under way, against my expectations it must be said. I knew that it would be hard to sit in the dock listening to the prosecution evidence. I didn't know what to do for the best. Should I look across at the jury from time to time? Would it show to them that I wasn't hiding anything, or would they see it as intimidation? I couldn't win and so I just sat there without moving, and without making any reaction or facial expressions to the evidence I heard against me.

I remember one of the witnesses said I had jumped up and

down on my assailant's head whilst he was on the floor. The witness went on to say that I then picked him up and started punching him in the face before discharging my CS spray at him. If this had been true, then I think the judge would have been considering a far more serious charge. Fortunately, the medical evidence would completely discredit this account and when the doctor was asked to make comment about it, his exact words were, 'I completely rule that out.'

Another witness admitted that a number of the prosecution witnesses had openly discussed the case with each other. One by one, the witnesses entered and one by one, conflicting tales were put forward. They seemed to be making a poor case against me. None of their stories was anywhere near to being consistent, despite the collaboration. Two of them described me as short and stocky with spiked blond hair. I'm actually 5 feet 10 inches, slim and have dark hair. I became slightly more at ease as I realised that the case against me included some people who clearly didn't like authority, and were seeing this as an opportunity to do a police officer a disservice.

The days passed and I sat and listened to the evidence being presented against me. I knew I would have my say in time and that I would take that opportunity to look the members of the jury in the eye and explain to them what was running through my mind at the time I kicked my assailant. Before I got my chance, however, the prosecution produced their 'ace card'.

Police Sergeant Milburn had been present at the incident and her evidence was deemed to be useful to the prosecution. I had seen her outside the courtroom talking with my assailant, which I had found to be unusual. He was a convicted criminal, after all. He'd been convicted of assaulting me. She told the court that she'd thought I'd kicked my assailant three times in the head with the same force as that used for kicking a football. Her account flew in the face of the medical evidence. Two doctors giving evidence said the fact that my assailant was uninjured clearly suggested that this level of force had not been used. One even went so far as to say that had the victim been kicked in the head repeatedly as claimed, he would have expected significant injuries to be present, including substantial haematoma. There were no such injuries. Whilst it was far from helpful, I didn't see it as a major problem because her account was so far-fetched that I knew the jury would dismiss it. Nevertheless, her evidence was regarded as being extremely valuable by the judge. He made her out to be the key witness in the case and informed the jury that her account should be highly regarded. I was worried by his handling of the jury who, as you would expect, sat and nodded to everything he said. It was at this point in the trial that the judge charged me with common assault in front of them. He also commended Milburn in open court as well.

After having heard four days of evidence against me, it was finally Mr Stewart's turn to put my case forward. Each day, Dad, Tim and Cath sat in court, listening intently. Some of my other friends came when they could, but my police friends had been told that they weren't allowed to support me so they had to stay away. The media was present every day and, every so often, a report on the progress of my trial would appear on the radio and in the newspapers. An article is rarely objective and cannot provide insight into the fear which I experienced during the attack; I found such coverage very frustrating and I was unable to read it at the time, as it was too much to handle.

My spirits were raised over the next few days, as the weight of evidence tipped in my favour. The best came in the form of a medical analysis from the force doctor. He stated that if any of the prosecution witness accounts had been accurate, then the level of injury to my assailant's head would have been significant. Not only was this good evidence to acquit me of the assault charge, but it also discredited the prosecution witness evidence. I thought that this in itself was enough to acquit me, because it did more than cast a doubt over the prosecution case. An eminent toxicologist said it was unlikely I could have formed the *mens rea* (criminal intent) for assault following my exposure to the CS spray and, in addition, the effects of the gas radically influenced normal powers of rationality. It was the job of the prosecution to prove that I had intended to do what I did and with this evidence, they would find it hard to do that.

Things were looking good for me, with additional evidence given by the eye specialist, who said that the only reason I didn't sustain a very serious injury was because of my naturally deep-set eyes. The dental evidence confirmed the high power of the punches my assailant had delivered to my head and face. I was convinced we were winning the jury over, but I still didn't dare to look at them.

After hearing the summing up, however, I left the courtroom expecting the worst. I remember thinking to myself that if I'd been a member of the jury, I would have convicted. He started with a potted history of the police service and even went back to the days of Sir Robert Peel. This bore no relevance to my case whatsoever. He'd also shrewdly informed the jury that I was a 'special' case and therefore should be viewed differently. He failed to highlight the parts of the evidence which were helpful to my case, like the medical facts and my state of mind. He focused on Sergeant Milburn's account and all but told the jury that she had given them the true version.

To make things worse, he failed to explain the law relating to self-defence, despite desperate pleas from Mr Stewart. There are numerous laws in England which allow a person to use reasonable force to protect him or herself from violence. There is another law allowing a police officer to use reasonable force to pursue a lawful arrest. My case was based on these laws relating to self-defence, yet the jury was not presented with this information when they went out for their deliberation. I felt it was a crucial flaw in the judge's summing up.

As a result, there was only one verdict which the jury could have arrived at following the hearing. Just one hour later, I was invited back to the courtroom where the jury delivered a verdict of not guilty to actual bodily harm, but guilty on the charge of common assault, the one the judge had added in the trial. The instant the verdict was announced, there were gasps in the courtroom comparable to a scene from a film. My dad remained still and expressionless. Cath looked across at me in the dock. I will never forget the look of disbelief in her face. The jury had just condemned me and even though they probably didn't realise the consequences of what they had just done, I did. But we have to abide by the judicial system which is, purportedly, the envy of the world. I can honestly say, hand on heart, that the system had got it wrong this time.

Once the courtroom had settled, the judge turned and looked at me quite menacingly. I knew he was not going to be easy on me. He started by saying that there was little doubt the assault on me had been unprovoked and brutal. If only he'd said that earlier. But then he stated that my response to the attack was equally brutal and was as a result of my uncontrolled anger. He said that the fact that I was a police officer made the offence worse and he had to be seen to take a hard stand on such intolerable behaviour. He told me he would defer sentence for five weeks so that pre-sentencing reports could be completed.

Just before he allowed me to go, he fired a last shot. 'I want you to be perfectly clear that when you come before me again in five weeks' time, I will be dealing with you by way of custody. That is the only appropriate sentence in this case. I want you and your family and friends to be aware that you will be leaving this courtroom through the back door downstairs, in handcuffs. You will be going to prison for some time.'

The jury gasped as they realised exactly what the guilty verdict signified. From their reaction, I thought that they hadn't understood the significance of the conviction. My worse nightmare had come true. I felt the trial was heading towards a conviction from the start. Even though I had been acquitted of the original charge, I wasn't surprised when the verdicts were read out.

I gave no reaction. The five weeks' bail would either give me time to mentally prepare for my prison sentence, or it would send me mad thinking about it. Either way, I had no choice in the matter. The date was fixed and I was allowed to leave the court. I stepped out of the dock and took my last look at the jury. They looked sorry, regretful even. I couldn't bring myself to bow to the judge. My dad followed me. As I walked out, I saw Sergeant Milburn standing with some of the witnesses. She seemed to be chatting with members of the prosecution case (including the wife of my assailant's co-accused). I was bemused by her behaviour. Sergeant Milburn was promoted just weeks after the trial.

Tim and Cath were waiting outside. Cath was crying. Her eyes were red and she was unable to control her tears. Tim's face was white. He seemed dazed by everything. Cath ran across and hugged me. Tim joined in.

'I guess we won't be having the piss-up after all,' I said, trying to lighten the moment. They shook their heads in dismay.

My dad's outward appearance didn't change, but I knew what this would be doing to him. We left the court building, trying to ignore the barrage of press, and went home.

A couple of days after my conviction, I was suspended from duty. Having been through the ordeal of the court trial, I would have to face a disciplinary hearing at some point in the future. My career as a police officer would be decided at the hearing, but I knew it was a long way off. I also knew there were officers serving in the force with convictions of common assault and so I tried to remain positive. My main concern was the threat of a prison sentence, which was almost certain to happen.

The five weeks leading up to my sentencing hearing were tortuous. I spent the whole of the time trying to imagine my future life in prison. I tried to keep optimistic by telling myself that the judge had done this just to frighten me and that he would seek an alternative method of punishment upon my return to court. I knew in my heart of hearts, though, that this was unlikely. He wasn't bluffing; I was going to prison.

Tuesday, 7th September 1999, was the night before sentencing and ironically my 26th birthday, too. I was determined to have a good time and so I invited a few friends to my local pub, the Old Griffin Head at Gildersome. Once again, Tim and Cath made the journey from the Isle of Man. My mum and dad came, too, but both were subdued. I tried to put a brave face on things and enjoy a birthday drink with my friends. All things considered, it was actually a good night. When the bell rang for time, the enjoyment ended and the realisation of where I would be in just twenty-four hours' time hit me hard. I went home with little hope. I can't put into words exactly how I felt by the end of the night, but it was an overwhelming feeling of being out of control, which frightened me.

As I got out of bed on Wednesday, 8th September, I prayed the judge would show mercy on me. I waited for Dad to arrive; and this time Mum was coming to court, too. She knew what to expect, but she couldn't leave her son to face going to prison alone. We left and I locked the door to my house. It was a very strange feeling not knowing when I would be entering it again.

Tim and Cath were already at court when we arrived. Cath hugged me and Tim simply put his hand on my back. Mr Bell and Mr Stewart arrived and told me to prepare for the worst. How does a policeman prepare to go to prison?

My name was called out and Tim and Cath decided not to come in. Mum and Dad followed me in and we already knew that too many supporters wouldn't be appreciated by this judge. He had taken the notion of a public trial away from my hearing, of that there was no doubt.

We had our last embrace. 'It'll take more than this to finish me,' I said. 'Thanks for everything and I'll see you when I'm out,' I whispered. They didn't reply. They didn't need to.

'We love you,' Mum said. She was remarkably in control.

We entered the courtroom and I was immediately placed in the dock. Security officers surrounded me. The judge entered and the short proceeding began in which Mr Stewart put evidence of mitigation to him. He also read a number of letters from people who had provided character references for me, one of which was a letter of my good character written by a magistrate. He, a long-standing family friend, and his wife, a vicar, made a compelling case that custody was not the appropriate way of dealing with me.

The judge was unaffected. Once again, he turned to me. He made comment on my previous character, stating that he didn't doubt that I was a good citizen. He said I had achieved my life-long ambition by following in my father's footsteps into the police service and that I had even been given my father's old collar number, 451. However, he went on to say that the offence was a serious one which could only be dealt with by way of a prison sentence. He sentenced me to four months' imprisonment, almost the maximum sentence available for this offence.

I was too shocked to do or say anything, but there was no way I would let him see a reaction. I looked straight at him, but he didn't look back. I was incensed by this man. I had dealt with dozens of common assaults as a police officer and never known anyone get prison before. Here I was with almost the maximum. I turned to one of the Group 4 security officers. She smiled sympathetically and led me out of the dock through the back doors. I *was* going to prison.

Part II

Prisoner DK 8639
Michael Bunting

Chapter 9

My Mate Tony

8th September 1999 (continuation from 'The Beginning')

Minutes in prison really did feel like hours, and hours like days. With nothing to do for weeks at a time, some prisoners are unable to cope. Many suicides in prison are related to depression and boredom, not to mistreatment, which is a commonly held belief. It can lead even the most stable person to contemplate suicide. I know this, I've been there. The mental torment that goes on when you're locked in a cell is hard to describe, but I'll try.

I remember I had only been in my cell at Armley for about four hours. After the shock of receiving my sentence had subsided, I realised that there would be no more moves to other cells and therefore the attention from prison officers would be reduced. In fact, no one returned to my cell for the remainder of the day, apart from a prisoner who brought me a meal at teatime. I gathered that word had still not got around that I was a policeman, because he was quite friendly towards me. He asked how I was and told me that the screws would have me on a wing as soon as I was fit. He obviously thought I was suicidal or something. I feared that his ignorance of the real reason I was there would be short-lived and the drama would soon begin. As he put the plate on my hatch, his dirty thumb and finger went into the food.

The meal consisted of sausages, baked beans and mashed potato and it came on a paper plate with a plastic knife and fork. I was given a cup with some hot water in it. Upon my arrival at the prison, I had been given a sachet containing two tea bags and two little wrapped squares of butter. I was quite thirsty and so I carefully opened the sachet and placed one of my tea bags in the hot water. This bothered me as I realised that I couldn't even have a cup of tea when I wanted one. What did I expect, though? I was in prison. Never in my life had I anticipated being in this position.

I wasn't hungry, which was fortunate really as I eyed up the food on my plate. The beans had a crusted layer on top of them and had moulded together, as they had obviously been heated in the microwave and then left for some time. The lumps in the potato were the size of my fingernails. The sausages leaked fat from each end. I picked up my fork and prodded one of them. As I pushed it deeper into the middle, both ends of the sausage came up off the plate into a 'V' shape. The fork wouldn't penetrate the tough skin. More fat oozed out of the ends. It was disgusting. I didn't even try a single mouthful. I placed the plate back onto the cell hatch hoping that it wouldn't be too long before the prisoner would return to collect it.

I carefully stirred my tea with my little finger. The water was only lukewarm by now, anyway. I cradled the plastic cup with both hands as I sat on my bed and took small sips from it. It had an unfamiliar flavour, a sort of perfumed taste. It wasn't pleasant, but I managed to drink about a third of the cup. I placed it on the cell hatch with the plate, looked at the food again and sighed, then got back on my bed and stared at the same piece of ceiling.

I had spent the whole of my first afternoon in prison dreading the arrival of dusk, as the thought of actually getting undressed and going to bed in this establishment scared me: it would confirm that I wasn't going home and even though I'd lost all hope of getting out, I didn't relish spending the night with a thousand rapists, drug dealers, murderers and the like. However, another part of me wanted the time to pass as quickly as possible, for obvious reasons. These contrasting thoughts actually had the effect of making the time pass at snail-pace. It was painful.

The same prisoner came to collect my plate and cup. He looked at the untouched food and then made eye contact with me through the hatch, as I lay motionless on my bed. 'Not up to much is it, Bunting?' he said. How dare he refer to me as 'Bunting,' I thought. 'You'll get used to it. It usually takes about a week. When you're fucking starving, it looks superb,' he continued.

'Thanks, mate,' I replied, as I tried to establish a pretentious camaraderie for my own protection. I knew it wouldn't last, but the longer I could maintain it, the less time I'd have to endure the 'policeman in prison' treatment. I began to think of the prisoners' reaction to me once they'd realised I'd been lying to them. Would this make it worse? Should I tell them now and get it over with? I have to be honest, it was irrelevant as I didn't have the courage to do that.

My cell overlooked the exercise square, which was surrounded by high walls. Litter swirled around in the wind and landed in a heap in one corner. It was a depressing sight and one that, if I had allowed it to, could quite easily have made me lose hope at a very early stage in my sentence. I watched the sun sink beneath the building opposite my cell. The exercise square filled with darkness in a matter of minutes and I noticed a number of cells light up across the yard. I saw prisoners as they forced their heads right up to the bars on the window. They began something which I would learn was a nightly ritual. Once they had been locked in their cells for the night, they would spend hours, and I mean hours, shouting to each other between cells. They would talk about nothing, or what seemed like nothing to me, anyway. Every so often it would go completely quiet. I welcomed this, as the solidarity between the inmates felt threatening to me. My stomach would sink as the next 'Oi!' bellowed from a nearby cell. It would spark off a conversation that, with twenty or thirty hardened inmates participating, sounded extremely harrowing.

Occasionally, if one of the prisoners crossed another, a threat would be given out, usually quite a nasty one. Something as innocent as boasting about having a cigarette to smoke for the night could trigger a torrent of dreadful intimidation. Having been a police officer for several years, you might think I'd have been ready for this, but nothing can prepare you for something as bad as this when you actually have to live in it. I was beginning to realise just how naive I really was.

It got darker. The light in my cell came on. The bulb was faulty and the light flickered annoyingly. I didn't dare ask to have it looked at. There was no one to ask, anyway. The jangling of keys in the corridor was getting less and less frequent and I assumed that the nightshift was coming on duty. If the prison service was anything like the police, then there would only be a skeleton staff. I had no idea what the time was, so my next dilemma was to decide when to go to bed. This may sound like a strange thing to say, but when you've spent all day in a cell and you have no idea of time or when you are next going to have human contact, deciding on the right time to actually take off your clothes and get under the covers isn't easy. Should I wait until I was tired, or until it had been dark for a few hours?

My mind was beginning to race so I got onto my bed. I knew that I wouldn't see anyone again until the morning and if I did, then it would be a bonus. Tony Adam's biography was right next to me as I needed it close. I didn't want to start reading it yet, as an unread book in my cell was something to be cherished, but it was holding me together. Reading it was something positive to do in the future and it was the one and only thing in my life that I had control of. If I finished reading it, then I would lose this feeling. I put my hand over it and closed my eyes, as the flickering light was starting to make me feel nauseous.

I didn't allow myself to fall asleep, though. The thought of waking up in the early hours scared me. I don't really know why, though, because the only difference between night and day in prison is that at night it's dark, and by day it's light. Everything else is the same. There's nothing to do, twenty-four hours a day, and so whatever time I woke up, the boredom would strike instantly.

I wanted to keep my mind active in order to keep awake. It may seem silly, but the first thing I did was to try to remember all the pupils' names who were in my first ever class at infant school. It was over twenty years ago, and therefore took some doing, but it was something I could do without any resources whatsoever; I didn't even need light. I tried to think of other equally simple pastimes.

Occasionally, I would be interrupted by more shouting from prisoners. 'Dave!' bellowed a hard voice. 'Dave, I know you can fucking hear me.'

There was a hostile tone to the man's voice. I got off my bed and peered out through the bars into the yard. It was impossible to tell who it was, because by now there were literally hundreds of prisoners with their faces up to the bars in their cell windows. 'Dave,' he persisted. 'Dave, I know you can hear this. I'm gonna fuck your mother when I'm out of here tomorrow. There's fuck all you can do about it. She's a fucking slag, and I'm gonna fuck her. Do you hear me Dave, you fucking wanker?'

I began to walk up and down the length of my cell. I was becoming increasingly frustrated with not knowing the time. It was now completely dark outside so I guessed it was around nine or ten o'clock. It was still very quiet in the corridor. The prison officers had probably settled down in their office for the night and would only be seen or heard on the corridor when doing their mandatory one-hour checks. Every so often I would hear the man in the next cell to me shouting. I gathered, by the bizarre things he was saying, that he was in the hospital wing because of mental health reasons. He was talking as if he had pet animals in his cell.

'Butler, shut the fuck up,' came the command from the prisoner in the opposite cell. At this, I heard a loud bang from Butler as if he'd suddenly jumped up from his bed.

'Take your hands off me!' Butler shouted. 'Rape ... rape!' he continued. Again, I knew this was fictitious because it was one man to a cell. His voice was strangely high-pitched yet it didn't lack aggression or volume. His outburst triggered some immediate attention from the prison officers, and the sound of jangling keys approached. I watched through my cell hatch as they ambled past.

'Butler, go to sleep,' said one of the officers.

'Argh!' he screamed. 'Get away from me. I know what you're trying to do. Get off! Get off!'

'Just settle down, or you'll be having one of your injections and you don't want that again, do you?'

'Don't care! Do what you like to me ... Rape!' he screamed.

The prison officers were obviously familiar with his outbursts and once they had seen that Butler was okay, they casually walked back, seemingly quite amused. They peered into my cell as they walked past. 'You okay, Bunting?'

'Yes thanks. Ummmm ... what time is it?'

'Bed time,' came the distant reply from down the corridor.

I sat on my bed. 'Wankers,' I muttered to myself.

I decided the time had come to start to read my book, despite the flickering light. I began by reading the comments on the back page. The very first words, written by Tony Adams himself, were the most inspiring I'd ever read. *Prison had told me I was a survivor.*

I focused on them and read them over and over again. It was as if the book had been written just for me. Tony Adams had served a prison sentence for a driving-related offence. If you've never been to prison, you probably wouldn't fully understand exactly what Tony Adams meant, but *I* did and I still do. I didn't feel quite so alone now, knowing that somebody as successful as Tony Adams had felt as desperate as I was now feeling. I thought back to the 1998 World Cup quarter-final in France, in which England played Argentina in a thrilling game. I thought England had deserved to win. The player who stood out in that game for his determination, fitness, contribution, leadership and, most importantly, passion was Tony Adams. I took comfort from the fact that this brilliant performance took place after his prison sentence. I had seen Tony Adams rise to the heights of captaining his country, the highest honour for a footballer. Thanks to his book, I believed that when I was eventually released from prison, there was hope. For the first time, I began to think of my future. I opened the book and began to read.

For about the next hour or so, I lost myself in another world. That's the beauty of reading, I suppose. I purposely read very slowly so that the book would last for as long as possible, but I knew it would only be a matter of time before I would be re-reading the back page again. On this particular night, however, I only read the first chapter and I wouldn't allow myself to read any more until the following day. The constant interruptions I'd had from shouting in the other cells had actually helped me to read more slowly than normal.

I put the book on the floor, fanned open on the page that I was up to. I gazed around, realising that the time had come to go to bed but delaying removing my clothes for as long as possible. I read some more of the graffiti on my cell walls. I really wanted to sign my name and protest my innocence as a lot of other prisoners had done on the back of the cell door, but I resisted. I would never allow myself to be drawn into the criminal's way. I must admit, though, it was tempting.

Once again, the feelings of injustice surfaced, but I tried to push the thoughts aside. I collected my senses and washed my face with freezing cold water in the stained tin sink, then used the toilet which was made of the same metal. I had to close my eyes as I did so, because it was so filthy it made me feel sick again. There were pieces of excrement up the inside of the toilet. It had obviously only ever had a superficial clean, if any at all.

After that, I brushed my teeth. The prison issue toothbrush was inadequate, as the head was very small and the handle would bend even when I applied just the slightest pressure. I had been given a tiny tube of toothpaste when I arrived in my cell, probably enough to last four or five days. I had been told that I wouldn't be issued with another one for seven days so used just a minuscule globule of paste. I had always looked after my teeth, and the fact that I wasn't being allowed to take proper care of them annoyed me. I slid my tongue over my damaged tooth, the one broken during the assault. It had been repaired but it still didn't feel right. It seemed to magnify the injustice of my prison sentence, and this escalated my anger at the judiciary.

I diverted my mind from thinking this way, as I knew that it wasn't productive. I felt my heart begin to beat faster and harder in my chest. This wasn't healthy. My attention was then caught by a big spider, which ran across the bare floor of my cell. I began to search for other creatures. I looked under my bed but, fortunately, all I found was dust and dirt. The previous occupant had not excelled in personal hygiene, given the state of the floor and the toilet. I pulled the bed covers down to check inside my bed. Even though they smelt clean, there were a number of stains of varying colours. I rearranged them on the bed to make all the stains face outwards so I was effectively getting into a clean bed.

Amazingly, the next thing I heard was the sound of my plastic cutlery being placed on the cell hatch by the same prisoner as before. The night had passed. I opened my eyes and was immediately struck by a terrible sinking feeling as I realised exactly where I was. The prisoner looked at me with a fierce stare: different from how he'd been before. Had he found out I was a policeman?

'Thanks,' I said. He just screwed up his face and walked away, making as much noise as he could with the trolley. I knew it was too early for the newspapers to be in circulation so if he did know, how had he found out? What was going to happen to me now?

I assumed breakfast was always served at about half past seven, so I looked out of my cell window and made a note of the position of the sun. This would help to estimate the time on subsequent days. Not knowing the time had been unpleasant and I wanted to avoid this happening again. I would note the position of the sun at each mealtime in order to have three accurate reference points from which to gauge the time.

I took my cutlery and waited for my food. Even though I

had no intention of eating it, its arrival at my cell was an event I could focus on in the future and it kept my mind relatively active. I sat on the fragile wooden chair, which was pushed under an equally flimsy looking writing table. My book was still fanned open on the floor next to my bed. I thought it would be an achievement if I could resist touching it until after lunchtime. I doubted that I'd manage it, though.

I began to worry. Who knew about me? I knew I couldn't drop my guard now until the day I left prison. I anticipated my first beating in the shower block, trying to imagine what the prisoners would do to a policeman when they got the chance. I shuddered. I felt dirty and I was in need of a shower, but if offered the opportunity, I would refuse out of fear. Remaining dirty was by far the better option, but how long could I go?

The same feeling of desperation and helplessness I'd had the previous day ensued. I urinated in the dirty tin toilet. My urine was dark yellow, concerning me that I was dehydrated. The first signs of prison life being detrimental to my health had started and I'd only been in for a day. I buried my hand deep into my jumper sleeve and pressed the flush button. A violent burst of water shot down the side of toilet for about two seconds and that was it. I tried to flush again, but it wouldn't this time. I guess the water was rationed to prevent deliberate flooding attempts.

I walked back to my window and gazed at some pigeons on the ground in the exercise yard. Then, hearing a loud bang on my hatch, I turned round to find that breakfast had arrived. It wasn't the same prisoner this time. This one's facial expression was of pure indifference. The not knowing was beginning to perturb me. If he did know that I was a policeman, then surely my food would have been tampered with?

'Thanks,' I said softly. He didn't change his expression and walked off up the wing, dragging another trolley, which was equally loud, behind him.

I took the plate and looked at what was on it. There were scrambled eggs which looked like shiny plastic and two soggy pieces of toast which had been soaked by the liquid leaking out of the eggs. It looked as unappetising as the previous night's meal and so, using the plastic knife, I simply pushed all the food to one side of the plate as a gesture that I had at least tried to eat something, put it back on my hatch and lay on my bed. The waiting game began again. I didn't know what I was waiting for, but, nevertheless, I was waiting. I listened to the different noises coming from the corridor: shouts of desperate prisoners wanting to get out of their cell, the banging of food trolleys, stiff brush heads sweeping the floor, running water in the shower block, a distant radio and, of course, the ever-present jangling of the keys.

Yet another prisoner removed my breakfast. He was hard-featured and stared right through me as he collected the plate. I had given up trying to work out whether or not it was known who I was. I was too busy walking up and down my cell as part of my new ploy to pass the crawling time. I'd decided I needed two separate routines – one for daytime, one for night time. Lingering in my cell for twenty-four hours a day without a routine would be dangerous and it would only be a matter of days before it became intolerable. With a good knowledge of personal fitness, I knew a lot of different exercises where I needed no more than a wall and a floor. Of course, I had both of these things. I decided to spend approximately one hour walking up and down the length of my cell. This would keep my legs active, and keep my muscular atrophy to a minimum. Atrophy is common amongst prisoners who are kept in solitary confinement for long periods and is used to describe conditions when muscles decrease in volume because of reduced use.

After the hour or so had elapsed, I would then reward myself by reading four pages of my book. I would read as slowly as possible and at times I'd try to memorise whole paragraphs. I'd then follow the reading with about half an hour of hard physical exercise, including press-ups, sit-ups, dorsal raises and tricep dips, using the bed. I'd rinse my face in the sink and start the process again, walking up and down my cell for an hour and so on. I had no real way of knowing if my timings were accurate, but I guessed as best I could. After the anguish of my first day in prison, I knew that this routine was my only chance of keeping my wits together. I knew that at some point I would be given some writing paper and envelopes so that I could send letters to my family and friends and I planned to incorporate writing these letters into my daily routine. My night routine was far simpler; I would simply concentrate on thinking ahead to my future when I got out of prison.

Time would tell whether this plan would work, but if the morning of my second day in prison was anything to go by, then it wouldn't. I had meticulously gone through a complete cycle of my daily routine. I was feeling quite pleased with myself until I heard a prison officer shout, 'It's nine o'clock. Get ready for your showers in the next five minutes, please.' This shattered my feeling of achievement – I'd thought that it was at least eleven o'clock. My perception of time had gone astray within just one day of being inside. I aborted my routine, sat on my bed and buried my head in my hands. I was becoming more desperate.

I needed to find out exactly what would be happening to me and began to think of my family, especially my mum, as she wasn't well. If only I could have a ten-second phone call to let her know I was alright, I thought. Even getting out of my cell to make a call would be risky, but there was no way on earth that I wasn't going to ring my mum and dad. The thought of getting a chance to speak to them cheered me up. And then I heard a most welcome sound. It served as an immediate release to all my desperation. I felt as though the world had suddenly remembered me. It was the sound of the prison officer's key turning in my cell door lock. The door creaked loudly as it slowly opened.

The prison officer standing there was young and very smart. His face was strikingly benign and the fixtures on his epaulettes suggested that he was quite high in rank, yet I didn't feel that he was displaying any show of authority over me. He left the bolt out and entered my cell. (Prison officers always leave the bolt out so that the prisoner can't shut the door and trap the officer in the cell with them.)

He pointed to the lock. 'Sorry, we have to do that with 'em all. I know you're not a problem, it's just procedure.'

'No problem at all,' I said. 'I understand.'

'How are you?' he asked.

'Not too good, to be honest. I'm finding it hard being in this bloody cell all the time.'

'You know we can't let you out with the others, don't you?' he said. 'They'd kill you in here.'

'Oh, I know, but will I get out at all? I'm going mad.'

'I'll try to get you ten minutes when we have our meal break.

You can come and sit with us. We can't give you much more than that. If we give anyone favourable treatment, it just kicks off. We all think it stinks, you being in here locked up. We see what these bastards are like when they kick off.'

'I know, but I've got to get on with this now. I'm still finding it hard to believe I got time for common assault.'

Although our conversation was brief, Senior Officer Butt had raised my morale. I now had a point of contact on the wing; at least for the times he was on duty, anyway. He gave me my canteen list and told me how much I was allowed to spend. The prisoners' canteen was a list of items on which they could spend their weekly money. It ranged from tobacco, phone cards, biscuits, stationery to a whole host of other things; in fact, just about anything you could imagine buying from the corner shop. I only had about £5 to spend. I wrote down my order straight away: two phone cards at £2 each and some stamps. Buying biscuits and the like didn't even cross my mind; I was now equipped to communicate and that was all that mattered.

I lay on my bed feeling a little better than I had done earlier, but the feeling was quickly overpowered by frustration as I realised that I hadn't asked SO Butt the most important question of all: did the inmates know who I was?

'You idiot,' I mumbled to myself. 'You stupid idiot.' And then I realised that I had also missed my opportunity to ask for some library books as well. I wanted to cry. The muscles in my face twitched involuntarily as tears tried to force their way out. I shut my eyes tight, rubbed them and took a deep breath; I was not going to cry for anyone. I forced myself off the bed and began walking around my cell again.

I started repeating the lyrics to one of my favourite songs;

written by Tupac Shakur. The lyrics were most apt for my circumstances as he had written them about prison life in one of America's gaols. I must have looked mad to anyone walking past as I shouted the same line of the song repeatedly.

These are not the most intellectually challenging lyrics but I tell you, it feels good to say them to yourself when you *really* do think you are going out of your mind. I can imagine how I must have seemed to someone walking past. After some minutes, SO Butt poked his head through the hatch. He just smiled at me in a way that made me realise he knew my game and understood what I was going through. I had found a friend. He didn't stay long enough for me to ask him my questions, but suddenly I was doing fine in my own little world. I continued reciting the Tupac lyrics. The cutlery eventually arrived. I took this as another achievement – I'd managed to get through another half day. I had now been in prison over twenty-four hours and I profoundly hoped that the worst was over.

And then, to my delight and surprise, the key went into my door again. It was SO Butt. He told me to sit down on my bed. He remained on his feet. I looked up at him.

'Good news for you, Mick,' he said.

'Didn't know you got that in here,' I replied wryly. I knew he'd take it as intended.

'You don't. You're getting out. You've got a Category D prison. North Sea Camp at Lincoln.'

A surge of energy frenzied up my entire body and, in an instant, everything seemed different and better. The excitement of the news hit me as I tried to tell myself that my nightmare in Armley was coming to an end. I began to shake almost immediately as I tried to talk. 'What's that like?' I enquired.

'Better than here. You'll be mixing with the other inmates,

but they'll not know you're a copper. You'll be out of your cell, though, and that's the main thing. I think they've got you a job picking potatoes in the fields.'

'Oh, brilliant!' I shouted and this time I wasn't being facetious. The thought of being allowed out of my cell for sustained periods was more than enough to compensate for the not so pleasant thought of picking potatoes all day.

'You'll be going tomorrow, Friday,' he said. 'There's a few from 'ere going, so you're gonna have to have your story ready for 'em in the sweat box.'

'I will. Thanks a lot,' I said, 'Do they know about me yet?'

'Not that I'm aware of. That's why we want you out of 'ere before they do find out, because you're all over the papers today, so it won't be long until they do know. Then we'll all 'ave problems.'

I didn't properly digest what he told me about the newspapers, as the elation of getting out of Armley suppressed any other emotion, including, for a short time at least, my fear. The prisoners would know who I was before nightfall, because super-enhanced prisoners were allowed to read the evening paper as a privilege. SO Butt left my cell as my food was placed on the hatch. One more meal to go, and then it would be nearly bedtime. I began to feel better.

I didn't pick up my plate this time; I'd given up trying to show willing. The stench of the food was abhorrent. There was, however, an orange and so I took it and put it next to my sink to save it for later. I now had a food supply in my cell and that made me feel a little bit more secure. Bit by bit, things were becoming more bearable. Also, my book didn't have to last quite so long now, as I'd be working in the potato fields all day and so occupying my time wouldn't be such a major task. It was the middle of the day, I had most of my book to read and I knew I was leaving tomorrow. I lay on my bed, opened my book and began to read more about Tony Adams, who had become my cellmate. I had a big smile on my face. This time tomorrow I would be out of here! My first proper signs of hope had arrived.

Chapter 10

Silver Service

My second afternoon in prison should have been a lot easier, as I had the luxury of unlimited reading of my book and I knew that I'd be moving on the following day. If only matters in prison were so simple.

I had been reading for about an hour or so and was still feeling relatively upbeat. The usual noises were evident, but I'd already learned to ignore them. Occasionally, I would get up and walk around my cell, because I wanted to and not because I had to pass the time. It was an indulgence, which meant a lot to me, and, compared to the previous day, I was beginning to cope quite well with my incarceration. I was drawing immense comfort from the smaller things in life, an essential skill that you need to develop in prison. Without it, you have no chance.

I looked down out of my window. Half a dozen or so prisoners in bright green overalls walked around the exercise yard with huge black bin liners. Occasionally, one of them would bend over and pick up a piece of litter, swirling wildly in the wind. None of the men showed any enthusiasm and they sauntered around the square lethargically. Their main concern seemed to be rolling up their cigarettes in Rizla papers. They were the epitome of institutionalisation, seemingly resigned to their fate of a life in prison. I could never be like that, I thought; I'd kill myself before it happened. Big puffs of smoke came blowing out of their mouths in turn. The pleasure they got from smoking was obvious, as they took long, deep drags on the cigarettes. Their lives seemed to me to be completely empty, as they robotically performed their worthless tasks. For the first time in my life, I began to think about the effects that this treatment would have on them. How could they be expected to offer society anything at all, once they were released? I realised they were trapped in the cycle of a fragmented life between prison and the outside. I was more fortunate. I had something positive to get out for: my family, my friends, my home, and a *future*, which I was determined to build as soon as I was released.

I began to pace up and down again, mumbling the lyrics to the Tupac Shakur song. This time, I wasn't feeling quite so desperate, but the song still had therapeutic qualities, which I was well in need of, despite my improvement from the previous day. There are never good moments in prison, but if you go from feeling completely depressed and dejected to just about able to cope, then you are on a good day. I got back onto my bed and looked at the offensive drawing on my trouser leg. It made me chuckle. I felt less angry towards the 'artist' than I had when I first saw it, as I now knew how bored he must have been to resort to drawing it. Nevertheless, I crossed my legs so as to cover up the illustration, and began the luxury of reading yet again.

I had barely read a page when the sound of the key turning the lock stopped me. I sprung on to my feet as SO Butt entered my cell. 'You're looking a bit better,' he said.

'I'm chuffed about my move, to be honest,' I replied.

'Ah,' he said, grimacing. I knew from his face that there was bad news. There was an immediate reaction within me. I had allowed my emotional guard to drop and this created an intense feeling of utter disenchantment. My body seemed to tense up and I braced myself for what he had to say. 'It's not good news,' he continued.

I knew straight away what this meant and the thought of more time at Armley petrified me. My new-found coping strategies were shattered in an instant. They had been so tenuous. I fell to my knees, unable to move for that moment. My heart began beating hard. I looked up at him.

'What?' I asked, already knowing what was to come.

'They think it's a risk sending you with the other prisoners. Everybody knows in here now, so I think they're gonna play it safe and look to get you somewhere else, maybe next week.'

Each word sent a wave of fear up my spine and my mouth went dry. I tried to think of a way to alter what was happening to me, but I couldn't. I couldn't face more time in Armley and I held my head in my hands.

'Please,' I begged. 'I can't do it. I can't.'

I dug my dirty fingernails into my head and sank to the floor.

SO Butt grabbed me under both arms and told me to get on my feet. The strength in my legs had gone, so I dropped straight back down again, looking up at SO Butt as I did so.

'I'm really sorry about this, Mick, I am. I'll keep you informed, but it's not looking good for tomorrow.'

He patted me on the back and left, slamming the door shut as he did so. I jumped as it reverberated down the corridor. Alone, on my knees in a prison cell with absolutely no hope for the future, I stayed in the same position for the next hour. My body shook violently, and my jaw seemed to lock tight shut. I felt very cold. I felt my strength drain away and desperation take its place. I hadn't thought it could get any worse in there, but it just had.

The following few hours are quite a blur to me. What I do remember is spending a lot of time with my head down the toilet, retching. There was nothing in my stomach to come up, which made it all the more painful. Eventually, the spasms subsided and my stomach felt as if it had been trampled on. I was in severe pain. Every time I coughed or sneezed, I would double over, cradling my belly. The retching had drained my energy. I knew I would need to start eating again soon or else I'd be in real trouble. I carefully lowered myself onto my bed and tried to rest. My heart was pounding; my fingers and toes felt ice cold and my teeth were grinding together. It hadn't even reached evening yet, but I got into bed. I couldn't focus on anything positive as I lay there and began the process of simply existing rather than living.

I actually managed to sleep through until teatime. Ironically,

Take that smile off your face, Bunting!"   (1)

It was, I have to say not as I expected, but I was here at last. I'd waited all my life for this moment and now here I was finally in my brand new uniform, standing in the freezing cold with ten other new recruits. I certainly wasn't smiling.

He stood tall. He was a big man. His smart appearance dominated. Every step he took echoed around the square. I knew that I would have to look like this one day. I still dare not move. I was intimidated by his presence but this feeling temporarily subsided to relief as occasionally Sergeant Wright would allow his emotionless face show a smile.

He walked behind the line that I was standing in. He went out of sight and I shut my eyes tight. I felt his stick hit the top of my helmet. The noise in my head was deafening. "STOP SMILING" he bellowed.

I couldn't understand this. I tried not to move but I felt my helmet coming from my head. I instinctively tried to catch it.

"Bunting. Stand still." His voice was penetrating. My helmet bounced on the floor in a puddle. It would be spotless again by tomorrow. I knew it would have to be.

My career in the Police Service had begun.
—— " —— " ——
I entered my room. The initial training period would be residential. One bed, one wardrobe

The drawings I did in my prison cell to pass the lonely hours.

A proud moment at my passing-out parade in September, 1993. (I'm standing directly in front of the female officer.)

HMP Armley, Leeds: 'Home' for the first part of my sentence.

Dad and me before his retirement in 1995.

It was always my childhood dream to follow Dad's foot-steps into the police service.

Dad and me.

With Mum, Dad, Grandma and Grandad as I am sworn into the police service by the magistrate.

Meeting Rachel has helped to give me some perspective on my past.

I'd had a nice dream of life on the outside. Even though this temporary escape from prison life had been a blessing, it made the realisation of where I was when I awoke much worse. The noisy trolley drew closer to my cell. My first confrontation with a prisoner who knew I was a policeman was about to take place. I heard him have a brief conversation with each inmate at their hatch as he left their cutlery for tea. Each time he spoke, I heard a little laugh and even though I didn't know what was being said, I felt extremely isolated, vulnerable and afraid. My emotions had had a hard enough battering already. My resistance was low. I started retching again. I got down onto my knees and held my head over the toilet and closed my eyes. I couldn't bear to look at the filth in it. The trolley stopped outside my cell door. I heard the sound of the cutlery on my hatch and I heard the same laugh again. It was at me. But he said nothing and carried on up the corridor.

I tried to stand, but my legs felt too weak so I crawled to my bed where I was just about able to climb up and lie down. I was beginning to worry about just how quickly my health had deteriorated in such a short space of time. My ability to focus had gone and I began to panic about my situation. I promised myself that I would eat some of the food that was brought to my cell, however bad it was. I took a small sip of water from the tap as I prepared myself to eat. I hadn't expected to have a supply of running water in my cell and I was grateful for it. My mouth had that nasty salty taste you get after vomiting and I needed to get rid of it if I was to have any chance of eating my food.

The prisoner arrived back with the trolley and placed the plate of food onto my hatch. 'Bunting,' he shouted pleasantly. I wasn't fooled.

'Thanks,' I said, as I walked across the cell to collect it. As I put my hand out to reach for the plate, he snatched it away. He held the plate to the hatch and peered through at me.

'*PC* Bunting, isn't it?' he asked ironically, and then took a deep breath to muster as much saliva from the back of his throat as he could. With one swift movement, he spat a big glob of phlegm into the middle of the food. The white phlegm floated around in the brown gravy. 'Hey lads, I'm feeding the pig,' he said.

With this, two other prisoners came to my cell hatch. They looked at me, sniggering, then they spat in my food, too. The first prisoner put the plate on the hatch and gestured for me to come closer. 'You're in our territory now, you fucking filth, and we're gonna fucking carve you up.'

I wasn't immediately afraid, as I had the protection of my locked cell door, but I knew that I would have to be on my guard every time it was opened. I just hoped that the problems with my transfer for the following day had been sorted out so I could get out of Armley. If not, then the next few days were going to be hell.

'You've been watching too many movies,' I replied. I wanted to show him that his threat didn't bother me, even though the reality was that I was terrified.

They disappeared, leaving me with the contaminated food. I didn't touch it. Adrenaline was then added to the cocktail of emotions that I was already experiencing, overriding the nausea. The strength in my legs had returned and I tramped up and down my cell, trying to think about my next course of action. I knew that having a shower would be a big risk, but I also knew that I could be in Armley for a long time. Even sitting with the officers, as SO Butt had promised me, wasn't without danger. My two options were either to spend the remainder of my time at Armley in my cell and run the risk of going insane with boredom, or to try to have some periods of human contact and run the risk of being 'carved up'. It was a no-win situation.

I began to shake more and I felt very cold again. I picked up the orange and frantically started to peel it. My hands trembled violently and I dropped it a few times. The pieces of peel that came off were minuscule, frustrating me even more and making the task all the more difficult. I put the first piece of orange into my mouth and bit into it. My mouth filled with orange pips and the juice was extraordinarily acrid. It was too unpleasant and so I immediately spat it into the toilet and put the rest of the uneaten orange on the plate, which was still on my cell hatch. I waited for the sound of the trolley so the food would be removed, and anticipated the next round of abuse. What would they have in store for me this time?

The sound of the trolley started again. I braced myself as it got closer. I stood at the far end of the cell and waited. It drew nearer and nearer. The same prisoner came to the hatch.

'Oh dear, aren't you hungry, Bunting?'

Using the back of his hand, he knocked the plate onto my cell floor. It upturned and the food went everywhere, on the floor, up the wall and all over me. He just carried on walking up the corridor, whistling, as though nothing had happened, leaving me with the repulsive mess. I had no means of clearing it up and so I waited for the sound of jangling keys so that I could summon assistance from an officer.

I got onto my bed and picked up my book. Even the simple pleasure of walking up and down my cell had been taken away from me because of the food all over the floor. I was also annoyed that I was now well over halfway through my book as a result of the reading 'binge'. Everything seemed to be going wrong. The day had started so well but was ending so badly.

I closed the book in a desperate attempt to save what was remaining of it for another day. I waited and waited for the sound of the keys to come. The darkness closed in; still no sign of a prison officer. I looked at the intercom button, a means of communication to prison officers on the wing. I had told myself I would only ever use it to gain attention in the most extreme circumstances and I didn't consider the mess on the floor to be such. I didn't want to become a nuisance to the officers. My only chance in here was if they remained on my side.

As it got darker, the ritual of the shouting between cells began, only this time it was even more sinister as it was aimed at me.

'Oi, copper. We fucking know you're in here, and we're gonna carve you up. Oi, copper, can you hear me? We're gonna fucking carve you up and watch you fucking bleed.'

I closed my eyes tight shut; I knew my time was going to come. 'Oi, don't fucking ignore me. I'm gonna fucking kill you. Watch your fucking back, Babylon.' (Babylon is a detrimental term that is often aimed at police officers by the criminal fraternity. I'd been called it many times in my career but I don't know where it comes from.) The threats echoed around the prison. The din was similar to a football crowd. I buried my head in my pillow and thrust my fingers into my ears, humming the Tupac Shakur song in an attempt to drown out the threats.

Not too long after the shouting had begun, SO Butt came to my cell. 'What the hell happened, Mick?' he asked, looking at the mess.

'It fell off the hatch. I'll clear it up. Can I have a mop and bucket, please?'

'Yes, but why didn't you get us on the intercom? Isn't it working?'

'I didn't want to bother you.'

'Don't be silly, Mick. You can bell us for something like this.'

'I didn't realise, but thanks anyway.'

'Leave it for the time being. I've got your phone cards here so I'll take you down to the phone now.' I filled with excitement and fear, all in one. I felt like I was about to be thrown to the lions.

'Where are the others?'

'They're on association in the games activity room,' he replied. 'Don't worry, they've been warned that if they so much as breathe on you then they're on a serious nicking.' I wasn't convinced I was safe. A lot of the prisoners wouldn't have the intelligence to anticipate the consequences of their actions. If they saw their chance to 'do a copper', then they'd take it. I'd heard before that if a prisoner has an opportunity to harm a police officer but doesn't take it, then he himself becomes the subject of a beating from the other inmates. I was about to put this theory to the test.

I walked out of my cell for the first time in well over a day. I had to squint as the lights in the corridor were so bright. It looked such a long way to the bottom, but that's probably because I wasn't used to the large spaces. Several of the cell hatches had pairs of arms hanging out of them as the prisoners in the cells looked at what was going on in the corridor. I followed SO Butt closely and another two officers joined us to escort me to the phone. As we walked, the prisoners started banging on the cell doors. The sound was overpowering. I looked into the activity room as we went by. There were about twenty prisoners inside, playing pool, watching television or reading newspapers. Some were just hanging around, seemingly dazed and locked in their own world. This was the hospital wing, after all. Everything seemed to stop as I walked past, and all of the men in the room stared at me. A few anonymous comments or pig snorting sounds were aimed at me, but I believed the prisoners had decided that this was not their moment to do anything. I looked straight ahead and carried on walking.

'You alright?' asked SO Butt.

'I'm fine, thanks,' I replied. 'But it's like a bloody zoo in here.'

'Yes, I know. We're not renowned for our high class clientele.'

'Thanks,' I joked, as he'd inadvertently just made a comment about me.

As we walked around the corner, there it was. The phone was hanging on the wall. It was a quiet part of the wing for which I was pleased, because if my mum had heard the comments from the other prisoners, then my call would probably have done more harm than good.

'There you are, Mick. We'll leave you to it. You'll be alright here.'

I picked up the receiver and inserted the card. I was hit with another rush of apprehension as I heard the dialling tone. I began to dial the number, looking around and behind me to make sure I was still safe. After about three rings, my dad picked up the phone. I froze. I couldn't believe that after what had seemed like an eternity locked up in my cell, I was now actually able to talk with my mum and dad in their house. My mouth and throat seemed to seize up; for a moment, I couldn't manage to say a word.

'Hello?' my dad said.

'Dad, it's me,' I eventually managed to force out.

He immediately shouted to my mum to pick up the other phone. 'Are you okay, son?' he asked.

'I'm okay. It's bloody horrible in here, but I'm safe and I'm bearing up.' I knew that I probably wasn't safe and I certainly didn't think that I was coping well, but there are things you should keep from your loved ones, especially at a time like this.

'We love you,' said Mum. I'll always remember hearing my mum's voice at that moment when I felt so vulnerable and needy.

I fought back the tears once more. 'Me too,' I replied. I couldn't compose longer sentences.

'We're doing everything we can to get you out,' my dad said. 'Are you managing to eat anything?' he added.

'A little bit. I'm okay.'

'Your sister sends her love, too.'

'Cheers,' I said, desperate to say more but I couldn't. My eyes were soaked with tears and all I wanted to do was sob, but there was no way I could let that happen. It would be unfair to Mum and Dad, though I think they would have understood.

'I'm gonna have to go now,' I said. 'I want to ring again tomorrow, so I'll save some of my units.'

'Okay, remember we love you,' Mum said again. She was close to tears as well. 'We're sorting out how we can come and visit you and we'll be there as soon as they'll let us.'

'Look after yourself in there, son,' Dad said.

'I will, don't worry.' Tears were streaming down my face.

'We love you,' said Mum for a final time. This time she was crying.

'Me too. Don't worry, Mum. I'll look after myself. I'll ring you tomorrow.'

I put the receiver back down. I had never known the power of a simple conversation up until this point in my life. I tried to imagine the pain that Mum and Dad were going through and there was absolutely nothing I could do about it. SO Butt approached. I was still desperate to keep control of my emotions but again my eyes were soaked with tears. My face quivered with emotion. I used my sleeve again and I looked down to the floor, embarrassed. He looked at me, and for the first time seemed quite cold, I don't know why.

'Come on, let's get you back in your cell,' he said.

The prisoners were lined up as we walked back up the corridor past the activity room. They jeered at me and made pig noises. They revelled in my misery. They would never show me any mercy and this was an early lesson that any sign of weakness would be attacked from all angles in prison.

I turned and looked at the inmate who seemed to be the leader. He sniggered. He was very pale and covered with tattoos: ironically, there was a tear-shaped one on his cheek. He casually rested his chin on a pool cue. I didn't have the courage to say anything, but to some degree I pitied him as his life seemed so pointless. My pity was short-lived, however, as he approached me and spat in my face, to a loud cheer from the other inmates. Before I could do anything, or more to the point, before *they* could do anything, SO Butt grabbed me and ran me back up the corridor. He hastily pushed me into my cell and slammed the door. He said something into his radio and then ran back down the corridor towards the other inmates, telling them to settle down. Maybe he'd been cold with me in anticipation of such an incident.

'We know he's the filth,' came a shout from the corridor. I washed my face to rid myself of the saliva, and once again I pondered on my situation.

I got onto my bed and reflected on the phone conversation I'd just had. I was grateful for it, but I was increasingly worried about my mum. To be honest, I had expected it, but to actually hear your mother cry in such circumstances is an experience I wouldn't wish on anyone.

Within a couple of minutes, I had a visitor. It was one of the other prison officers, checking I was okay. I explained that I was used to being spat at, as it had been an occupational hazard. He also brought me the telephone call booking sheet and I booked my call for the subsequent evening. I hoped I wouldn't still be in Armley by then, but if I was, then at least I had the call to look forward to. My troubles in prison had begun.

Chapter 11
I Need the Doctor

Early the following morning, my second in Armley, I was woken by the noise of my cell door opening. Two prison officers entered. One of them shone a torch in my face. It was still dark outside. It puzzled me that I was being woken a lot earlier than normal. I rubbed my eyes and was thankful for the good night's sleep. Either Butler had had a very quiet night, or I had become immune to his voice and slept through it all.

'Bunting,' said one of the officers.

'Yes,' I replied in a rough voice.

'Get a shower, you're leaving us today.' As he said this, he threw me a small bar of soap, a razor and a sachet of shampoo. I couldn't believe it. Not only was I getting out, but I was getting a shower as well!

'Are the other prisoners locked up?' I asked.

'Yes, you're okay to get a shower. Be quick, you're needed in reception by seven.'

'What time is now, please?'

'Six thirty.'

'Okay, thanks.'

'We'll leave your cell door open. Come back here when you've cleaned up.'

A good start to the day – I was going to be out of there without any of the prisoners even knowing about it. I almost ripped the sheets off as I rushed out of bed. I grabbed my towel and ran down the corridor towards the showers with nothing more than the towel to cover me. I almost broke into a little dance, I was so pleased.

It must have been the quickest shower I had ever had in my life. I was in and out within two minutes. I grabbed the towel and ran back to my cell clutching my bar of soap and razor. I shaved in my cell. After about five minutes, I was sitting on my bed, ready for off. In fact, I waited for about half an hour so the rush had been in vain. It felt much longer. I didn't know what was going on because the prison officers seemed to have vanished. The surrounding noise level gradually rose, as the daily prison life began to resume. I was worried because my cell door was still open, so I decided to pull the door to and lock myself in my cell. I folded my bed sheets up and took hold of my book and placed my remaining phone card in the pages so as to guard against theft by any other prisoners in the sweat box which would be used to take us to the open prison. The din outside became louder and louder. A radio came on with the over-the-top joviality of a local disc jockey. The clatter of trolleys started, as did the shouting. I tried not to lose hope about my transfer. Where had the prison officers gone?

I waited and waited, but I was rather pleased when the prisoner with the cutlery ignored my cell as if it were empty. He had probably been told that I was going. And then another prison officer came to my door.

'Come on then, Bunting. Let's go,' he said.

'Is it still on?' I asked.

'It is as far as I know.'

'Fantastic,' I mumbled to myself. I grabbed my book and followed the officer out of the cell.

On the walk down the cell passage, the usual jeers and pig squeals rained in. I wanted to return their insults, but I didn't want to risk anything or reduce myself to their level so I put my head down and braced myself through the avalanche of abuse. The more I thought about my transfer, the more their comments eluded my attention. We eventually got to the end and the officer unlocked another door and the journey through the maze of passages and corridors began. It was nice to stretch my legs properly.

When I eventually arrived at the booking-in desk, I was greeted by the same officer who had booked me in two days earlier. He lifted a large box from under the desk and placed it in front of me. 'Check it and sign here, please,' he said, thrusting a piece of paper in my direction. On the side of the box was my prison number *DK8639* in marker pen. I opened it and pulled out each piece of clothing. My suit was dirty and creased and a large spider had decided to use it as its home. Everything was there and so I signed the paper and changed into my own clothing. I was then led to a holding cell in order to wait for the sweat box to arrive.

I was horrified when the officer opened the cell door to let me in. There were about twelve other prisoners in the cell and as I entered, conversation ended, as each man turned and stared at me. I wanted to tell the officer that I was a policeman and ask to be placed into another holding cell, but I couldn't do it, as any cover that I had left would be blown. These prisoners may not have known who I was and so I couldn't risk saying anything. If I had, my move would almost certainly have been cancelled.

Every one of the men seemed to smile in a sinister and mocking way as I looked at them. Some were lying flat on their backs on the benches, whilst others sat with their feet curled up onto them. A few walked around the cell like animals marking their territory. I think just about every one of them had a rolled-up cigarette burning, filling the cell with noxious fumes. They were dressed in scruffy tracksuits or jeans with dirty trainers. Most were unshaven and there was a gallery of tattoos on show. And there was me, a non-smoker in a suit with not a tattoo on my body. I was instantly recognised as being different and so the silence and the staring continued.

I was terrified as I cautiously entered. The cell door slammed shut behind me. I was now locked in with them. I held my book tight and tried to find a place on a bench. I sat down next to the (seemingly) least threatening one of them. Finding such a man wasn't easy as the cell oozed intimidation. I sat on the edge of the bench. Did they know who I was? I was surely going to find out one way or the other, but gradually the prisoners began to chat amongst themselves again and the intrigue of my arrival subsided.

I remember one of the prisoners in particular. He was tall and thin and his tattoos were a stark contrast to his ashen-looking skin. His hair was shaggy and greasy and he looked generally unhealthy. However, he was very sure of himself and he appeared to be the main talker in the cell. I sensed the other prisoners were frightened of him. I can't say why, but he looked potentially violent. Maybe it was his eyes. They were sinister and made him look fearless. He ridiculed the prison service for granting him a move to an open prison and told his friends how he was going to simply walk out and escape on the very first night of his transfer.

My perception of this man intensified my anxiety. The containment in this cell was still like a game of cat and mouse to me. I tried to figure out whether they knew and, if they did, when they would strike and who would make the first move. Several of the men carried transparent bags containing their possessions and I saw that at least a couple had razors. I was prepared for these to be used for violent purposes – on me. I found it incredible that they were allowed such things, but they had earned the right to be transferred to open prison and this showed the level of trust the prison service had in them. Any slight deviation from perfect behaviour would have inevitably resulted in a move back to a closed prison and not many prisoners would risk that. However, I didn't need reminding that this situation was different. They were now in a cell with a policeman and if they had known that, they would have seen it as their duty to jeopardise their transfer, in order to hurt me.

I subserviently eyed them, as the initial attention I'd attracted steadily faded. The cell door opened again and I thought my anguish was over. But, instead, a brash-looking inmate strutted in. He held his hands aloft with the victory sign and nodded his head arrogantly, wearing a supercilious smile. A cheer erupted and several of the prisoners went and greeted the man and shook his hand, but not in the normal manner. They would link thumbs or bang their fists. Others simply patted him on the back. I tried to work out how he had achieved this apparent hero status. Had he committed an unusual crime to get in prison in the first place, or had he challenged the authorities in a way that would appeal to these people? The door slammed behind him. I continued to listen to individual conversations. Most revolved around drugs and where the next fix was coming from.

I was completely bewildered by what took place next.

The late arriving prisoner took out his tobacco bag and filled a Rizla paper with tobacco. Then the reason for his popularity became apparent, as he removed a small block of cannabis about the size of a thumbnail. He began to burn it with his lighter and scrape the residue into his roll-up. He was making a cannabis-laced cigarette right in front of us and, more to the point, virtually right in front of the prison officers. With careful precision, he spread the bits of cannabis along the full length of the cigarette and rolled it up perfectly. He placed the remainder of his cannabis into the tobacco pouch and placed the cigarette into his mouth. He lit it, inhaled, sat back and cockily nodded his head again. 'Fucking heaven!' he said.

One by one, the other prisoners took a turn to inhale, and the cell quickly filled with the sweet smell of cannabis. I prayed that they would not expect me to take a turn, because I didn't smoke anything and, more importantly, I didn't want the 'nicking' that they seemed to care so little about. Inmate by inmate, the spliff came closer to me. I battled to think of excuses, but maybe I wouldn't get asked, as I wasn't one of the 'gang'. But my turn did come and the prisoner next to me handed it over.

'No thanks, mate,' I said.

'Take a drag,' he said.

'It's okay, I can't.'

Everyone in the cell exploded into laughter. 'What the fuck

do you mean, you can't? You're in prison, what else is there to do?'

'I'm ill,' I said spontaneously.

'You wouldn't be getting a move if you were that ill,' he replied. He had a point. Prisoners with any kind of health problems would not be transferred to an open prison. I had made a mistake and he'd spotted it. 'Now fucking have some!' he shouted.

I took the spliff and handed it straight to the next man. As I did so, I felt a thud on the back of my head. It sent a pain into my ears and momentarily panicked me. I turned around with my arms in the air. The prisoner who had given me the spliff had his fists raised and before I could react, he punched me full in the ribs, which instantly took my breath away. 'You ungrateful twat,' he snapped.

Everyone laughed again. Even if they hadn't realised that I was the policeman in the jail, they had certainly worked out that I was very different to them and I became the focus of their hostility. I stood up and raised my fists. It was a gamble. I wanted to show I wasn't frightened of them and demonstrate to him that if he tried it again, then I wouldn't just take it. Fortunately, it seemed to work. He laughed at me, but didn't hit me again. I tried to control myself. I had never shaken with fear as much in my life. I sat back down and looked at my assailant again. He was small and thin-looking, and he had a lot of scars on his arms and wrists. One on one wouldn't have been so bad but, with his army of support, he was someone to be very wary of.

Moments later, a prison officer came into the cell. 'Can you all keep the bloody noise down? It's like a bloody circus in here. Now, I'm afraid I've got some bad news. There's has been a cock-up with the transport – I'm sorry, but you're not transfer-ring today so we're going to have to book you all back in and you're back to your cells. Sorry, fellas.'

It hit me hard because of the state that the attack had left me in. My stomach sank and everything around me seemed to dis-appear into a blur. I couldn't even focus on the inmates. I felt a pulsing sensation around my whole body and I seemed to go numb everywhere. This was the worst possible news for me as it meant more time in Armley and my enemy list was growing by the minute. The mood in the cell changed, too, as the inmates became angry.

'You fucking can't do this, boss! This is fucking stupid!' shouted one prisoner

Several others said similar things, but it was all in vain. We were marched out of the cell and given a new set of prison clothing. I felt as though I was marching to my death. Never in my life had I experienced such a feeling of dejection. It was as though I was alone in a world that was determined to break my spirit. I had no one to turn to and this magnified my hopeless-ness. I began to lose myself in my own world and I didn't even care about the other inmates any more. In fact, I wanted them to attack me again and put an end to my misery.

For the five minutes or so that it took to get changed, my emotions plunged. I lost all awareness of my surroundings and I was no longer intimidated by the other inmates. I didn't care what happened to me. The worst thing possible had happened: condemned to my Armley cell again. I slowly folded my suit into another box, and my prison number was penned onto it. A prison officer gave all of us two units each of a phone card so that we could let our families know that the move was off and we would be staying at Armley Prison.

We queued for the single phone that was at the booking-in desk. There was a lot of hustling, but again I wasn't bothered. However, I was eager to get to the phone, but I didn't really know why. I knew the news was going to be as shattering to my mum and dad as it had been for me. Nevertheless, my turn came and I dialled the number. My mum answered. I completely lost control on the phone and for the first time I showed real signs of weakness to her. I'll never forgive myself for that as I now know what that call did to her.

As I was taken back to my cell, the guilt impinged itself onto my other negative feelings. For a moment, everything piled on top of me. I looked at the escorting prison officer. 'I can't cope with this,' I said, 'I'm gonna do myself in.'

'Sorry?' came the reply, as he tried to clarify what I had just said.

'I can't stay in that poky fucking cell any longer. I'm gonna top myself.'

He looked at me inquisitively and then said, 'Right, come with me.'

We walked all the way back to the reception area and he pulled out my file. He added an entry with the date and time saying that I had threatened suicide. This wasn't good, for I knew another prison wouldn't accept me with such an entry on my record. My outburst was going to cost me dearly and getting it written off to keep the possibility of a transfer alive was not going to be easy.

This realisation became a leveller and I instantly began to regain some strength. 'I didn't mean it,' I insisted. 'I'm just in shock.'

'I have to act on stuff like that,' he replied, 'it's more than my job's worth not to.'

This was a disaster, as nothing would change for me. I was still bound for the same cell in the hospital wing, only now I had the added burden of proving that I was not suicidal, in order to get my transfer. Things were getting worse and worse. The walk back to my cell recommenced. I was a mess. I felt that my sanity was in the balance.

As we got to the hospital wing, the prison officer gave the paperwork relating to my potential suicide to SO Butt. SO Butt read the notes and shook his head. 'Mick, what's going on?'

'I didn't mean it. I'm just feeling the strain,' I replied.

'We can't write this off without the doctor, so I'll get him to see you.'

'I need him,' I said. 'I really need him.'

SO Butt walked me to my cell. This time, he gently pulled the door to to lock it. He looked at me as I went across to the bed. 'Hang in there, Mick. Hang in there.'

I nodded, got onto the bed and began yet another wait, this time for the doctor. My head was in turmoil; I began to think about ways of ending my life with the minimum amount of suffering. There is no easy way to do it, but I figured that it had to be quick. The quickest way for me was to use the razor blade.

Chapter 12

A Pig in the Zoo

As I dwelled on the catastrophic events of that morning, everything else in the prison ran as normal. I looked out of my cell window and watched about a hundred prisoners or so strolling around the exercise yard. Again, they clustered in their little groups. I wanted to know what they were talking about. Occasionally, a prisoner from one group would walk across the yard to another and hand over something. He would then walk back. It was all very mysterious. I saw two of the prisoners who had been in the holding cell earlier that day. They walked around the square futilely. They didn't realise it, but they were lucky. At least they were allowed the freedom to walk about. It seemed unfair that I was being punished more than the other inmates. I couldn't make any sense of the level of my punishment. I looked at my book. I had already nearly finished it and that distressed me even further. What would I do for the whole of the weekend? I knew that my handling of the next few days would be crucial to my welfare.

The sound of the trolley started again. I was getting used to it now and I was becoming accustomed to my surroundings, but that perturbed me a little, as I wanted to keep it firmly in the forefront of my mind that my time in prison was only temporary. Trying to acclimatise to the conditions made me feel that my stay was more permanent. It was very difficult to deal with. I needed a plan to get me through the weekend, but I also knew that I wasn't in the right frame of mind for clear thinking, as I was still distraught about the cancellation of the transfer. I paced up and down my cell once again. The sound of the trolley got closer. The joviality amongst the other inmates in the wing was menacing, intensifying my loneliness. The fact that they seemed to be handling their sentence better than me and the fact that they all seemed to be friends, made me feel even worse.

The trolley arrived. The same prisoner who had spat in my food on the previous day glared in at me. He smiled triumphantly. My pain gave him enormous pleasure. 'You staying with us now, are you? Does nowhere else want to take in a pig?' he said.

I felt a sudden surge of adrenaline. The accumulation of events and emotions had built up to such a level inside me that his comment triggered a release. I walked up to the hatch, put my nose right up to his and looked directly into his eyes. I didn't say a word, but I snatched the cutlery from his hands and held the stare in an attempt to outface him. After a few seconds he stood down. I'd beaten him. He turned his head away and carried on walking up the corridor. I felt content that I had peacefully won a battle, then sat on my bed and began to shake violently again.

After a further five minutes or so, the prison doctor arrived at my hatch. He looked in at me and then looked down to the keyhole as he entered my cell. He held out his right hand for me to shake. He shook his head as he looked at me. I knew straight away that he was sympathetic to me and it filled me with relief.

'Hello, Michael, I'm Doctor Ferguson. I'm here to make sure you're okay.'

He spoke quietly. He had a stethoscope hanging around his neck and he was carrying several very thick files. His tie was loosened, as was the top of his shirt, which gave me the impression that he was a very busy man. However, there was warmth about him and despite his rushed appearance he seemed to care about me. He put the files down, sat on my bed and began to talk.

'I've been called to see you because there is some concern about your welfare,' he said. 'It's been noted that you're very down and that you've threatened to kill yourself. Can you tell me a bit about it?'

'I'm not gonna do myself in,' I insisted. 'It was just a big shock knowing I'm gonna have to stay here for longer. I know I said all that, but I didn't mean it. It all just came out.'

'We just have to make sure, Michael,' he said. 'They're a bit eager to mark things like that down on your record in here.'

'I appreciate all that, but they don't need to do this just to cover their backs. I'm not going to do owt.' I could see why it had been done, but I needed it clearing from my record as soon as possible so that the transfer could be rearranged. I was desperate.

He put the stethoscope into his ears. 'Just take your jumper off for me, Michael, so I can take your blood pressure. I just need to check that everything's okay. How are you feeling?'

'A bit rough, to be honest, but nothing to worry about. I've just found it hard with the lack of contact. It's good to have you here. Will you be coming back?'

'Yes, I'll keep my eye on you, don't worry.'

Dr Ferguson wrapped the inflatable pad from the sphygmomanometer around my arm. It tightened and he looked intently at the mercury column.

'Mmmm, it's very high indeed. Have you been eating and drinking properly?'

'I can't. The bastards are tampering with my food.'

He pushed the cell door almost shut and told me that he'd visit my cell as often as he could in order to keep an eye on me. He showed me a relaxation technique to try to help with my high blood pressure. I can't remember all the details but I had to lie on my bed and imagine that I was on a beach somewhere nice. I have to say I was sceptical. It didn't sound as if this was the answer to my problems, but I was prepared to try anything for a man who had become a lifeline. I had found my second friend in prison. He told me that he was working for the whole weekend and this made me feel slightly easier, as I knew he was concerned about me and, more importantly, he seemed genuinely compassionate. I now had something to look forward to, his visit the next day.

My lunch arrived. I hadn't heard the trolley this time, as I'd been so engrossed with Dr Ferguson. I was annoyed that the same hostile prisoner served the food as if I was royalty, as he pretentiously showed Dr Ferguson that he was trying to help me. I didn't say anything, but the doctor shook his head as the prisoner left.

'He doesn't fool me. Has he been giving you a hard time? He's one of the hard-nuts in here,' he said.

'Oh no, not really. Nothing I can't handle,' I said – unconvincingly, it seemed.

'It's okay, Michael. You can admit it if you're getting a hard time. It'll help me to help you if you're honest.'

'Okay then, doctor, he's a real bastard, but I don't want anything done about it. I'm about the most unpopular man in here as it is, without being a grass as well. A copper and a grass, they'd bloody kill me.'

To be frank I thought that they were going to anyway, but telling tales wouldn't have been a healthy move and would almost certainly have sealed my fate. At least, for the time being, I was managing to avoid major conflict and, in my forty-eight hours inside, I'd only taken a couple of minor beatings. I felt the back of my head where the punch had landed and grimaced as I felt a small lump. I looked at my fingers to make sure there was no blood. There wasn't.

'Let me take a look,' said Dr Ferguson. 'Did they do that to you?'

'It's nothing, really,' I replied.

'I'll have a word with Mr Butt. I'll tell him what's happened so that his officers can keep an eye on you.'

'Thanks, but don't make a fuss, I'm okay.'

He walked to the door of my cell. 'I'm going to have to do the rest of my rounds. I'm finishing at four today. If I get chance, I'll come and see you again for a chat. If not, then I'll definitely see you tomorrow.'

'What time?' I asked desperately.

'Late morning.'

'Thanks, Doctor.'

'You can call me Steve, I don't see you as a proper prisoner. I don't know what they were thinking of, sending you in here.'

'Thanks, Steve,' I said humbly. In my very lowest moment so far and at a time when I had truly contemplated suicide, Dr Ferguson had appeared in my life and literally, within minutes of my meeting him, he had become my saviour.

I picked up my plate of food and decided that this was the moment when I was definitely going to eat at least some of the meal. But the pathetic-looking omelette was soaked in what looked like saliva. This time, the prisoners had sneakily tampered with my food in the hope that I would eat it. I didn't. Despite this, I was managing to stay comparatively upbeat. Meeting Dr Ferguson had certainly come at the right time.

Then, to my delight, one of the officers delivered my first lot of mail plus some writing paper and envelopes. The prison issue pen was bitten at the end and the ink seemed to have spilled out of the cartridge a little, but I didn't care. I felt as if I had been given a winning lottery ticket. I now had an extra activity to add to the routine that I would adopt again to get me through the rest of the day. Never before had I experienced such rapid alterations in my state of mind, as I began to feel slightly less anxious about the forthcoming long and lonely weekend.

I had been sent two letters. I recognised the writing as my mum's on one and so I opened it like a child pulling away at wrapping paper. I sat on my bed and read her words and, once again, tears streamed down my face. She told me that everything possible was being done to secure an appeal. She told me to keep strong and reiterated her and my dad's love for me.

With every couple of words I read, I had to wipe the tears away. I pictured my mum writing the letter, no doubt shedding tears, too, and I visualised my dad sitting quietly devising a considered plan of action for me. That's the kind of man my father is – cool under pressure, making the right decisions in tough circumstances. I knew they would be doing everything in their power to help me. Deep down, though, I knew that there was no hope at all of an early release.

I opened the second letter and was pleased and moved that an old friend from work had taken the time to wish me well. I put this letter with the one from Mum and Dad.

I picked up my Tony Adams book and flicked through the pages and realised that there were three photograph sections in the book containing action shots of Tony playing football. I sat at my desk, opened the book at a page with a picture on it, picked up the pen and meticulously began to copy the picture. I had found a new hobby. I looked around the cell. 'Yes,' I said to myself. Time would surely pass quicker now. I smiled as I remembered that I was able to write a letter now, too.

The next set of cutlery arrived for tea. I didn't want to look at the prisoner who brought it to me. I knew I'd receive an abusive comment or an aggressive stare and I didn't wish to give him the satisfaction. Instead, I stood and stared out of the window with my back to the hatch. I could sense him waiting for me to turn around. He waited for a minute or so. Then, finally, I heard the trolley move away and I smiled to myself, as I knew I had won again. I felt a little more in control as my fighting spirit returned slowly. I walked over and examined the cutlery. It all seemed okay, but I rinsed it under the tap anyway. I was determined to eat something and I had devised a plan if the prisoners tampered with my food again.

Just then Butler started another one of his outbursts.

'*Aargh!*' he cried. There was a brief pause and then he shouted it again and again.

I knew that there was no one else in his cell and I thought it was just another of his attention-seeking tantrums. But I was wrong. The shouting subsided conspicuously. He would usually start banging something or shouting more abuse or threats, but this time there was nothing. I knew something was wrong and I went to my cell hatch in order to look as far up the passage as the angle would allow me to.

The eerie silence continued until three or four officers sprinted up the passage towards Butler's cell. I couldn't see anything, but I heard the door fly open. The officers whispered frantically to each other. One ran back down the passage, shouting into his radio for an ambulance. Another two officers ran into Butler's cell. I waited to hear one of his familiar yells, but it didn't come.

As other prisoners became aware of what was happening, they started banging on their cell doors in time with each other. I didn't understand why they were doing this. I kept quiet and tried to see what was going on, but all I managed was the occasional sight of one of the beleaguered prison officers. They wore surgical gloves and the officer who had run from Butler's cell earlier returned with a large green first aid kit. It was obviously a serious situation, but I couldn't work out exactly what Butler had done. The noise from the synchronised banging on the cell doors amplified. Prisoners had been locked away in their cells whilst the incident was being dealt with.

The ambulance crew arrived and ran to Butler's cell with all manner of equipment. Ironically, I recognised one of the crew from a road traffic accident that I'd attended a few years earlier.

'Hello, Mr Butler,' said one of the crew. 'Can you hear me?'

Silence.

I heard more worried whispers amongst the prison officers. I knew that something as innocent as the illness of a prisoner had the potential to over-excite the inmates, which could escalate to violent outbursts. Most didn't need excuses, but I'm sure they would have seen this as good enough.

As I contemplated the consequences, the ambulance crew wheeled Butler down the cell passage. He was in a wheelchair, covered with a blanket and restrained by two ropes tied across his body. His eyes were closed and his mouth open, but his head was upright so I realised he was semi-conscious. There was a small patch of blood on his forehead and I saw his hands hanging from underneath the blanket. They, too, were covered in blood. I never saw Butler again.

I lay back on my bed. I knew that tea would be delivered very shortly and so I continued to develop my plan. I wasn't really very hungry, but I was determined to eat. I closed my eyes and waited for the sound of the trolley. All I could hear were occasional verbal protests from prisoners claiming that Butler had been the subject of a beating from the prison officers.

I didn't have to wait long for the trolley. Any disruption to normal daily routines in prison is avoided as much as possible and quickly corrected, so as to prevent the inevitable chain of rumours which could spark a riot. The plate landed on the cell hatch. I got off my bed and eyed the prisoner. He stared back at me. I approached the food and as I did so he spat into it and laughed.

'There you are, pig. There's your swill.' He began to walk away, laughing even louder.

'Oi, come here,' I said authoritatively. As I did so, I discreetly pressed the button in my cell to attract the attention of a prison officer. As it was the first time I'd used it, I was confident they'd respond promptly.

The prisoner, unaware that I'd done this, approached me warily with a rather gormless expression. This time *he* was the unwitting prey, walking right into my trap. Just as he got back to my cell, I poured the food down myself and threw the plate down. It made a loud, echoing bang as it hit the bare floor.

'Oi!' I bellowed as loud as I could. I projected my arms out of the hatch in a defensive stance as if I was trying to push the prisoner away. 'Get off me!' I screamed. 'Get back!'

Two officers came running up the passage. They immediately looked through the hatch. I was covered in food and so was the cell floor once again. I rubbed myself down, shaking my head as I did so.

'You okay, Bunting?' asked one of the officers, as the other escorted the prisoner away. Surprisingly, he didn't even attempt to protest his innocence.

The first officer unlocked my door. 'What happened then?' he asked.

'It was just a misunderstanding,' I answered.

I didn't want to create more problems for myself by getting the prisoner into more trouble; I just wanted to prevent any prisoner coming into contact with my food again.

'Did anything happen that we need to know about?'

'No, nothing, but I would prefer it if I could have my food delivered by an officer if possible. They're tampering with my food.'

'What have they been doing?'

'I don't want to cause any trouble, but I haven't had a clean meal since they found out I'm the Old Bill.'

'I'll get you a replacement meal right away,' he said sympathetically.

'Cheers,' I replied.

'I'll sort you some clothes out, too,' he said.

'Thanks.'

'Not nice in here, is it?'

'They're a bunch of fucking animals,' I said. 'It's more like being in a fucking zoo than a prison.' I was beginning to let the pressure show again.

'I'll sort these things out for you, Mick. Try to keep on top of things.'

'Yeah, I know.'

I stripped off my dirty clothes. My mission had been successful and I waited for my first untampered-with meal in a long time, but my hunger had been stemmed once again by the surge of adrenaline. The sound of the officer's footsteps coaxed me off my bed. I knew it was the same one as before because of the noise his heels made as the segs made contact with the floor.

'There you go, Mick,' he said, placing a plate of steaming food on the hatch.

'Thanks a lot,' I said as I collected it, wearing just a T-shirt and a pair of dirty boxer shorts.

'I'll get you some clean clothes when I get a chance.'

'Cheers.'

I shifted my book and drawings to one side and placed the plate of food onto the table. I picked up my knife and fork and sat on the chair, staring at the food. This meal was rice with what appeared to be chicken in a sweet and sour sauce. The rice had stuck together in big lumps and the sauce looked repellent. Large pieces of fat accompanied each piece of chicken. The only thing the meal had going for it was that it was hot and not swimming in saliva. I cautiously pushed my fork into the sauce and chicken. I closed my eyes and placed a small amount into my mouth. I sank my teeth into a piece of chicken and immediately spat it out again as I realised it was mainly gristle. I grimaced as a feeling of nausea took hold of me. I walked over to my sink and swilled my mouth with water to expel any other stray bits of food that were present. I knew that I couldn't afford to waste any toothpaste for such non-essential use, but it would have been nice. I shovelled about half of the plateful down the toilet so that it appeared as if I'd eaten something. I didn't want the prison officer to think that I was being ungrateful.

The sun dropped behind the building and the cell lights came on. I mentally prepared for this unexpected and certainly unwanted third night in Armley Prison. I knew that the novelty of drawing would wear thin after doing it for the whole weekend, but I had no choice. At least it was better than the routine I'd devised for myself the previous day. I decided I would write some more letters later that night so that I had something to look forward to. Actually, I was beginning to feel slightly better as I tried to structure my time again. Little things like writing letters to family suddenly became very big in the position that I was in.

I also began to think of how I could persuade the prison officers to remove my suicide marker from my prison record so that they could consider my transfer again. I knew it would take some doing. If they removed it and then I went ahead and carried out my threats, someone would be in deep trouble. I knew they wouldn't be willing to take any such risk and so convincing Dr Ferguson that I was mentally fit for a transfer was my only chance. Without it, I was doomed to stay at Armley for the whole of my sentence. This was an unthinkable scenario. If the inmates didn't kill me, then desperation would. I began to worry and once again the stability of my emotions was in question as my mood rose and fell in a matter of minutes. This is what prison does to your mind and the frightening thing about it is that there's absolutely nothing you can do, even when you know that it's happening.

I spent the whole of Friday night dwelling on what *could* have been and what actually was happening. I was in a worse position than I had been in since arriving in prison: not only was I stuck in Armley for at least the rest of the weekend, but I also now had the black mark against my name. Working on pure adrenaline, I lowered the palms of my hands to the floor and frantically started a set of press-ups. Once again, I growled the line from the Tupac song. I repeated it on each press-up, as beads of sweat began to drip from my nose. The adrenaline was compensating for my lack of food, because my body couldn't normally have performed this task on the little fuel it had available.

Suddenly, I heard a voice from behind me. 'Night, Mick.'

It was SO Butt. He winked and smiled at me. I felt a certain amount of admiration and respect from him, maybe because I was a policeman doing time and there was I doing press-ups in the middle of my cell floor. I was determined not to be beaten. He was wearing his civilian jacket and he had an empty lunch box tucked under his arm. He'd made a deliberate trip up the wing to come and see me. 'I'm on in the morning so I'll see you then.'

'Cheers,' I replied, as I got up from the floor with sweat pouring down my face. He put his thumb up and winked again. I clenched my fist and raised it, defiance on my face to show him that I would get through. His humanity generated a tear in my eye which mixed with the sweat as it rolled down my face. He was a good bloke. I sat back on my bed and used the towel to mop up the sweat. I then became mad with myself for getting into this state, as I didn't know when I would get the chance to have another shower and now I badly needed one.

All I could do was listen to the nightly ritual of the prisoners shouting between their cells, as it started once again. What they shouted still didn't fail to stagger me. Listening to them took its toll as most of it was directed against me. I turned the light off in my cell and curled up on my bed, putting my head under the pillow trying to block out the comments.

'Oi, filth, we know you can hear us, thought you were out of here, did you? We know you're still here and you're getting carved up.'

The intimidating tone was more than an act to frighten me. I could sense real hatred and the desire to badly hurt me. I knew that the beating I'd had earlier in the holding cell was nothing. I also began to realise that the chance of another face-to-face confrontation with a prisoner was likely at some time over the weekend, unless I was to remain in my cell for the whole time. This was not an option for me, as I knew that my ability to stay focused and sane wouldn't tolerate a whole week-end of absolute nothingness. This would do more damage than any blow to the head or razor to the cheek. Yes, these were desperate evaluations but it was how I felt.

I spent the whole of Friday night lying on my bed listening to the torments from the prisoners. I knew that it was definitely not a good idea to write any letters with my state of mind as it was, and so I decided to save that pleasure for the following day. I got into bed and tried to sleep but the shouts and the echoes around the exercise square were endless. It was as if the prisoners felt my desperation and relentlessly attacked it in an attempt to destroy my spirit. They succeeded on this particular night, as my ability to focus on my life in the outside world after my release was choked by their sickening coercion. I began to feel unbearably low again, each comment eating away at my will to live. I looked at my trousers, which I had neatly folded and placed on the floor, and calculated the best way of forming a noose. And this time I meant it.

Vision of my long-term future was being stifled by the short-term hell that I was living in. I climbed out of bed and looked up into the sky. In total contrast to my thoughts, the stars were beautiful. They glistened and seemed to communicate with me as I looked up at them. The enormity of space hit me, but my problems seemed bigger than space and I drew little comfort from the stars, despite their splendour. I picked up the trousers and held just one of the legs out in front of me. I pulled it taut. The material was strong enough for my needs so I wrapped the trouser leg around my neck and tied it loosely as I looked around for something to tie the other end to, that I could hang from. The shouting continued and the ventilation system, which made a soft, grating noise, had a musty smell coming through it. This all seemed irrelevant, though, and I felt strangely empowered by my decision. I tightened the trouser leg around my throat and tied the other leg around the bar on the top of my window. I spent several minutes meticulously making the knot fail-safe. I stood on my chair and tightened the trouser leg still further until it was painfully tight around my neck. I began to choke. One step from the chair and my neck would break and my problems would be over in a second.

I held this position for a number of minutes, with the airway in my throat partially obstructed. My pathetic body shook as I tried to step off the chair. Then I thought of Mum and Dad. I knew that if I did it, *my* problems would end instantly, but *theirs* would never end. It struck me that there was no way on earth I could do that to them. I untied the trousers and stepped down from the chair. Little did they know it, but Mum and Dad had just saved my life.

'You fucking idiot,' I whispered to myself, knowing how close I had come to death. I got back into bed and mopped up yet more tears. I didn't let myself burst out crying, though. I couldn't let that happen. Looking back, perhaps it might have been better if I had. I fell asleep in the most depressed state I have ever been in in my entire life. I wanted to die but couldn't kill myself.

The following morning I didn't bother even to consider eating. I ignored the jibes and insults that I got as my food was delivered. I just lay in bed, lacking the energy or the will to move. I was waiting for the doctor. I needed to tell him just how bad I was feeling. Usually, things seem better in daylight, but that rule doesn't apply in prison. Nothing had changed. I felt terrible.

I spent most of that morning in a numb state. I had given up trying to find relief from my desperation. The constant battle over the previous three days had taken its toll on me as I lay there motionless and purposeless. I didn't care about anything any longer. I didn't have the energy to overcome the negativity that was slowly consuming me. My eyes stared across the cell as I lay in the foetal position. I stayed like that for a number of hours as the constant din of prison life continued.

'Hi, Michael.' The voice was soft. I knew instantly that it was Dr Ferguson. He had kept his promise and had come to see me. My despair turned to delight as I leaped out of bed to greet him.

'Am I glad to see you!'

'Michael, you look terrible, are you okay?'

'No.' I couldn't manage to say anything else as the tears started again. My face shook as I desperately tried not to cry.

He sat on the bed and looked at me, shaking his head. He placed his hand on my shoulder and looked into my eyes. 'I won't allow any harm to come to you, don't worry.'

'I'm in a bad way,' I whimpered.

'I know. I'm going to take you down to my surgery now. I want to check your blood pressure and I think you need to get out of this grotty cell for a while. Can you get dressed?'

'Thank you so much,' I said. Not only was I going to be able to spend some time with a human being who didn't want to kill me, I was also going to be able to walk around for a short while.

I was elated and this overrode any fear of walking around the prison. Once again, the desperate low had been transformed. I got dressed quickly and I threw some water over my face and brushed my teeth. I used a larger blob of toothpaste; this *was* a special occasion, after all. He opened the cell door. This was a very dangerous move and I looked both ways as if I were crossing the road, before I dared to follow him out.

'It's okay. No one will touch you whilst you're with me. They need me and I can have them out of here in two seconds if I have good reason.' (He was referring to the hospital wing.) Nevertheless, I was still very edgy.

He slammed the door and shouted down the corridor to one of the officers, telling him where he was taking me. We began the walk to the surgery. Each door that we came to had to be unlocked and it seemed to take great strength from Dr Ferguson to open and close them, due to the weight of the steel. It was the epitome of the image of a hard prison.

We eventually arrived at the surgery, only a few hard stares to the bad. I entered. There were photographs of the doctor's family on his desk. Lavish paintings covered the walls. There was a kettle and even a television. I had entered civilisation, but to me it was much more than that.

'Sit down, Michael,' he said. I did as I was told. 'Roll your sleeve up for me, please.' Once more I complied. As soon as I had done so, he wrapped the large piece of strapping from the sphygmomanometer around my upper arm and with a few gentle squeezes on the air bag, the pressure intensified. He looked at the mercury level closely.

'That's very high indeed, Michael.'

'I thought it might be,' I replied, rolling my sleeve back down.

'I'm a little concerned about you, to be honest.'

'I'll be okay. I just need to get out of here.'

'Yes, I know, but the reality is that you're not getting out just yet, so we need to work out what will be best for your health.'

He sat in his chair and repeatedly banged his pen on the desk as if he were playing the drums. His look of concern remained.

'I'm going to have to put you onto dailies,' he said.

'What does that mean?'

'It means I will bring you down here each day to assess your condition. It just means I'll be keeping an eye on you.'

'What about my transfer? I can't handle it here much longer.'

'I'll be pushing for that, don't you worry. This won't affect the move.'

This relieved me, as I knew that I'd come very close to ending my life the previous night and I knew that getting out of Armley was the only chance of preventing me from getting so low again. Or so I thought.

I spent twenty minutes in the office and had the luxury of watching his Euro Disney animated clock, which hung precariously from the wall. I formed the opinion that DIY was not his strong point from the way it dangled at an irregular angle from the hook.

The walk back to my cell was depressing as I anticipated the hopeless feeling that I'd experience again once the door was slammed shut. I kept my head down and didn't speak at all.

Dr Ferguson kept his hand on my shoulder the whole way. I felt safe with him. 'I'll be in again tomorrow,' he said.

'I'm not going anywhere,' I answered, with a forced smile.

He smiled back, closed the door and walked away. I later found out that he had taken the trouble to telephone my mum and dad to reassure them. He was a good man. I settled onto my bed, thinking, with a feeling of resignation, that this was the last civilised human contact I would have until the following day. However, no sooner had I begun to plan the rest of my day when the door to my cell was opened again and SO Butt entered.

'Hi, Mick.'

'Hi.'

'I've just been speaking with Dr Ferguson and he's told me to have a word with you about your move.'

'Is it on or off? I need to know. I can't take another knock like yesterday.'

'It's most certainly on. We don't want to have you here, as you're a security risk for us. The only thing is that nothing can even get started until Monday, so it'll be well into next week before you get shifted.'

I immediately despaired, but then felt great relief. The move was *definitely* going to happen.

'There is another thing,' he said.

'Yes?'

'The prison chaplain is here now and he's asked to see you. Would you like that?'

'What for?'

'Just for a chat. It sometimes helps prisoners when they're struggling to come to terms with their sentence.'

'That'd be brill,' I replied. Any human contact was a bonus and the chaplain was more than welcome in my cell even though I wasn't particularly religious. In fact, anybody who didn't want to hurt me was welcome.

'He'll be here in a bit, okay?' he continued. 'And don't worry, your move will be sorted. You just need to be patient.'

'I'm developing patience pretty well in here,' I said, trying to inject some humour into the conversation for the second time that day. The truth is that I was trying to cover up my real feelings of dejection as a result of what I'd almost done during the night.

The chaplain was the next person whom I spoke with. He was older than I had expected, perhaps in his seventies. He wore the identifiable collar and clutched a book in a way that made me think it was precious to him. It looked too thin to be the Bible, though. He radiated warmth and compassion and the first thing he did as I stood up was place both of his hands on my shoulders. He closed his eyes and held this position for about ten seconds. It was surreal, yet extremely moving.

I didn't know what to do or say and so I just stood there as he held on to me. His eyes opened.

'Hello, Michael.'

'Hello.'

'Please sit down,' he said. 'I'm Bill Foster, the chaplain for the prison. I've come to have a small chat with you. Is that okay?' he asked.

'I'm glad to see you,' I answered, fighting back tears yet again.

'And I'm glad to see you, too.' He sat down beside me and looked at me. 'You must feel devastated by all this,' he said.

'It's turned my world upside down and inside out. I'm ruined,' I told him.

'I understand you're finding it hard to cope in here. Do you want to tell me how you feel?'

I *did* want to tell him everything, even what I'd nearly done in the night, but I knew that this could be potentially damaging to my transfer. I had to dispel any thoughts of suicide from my mind.

'I'm up and down, but I'll be okay. I just can't understand why I've been sent here. No one goes to prison for common assault, so why me? It isn't as though I went out and got drunk and got in a fight. I was trying to arrest a violent man. He should be in here, not me.'

'We all think it's wrong that you're here, but these feelings you have are too destructive at the moment. You mustn't ask why. You'll never get an answer, all you'll get is anger.'

He placed his hands on mine. He told me I should try to stop resisting the fact that I was in prison and, instead, accept it by giving myself to God. At first, I was dismissive, but he kept repeating it. He told me that by admitting to God that I was helpless and in need of His help, then He would answer my prayer. I had nothing to lose and so I told him that I'd give it a go.

He gave me a booklet called *Daily Strength*. It contained excerpts from the Bible. He told me to read it that night before I went to sleep. I took it and placed it on my pillow in readiness.

The following twenty minutes or so passed very quickly as we spoke about everyday things. I distinctly remember getting a very detailed progress report on Leeds United. I have a passion for football and just to talk about everyday things to do with my team came as a welcome break. I lost myself in the world of football. It was fantastic. The only problem for me came when he stood up to leave. This magnified my position once again and hit me hard and I begged him not to go.

'Michael, I have to go. I have others to see, but I'll come and see you next week.'

'Next *week*?' I questioned anxiously. 'I'll never last a week in here.'

With this, he took hold of my hands and we both sat down again. He bowed his head and so I did the same. He began to say a prayer.

'Lord, we ask that you come into Michael's life at this time when he needs you. We also pray for Michael's mother and father.'

My resistance against an outburst of tears gave way. I began to cry like a child. Unperturbed, the chaplain kept on praying. I can't tell you what he said as I'd lost control of my emotions and I shook violently as I cried aloud. I gripped his hands. My face and throat ached. I couldn't stop weeping.

He eventually finished praying and looked up. He had tears in his eyes, too; he really cared about me. 'Michael, you have found yourself,' he said. 'At twenty-six years old, you have found yourself. One day, you'll be grateful for this experience and you'll take it with you for the rest of your life. The Lord will look after you in the meantime.'

He wiped away his tears and hugged me. He told me to read the booklet and I promised him that I would. With one final hug, he departed. For the first time since entering Armley, I had completely lost my battle against crying and I lay on my bed and wept aloud for the following ten minutes or so.

I spent the remainder of the day trying to recover from the intensity of the emotions released by his visit. I wrote a couple of letters, but I had to read them again and again to make sure there wasn't so much as a hint that I'd lost hope. It would have sent my mum over the edge, I was convinced of it. For this reason I kept my letters vague, but I tried to show everyone that

I was positive about the future, as my move had now been confirmed for me. I completed another drawing to add to my collection and I attempted some exercises, but my body was suffering too much; it had been three days since I'd eaten anything and it was showing. I had lost a lot of weight even in this small space of time.

One more person visited me that day. Call it the first answer to my prayers; call it what you will, but it was the best news that I'd received since being put in prison. The food had just been cleared from tea and SO Butt came to my cell. Again, he was ready for home and carrying the same lunch box.

'Mick, I have some bloody good news for ya, mate.'

Now, I had to think hard about this comment. I wasn't used to good news. 'What? What?' I asked hurriedly.

'Your mum and dad are coming to visit you tomorrow afternoon.'

'Are you serious?'

'Yes. They'll be here at two o'clock.'

'Brilliant! How long do I get?'

'Two hours. I'll be on as well, so I'll make sure that you get a shower so you'll look alright.'

'Thanks,' I replied. I was reduced to tears yet again, but at least this time they were tears of joy.

'I'll see you in the morning. Try to get some sleep if you can.'

'Thank you very much.'

I lay on my bed and really thanked God. I actually spoke to Him and I felt that He was there. I spent the rest of the evening writing letters, as I thought that my jubilant mood would be evident in my writing. For the first time since coming to prison, I felt comfortable. I couldn't get to bed fast enough, as I wanted the next day to arrive as soon as possible.

That night, the routine threats weren't the focus of my attention. In fact, I laughed to myself as the prisoners tried to frighten me with more promises of what I had coming to me in the shower block. I picked up the chaplain's booklet. What I read will remain with me forever. I circled one particular passage, as it reflected what the chaplain had told me: Isaiah chapter 30, verse 19 helped me every time I read it from that day on. I probably read it on average fifty or sixty times a day while in prison. Each time I read it, my feeling of desperation would decrease and I'd feel a little more at ease. Maybe this was my inner strength at work, or maybe it was an act of God. I honestly don't know, but I really do believe God was by my side when I was in prison.

How gracious he will be when you cry for help. As soon as he hears, he will answer you. – Isaiah chapter 30, verse 19.

Chapter 13

Big Boys Don't Cry

My new-found faith wasn't a miraculous cure for all my problems. The following day demonstrated that only too well. I woke up very early, excited about the visit later that afternoon. I lay in bed for hours in the pitch dark and absolute silence. The prisoners were at rest and I tried to enjoy the respite from the torrent of threats and abuse. I didn't need to find something to do to occupy myself on this occasion, as I was more than happy to lie and think about the forthcoming visit.

The hours ticked by and still there was no sign of sunrise. I thought about Butler, but I knew that I'd never find out what had happened to him. It had looked serious, though. There was no chance of me getting back to sleep, as my heart pounded with eager anticipation, so I got out of bed and looked out of the window, hoping that it wouldn't be too long before sunrise. Eventually, the sound of birds singing graced my ears. The different tones that they made fascinated me as they communicated with each other. I had never taken the time to listen to anything like this before and it made me realise that there's a lot to be said for such simple life, with not a hint of hostility in their singing. The singing was complemented by a brilliant red sky as the sun began to rise. The beauty was dazzling and I thought that nature was playing its part in trying to take me away from my living hell. I didn't want the prison to wake up.

The trolley had now developed an annoying squeak. What annoyed me more was the fact that it didn't seem to bother the prisoner who was pushing it, as I heard him laughing with each inmate as he dropped off the cutlery. What kind of person could laugh in a place like this? Then I realised just how empty some of the prisoners' lives were and that to them prison life was quite acceptable and normal. I felt a sense of sympathy rise in me, as once again I was torn between pitying them and truly hating them. The balance was tipped towards hatred, though, when the prisoner spat on my bed through the hatch as he left me my cutlery.

'You fucking scum!' I shouted.

I realised I was past caring about the consequences of reacting and what could happen. He looked at me. I looked at him. He smiled. I smiled. He shook his head. I shook mine. I was not going to back down from this little duel.

'What did you just say?' he asked threateningly.

'You heard what I said, now fuck off.'

'You'll regret you ever said that,' he replied.

I looked at him. His face was pasty and damp and he had a very slight frame. He himself was not a problem to me. I wasn't frightened of him, but I didn't know who he knew in the prison. I still didn't really care. He walked off. I had won. I mopped up the saliva from my bed using precious pieces of toilet paper, washed my hands with all that I had available, cold water, then got dressed and continued to marvel at the beautiful sky as the sun appeared above D-wing.

My food arrived, but once again I made no effort with it. Instead, I gazed out of my window and drifted with my thoughts as the excitement of the day intensified, until I heard the sound of keys coming up the corridor.

'Morning, Mick,' SO Butt greeted me.

'Are they still coming?'

'They'll be here at two.'

'What time is it now?'

'Only eight o'clock, but the Doc wants to see you at nine. Get your stuff together and I'll take you down to the showers.'

I was glad of the opportunity to take a shower, but my previous one had been taken at a much earlier hour, before any other prisoners were out of their cells. This time, the passages were filled with working inmates. I began to regret my earlier bravery with the prisoner at my cell hatch. This was probably the moment the prisoners were waiting for. There would be only the minimum number of officers on duty as it was Sunday morning.

SO Butt stood at my cell door and held it open as he waited for me to get my towel. He handed me a small bar of soap. I cautiously stepped out of the cell. There were many prisoners sweeping, scrubbing, polishing and generally doing anything they could so as to be allowed out of their cells for as long as possible. One by one, they noticed me and one by one, they stopped working to stare at me. Some shook their heads as a gesture of disgust whilst others remained expressionless. The noise of work had subsided to deadly silence.

I stood motionless. SO Butt was close to me and he pressed

a button on his radio. This unnerved me somewhat, as pressing a button on the police radio was a way of summoning assistance and I assumed he was doing the same. And I was right. Within seconds, two officers hurriedly walked down the passage towards us. One shouted at the prisoners to continue with their work. The prisoners ignored the order and I saw one prisoner spit on the floor in defiance. I was petrified.

To my alarm, the prison officers began to walk me to the shower block. This was only about twenty yards or so, but I had to walk past prisoners and it seemed to take forever. Each time I walked by an inmate, I expected a blow to the back of my head, though I dared not look back. I had never experienced fear like this before. I was almost running a gauntlet. If they really were going to carve me up, then it was now or never. If they failed to do it, then they'd lose credibility with the rest of the prison inmates and risk a beating themselves, so I prepared for the worst.

As I walked the longest twenty yards of my life, I quickly tried to devise a plan of action in case of incident. But I couldn't. I would have to rely on instincts to save me. Sneers, jeers and pig noises came from all directions. Prisoners came to their hatch to spit at me. One of them got me in my face from eight feet away. Another inmate approached down the corridor. I wasn't sure what he was doing, but he wasn't working like some of the others. He was staring at me. He was big and muscular and as he came more clearly into focus, I saw he had many scars on his face and neck. He got closer. I had a feeling about this one.

The officers were well in front of me now and their complacency was about to cost me. The prisoner grabbed me by the throat and pushed my head into the wall. 'I'm gonna fucking bite your ear off,' he whispered, softly enough to evade attention from the officers who had by now turned the corner to the shower block.

I began to choke badly as his grip tightened. I managed to get an arm free and I thrust the heel of my hand upwards into his nose. This had the desired effect immediately, as he let go of me. I ran over to the corner where the officers had gone, to find them retracing their steps looking for me. I didn't look back. I decided that telling the languid officers what I thought of them was probably not a good idea, so I reluctantly kept my mouth shut.

We arrived at the shower block, which had a strong, dirty smell that made my stomach retch. If there'd been anything in to come up, I would have vomited. There was one other prisoner in the showers, but he was at least sixty and just smiled pleasantly at me. I sensed that he wouldn't try anything. I stripped off my clothes and deliberately filled my lungs with air as a show of strength to the old man, just in case. To my shock, as I stepped in the prison officers walked around the corner and back towards the door. Surely they weren't going to leave me? I was just one unlocked door away from all the other prisoners. I tried to watch the old man as well as the door, hurriedly rubbing the soap all over into lather as the water showered down my body.

Within about forty-five seconds of walking into the shower, I'd managed to wash myself thoroughly. The only thing that remained was for me to wash my hair. I looked at the old man. He leisurely rubbed soap under his arms. He was smiling to himself as he hummed some classical tune and his eyes were closed, but occasionally he'd open them and look at me. In a strange kind of way I liked him, because he was quite obviously detached from the rest of the prisoners who wanted to see me dead.

He threw a small sachet of shampoo my way. 'There you go, son.' He was extremely well spoken.

'Thanks,' I said hesitantly.

'Don't let these guys get you down in here.'

I ripped the sachet of shampoo open and carefully began to wash my hair. Not completely at ease, I watched him and the door. I couldn't trust anyone in here. The lack of attention that I was getting from the rest of the prisoners was unnerving. I suspected the door would fly open any second, signifying the end for me. I had no means of defence except my bare hands, so my only plan was to finish the shower as quickly as possible. Soap got into my eyes. I could either prevent the stinging by shutting them, or take the pain by keeping them open to watch the door and the old man. I was too scared to close my eyes despite the fact that they were agonising and frantically rinsed off the soap with them wide open. Then the door began to open slowly.

I ran out of the shower, grabbed my towel and began to dry myself quickly. The door opened fully and I was filled with dread. It was the prisoner who had delivered my food the previous day, when I'd got the attention of the prison officers after tipping the plate on the floor. He stood at the door and looked at me. I hurriedly pulled up the prison issue boxer shorts. I didn't fancy fighting for my life in the nude. The old man carried on showering and humming, either oblivious to what was about to happen, or choosing not to see.

The prisoner walked towards me. His casual demeanour was worrying. He had a haughty swagger. As he was alone, I knew that if I made a move early I could remove him as a threat. He, like many of the inmates, was small-framed and his pale features and staring eyes brought me to the conclusion that heroin or some other similar drug had played a major part in his life. I had spent the past ten years keeping fit and just when I needed it, I felt a surge of physical superiority. I looked to see if there was a way out of the shower block, but the door which he'd used was the only exit. This was what I had dreaded since I had come into prison: a face-to-face confrontation with a prisoner who wanted to injure me. I wouldn't let it happen. I would go down fighting and if that meant me getting into trouble, so be it.

I was confident that I had the upper hand, but the odds suddenly went out of my favour. The prisoner put his hand up his jumper and produced one of the plastic knives, now sharpened into a lethal weapon. I had about the same amount of thinking time as I'd had when my assailant from two years earlier had attacked me. I didn't think that pleading for mercy would be of any use with this individual. His eyes gave away his hatred for me; he wanted to seriously hurt me. He waved the blade in the air. Part of the fun for him was to see me scared.

I prayed that the prison officers would come in and overpower him. If that was going to happen, then they had about two seconds. He made a half-hearted attempt to thrust the knife towards me. As he stepped forward, he slipped on some water, which made him bend backwards at the waist in order to keep his balance. Without hesitation, I took the opportunity to keep his backward momentum going and pushed him in the chest. His frailty became even more apparent as I felt his ribs through his T-shirt. He fell back, losing his grip on the knife as he did so. It went spinning across the tiled floor.

I jumped on top of him and lay there and shouted to the

prison officers for help, hoping that the other prisoners wouldn't get here first. If they did, then it would be game over for me. Fortunately, three prison officers ran in almost straight away. I held my hands in the air to show I wasn't the aggressor, keeping my knee on the prisoner until the officers got by my side. I didn't know what other articles he had with him and I wasn't willing to let go until I was sure he was properly restrained. Two of the prison officers pushed me aside and took hold of the prisoner, whilst the other immediately recovered the knife. They took him away and I was escorted back to my cell.

The officer who brought my clothes back told me that the prisoner in question had been moved to another wing and that it was best that the other prisoners didn't find out what had happened or else there would almost certainly be more attempts at reprisal from them. I thanked him and got dressed, uninjured and not in trouble. In the circumstances, I considered that to be a good result. About ten minutes later, I saw the old man walking past my cell hatch. He had his towel over his shoulder and he carried his clothes as he was wearing just his boxer shorts. He was whistling. His ability to be wholly unaffected by his surroundings fascinated me. If it was a consequence of a condition or ailment, then I'd have been grateful to be afflicted by the same illness for my duration in prison.

After the shock of the morning's events had settled somewhat, I was swiftly taken over again by the excitement of the day ahead. I lay on my bed feeling relatively upbeat, though feeling happy in prison can't possibly be compared to experiencing happiness on the outside.

Moments later, Dr Ferguson arrived at my cell. The door opened. I tingled with exhilaration as I knew that he'd take me down to his surgery for a while. Maybe my lowest moment had passed; maybe my fortunes were destined to improve from now on.

'Come on then,' he said, looking at me with examining eyes. 'You any better?'

'I'm okay. I just can't wait for this afternoon.'

'You look very pale,' he said, which surprised me as I was feeling so much better. This made me realise just how poorly I must have been. The fact that I was feeling more optimistic didn't alter the fact that I hadn't eaten for the best part of a week. *And* I had almost killed myself a couple of nights ago.

'I'm okay,' I repeated, disappointed that my new mental outlook hadn't been an instant cure to my physical condition. I got up and we began the walk to the surgery. This time the passages were quiet and, to my relief, the journey passed without so much as a menacing stare from another prisoner.

As soon as we arrived in the surgery, Dr Ferguson took my blood pressure once again. He didn't make a comment and I didn't ask. I was too busy thinking of other things. I was fit enough to be able to withstand temporary high blood pressure and I wasn't concerned about it.

'Have they given you a shower?' he asked.

'Yes, thanks. I feel clean again.'

'Are you ready for this afternoon?'

'I am. I just hope that I can hold it together. I know that I'm probably going to cry when I see them.'

'Michael, it's important that you don't. You can cry all you like after the visit, but for your family's sake, you mustn't show them how you really feel. If you can show them that you're coping okay, then they won't feel so bad when they leave. If you cry, then they have to live with that until they next visit you, which could be a couple of weeks away. Promise me you'll be strong for them.'

'I will. I promise,' I replied. My eyes filled with tears as I said this.

'Good lad.'

I spent the next half hour with him. We talked about my career as a police officer and some of the things I had seen and done during it. I also told him I'd started writing this and that he'd already had a big impact in my life and would undoubtedly feature heavily in the story. He seemed flattered. He jokingly asked to have a signed copy of my book if it ever got published. He was at the top of the list and you can rest assured that by the time you're reading this, he will have his very own copy.

When I returned to my cell with Dr Ferguson, I was delighted to be greeted by something of immense value to me: an old radio. It was one of the most dated looking pieces of equipment I had ever seen, but it caused me great excitement. I raced over, plugged it in and switched it on. The poor reception was irrelevant; at least it worked. I felt as though I now had contact with the outside world again.

'Who got me this?' I asked, bewildered.

'It was the chaplain,' said Dr Ferguson. 'Now remember what I said about your visit. No tears, okay?'

'Okay, okay,' I said, not really listening as I fiddled with the tuner button on the radio. Everything was going right today.

'See you later then, Michael. Hope it goes okay.'

I suddenly realised how rude I must have appeared. 'Oh yeah, sorry, doc. I'm just chuffed about this bloody radio.'

He smiled and walked out.

In reality, the radio was a rather pathetic looking thing. The aerial was snapped off, the back was hanging on by the only remaining screw and tuning it into anything like a good reception was impossible, but this was a lesson in life for me because in my circumstances it was the world. I spent the next hour or so meticulously positioning the radio in the place with the best reception in the cell. It ended up balanced half on my bed and half on the back of the chair. I could just about make out each song as it came on. I quickly scribbled another drawing of Tony Adams and before I knew it, it was lunchtime. There were only a couple of hours to go until the big moment.

Eating was out of the question, but this time it was because of excitement and nothing else. I ignored the food and, more importantly, I ignored the prisoner who brought it. He ignored me, too. I stomped up and down as I made out one of my favourite songs on the radio above the crackling of the poor reception. I tried to turn the volume up but I was prevented from doing this by a nail that had been banged into the volume dial. I had been told not to publicise the fact that I had the radio. If the other prisoners found out, then they'd try their hardest to get it from me. I sat on the edge of my bed in nervous anticipation of seeing Mum and Dad, trying to focus my mind so as not to show any negative emotions when we finally met. That was going to be tough.

At long last, my cell door opened. The time had arrived. A prison officer smiled at me. 'They're here, Mick.' Magical words for me at that time. I tingled with excitement and I felt the strength drain from my legs. It took me some time to stand.

'We've put them in the library so that you're away from the others,' he continued.

This was good news, as I knew that I could spend the time enjoying the visit without fearing an attack from any of the prisoners. A revenge attack for what had happened in the showers was likely, but I could forget about that until after the visit.

I walked down the passage and this time there wasn't a soul in sight. Every single cell hatch was open and so, with natural curiosity, I peered into each one. Occasionally, a prisoner would come to his door as he heard the jangling of the officer's keys and the patter of our footsteps. Others were lost in their own world. I looked into one cell and what I saw was repulsive. The prisoner was laid on his bed wearing only his underpants. He stared at the ceiling and had his hands down his underpants, rummaging around in his pubic hair. He pulled his hand out with his thumb and forefinger clasped together, holding something. He then brought his hand up and placed whatever he had picked out of the hair into his mouth and smiled as he made an exaggerated swallowing sound. He was distanced from everything around him and he gazed aimlessly. My excitement at seeing Mum and Dad prevailed over my curiosity about this man, so I kept walking, though in other circumstances I could have watched him for much longer. I later found out that he had been segregated to the hospital wing as he was covered in contagious lice and he had persistently refused treatment because he saw them as his friends.

The atmosphere in the next cell down was rather more civilised. It was occupied by the old man who had been in the showers at the same time as me. His hair was perfectly groomed and he was clean-shaven. He wore spectacles precariously balanced on the end of his nose. His cell looked busy with piles of paper everywhere and he was writing at speed. Maybe he was writing a book about his time in prison, too. If he was, then I knew I'd like to see what he made of the incident involving myself and the other prisoner earlier that day. Not surprisingly, he was still humming. His contentment intrigued me but troubled me a little, too.

We arrived at the door leading to the library. The officer opened the door and nodded for me to go in. I took a moment to compose myself, took a deep breath and reminded myself that I had to keep it together. I entered the room. Mum and Dad were sitting at a table with an empty chair for me. What I had forgotten to take into consideration was the fact that my parents hadn't seen me in prison clothing before. I had had five days to get used to it, of course. The shock on their faces as I walked in was obvious. My dad just bowed his head. To see your father like this is about as bad as it gets. I'd never seen him cry before. He looked up at me and seemed shattered – his eyes were drawn and he was very pale. That was when I began to realise even more fully the effect that this was having on them. My mum's eyes glazed over, but surprisingly, she kept herself composed. She had probably told herself the same as I had, that she wouldn't cry until she was out of sight.

An uncomfortable silence between us continued for some moments. 'I'm okay,' I said. It was all I could think of saying and I was concentrating too hard on not crying. 'I'm out of here next week.'

After the initial shock of seeing me in this state, the atmosphere lightened. I did my best to convince them that I was in good spirits and the conversation became relatively normal as I caught up on everyday things outside. The subject of my being released early was not even mentioned; confirming to me what I'd already resigned myself to.

Our two hours seemed to pass quickly, *too* quickly. To the prison officer, it must have felt like ages. He had sat patiently in the corner of the room reading the newspaper while we talked. He finally looked at his watch and nodded his head to me as a gesture that my time was up. The fear in my stomach was heavy, as the imminence of the stark loneliness of life back in my cell hit me again.

'I think it's time,' I said. My mum gave me a hug. My dad gave me a look and nod of encouragement. He had composed himself following his earlier uncharacteristic show of emotion. The prison officer stood up, indicating that it was time for them to leave.

I didn't look into any of the cells on the way back. I was too busy trying to deal with the renewed low that I was feeling. I didn't know when or where I would see Mum and Dad again. Back in my cell, I cried for hours.

During my time in prison, I learned that whilst visits were something which would keep me focused and were just about the only part of the future worth anticipating, the depression they caused afterwards was unbearable. The hours crawled by; my head was filled with nothingness. I didn't even have the will to draw or write; my mind was wasting away in an empty world. I tried to get over the fact that the visit was over, but I couldn't. What did I have to look forward to now, other than having some pathetic heroin addict try to kill me because I was a copper?

The negative effects of the visit were clear. I was numb and I had lost my strength once again. I felt absolutely drained as my body took yet another battering of turbulent emotions. I put my forearm across my eyes and continued to weep. It was nearly teatime. I wasn't in the mood for bullies and so I got into bed and buried myself under the blankets. My stomach heaved. A little bit of vomit came up. I was in such a state, I couldn't even manage to be sick properly. At least my family would think that I was coping better than I actually was, as I hadn't broken down once during their visit.

I plugged my ears with my fingers as the noise of the damned trolley started again. As my cutlery was being placed on the cell hatch, I heard a loud bout of laughter from the prisoner who had delivered it. 'The fucking pig's crying,' he bellowed down the passage.

I heard the sound of hurried footsteps and sensed that I had an audience for my misery. I knew that the only reaction that prisoners had towards weakness was to attack it. Still underneath my blankets, I wiped my eyes using the sleeve of my jumper and then I cast the bedding aside. I got out of bed and went up to the hatch. Four prisoners huddled around as if they were watching their favourite programme on television.

I put my face right up to the hatch and smiled at them all. 'Did someone want a word with me?' I demanded. 'Well, come on. One of your lot has already fucked up one chance to have me in the showers. This is yours. Fucking hit me.'

I put my chin on the edge of the hatch and braced myself,

though I was reasonably confident that they wouldn't do any-thing; that would mean instant loss of privileges. Seconds passed, nothing happened.

'Listen to this, everyone!' I shouted down the cell passage. 'The lads giving you your food had the chance to do a copper. They didn't take it 'cos they didn't have the fucking bottle!'

I knew that this would, at the very least, cause them major embarrassment, but it was more likely that if a big 'player' found out, they'd get a beating. 'Who's laughing now?' I whispered to them, as I went back to my bed.

They walked off mumbling abuse at me. That meant nothing. I'd learned that most of the prisoners on this wing were all talk.

The day's events had done nothing other than suppress my appetite even further. When tea finally arrived, it looked as unappealing as ever. I decided that I would try to get an early night. I was very tired and I knew that the sooner Monday arrived, then the sooner my transfer would be able to take place. As the sun fell, I got undressed and into bed, still feeling clean from the shower I'd had. I thought of the visit and pondered on the week ahead. It had to be better than the one that had just passed. I was depending on it; I wouldn't survive a second week like this one.

Chapter 14

Game On

I spent some of the following week at Armley Prison. My hopes were raised and dashed on a few occasions, when I learned that transferring prisoners places a huge administrative burden on the authorities. I spent my time writing, drawing and thinking. I worried that the boredom would drive me insane. The hostility from the other prisoners remained constant, but as their attempts to break my spirits increased, so did my resilience. This animosity meant that another shower was out of the question for me until the morning of my transfer.

On the Wednesday evening, after having spent a week alone in my cell, I was told I was to be transferred to HMP Ford, West Sussex, the following day. I had never heard of this prison, but there were positive and negative aspects about going there. It was an open prison and that meant that I wouldn't be locked in a cell again. Open prisons are the lowest security, known as category D. They are intended for low risk inmates and prisoners approaching the end of a long sentence and in need of rehabilitation before their release. This means that each prisoner has his own key for his cell. Education courses are available in open prisons, and day releases for work experience are a way in which rehabilitation is structured for some prisoners. Of course my sentence was too short for any of this, but at least in such a prison I had the chance of relative freedom. I hoped that my true identity would be kept secret from the other inmates at Ford so that I could blend in as a normal prisoner. I already had my cover story ready. But the major downside to Ford was that it was at the other end of the country, meaning a round trip of well over five hundred miles for my mum and dad to travel on visiting days. I knew they would make the journey without question, but it was an extra burden which I didn't want them to have to endure.

On the evening before my move I was extremely nervous, as I knew that another failed attempt at getting me out of Armley could do irreparable damage to my spirits. I refused to allow myself to get excited, as I'd done on the previous Friday when the move had been cancelled at the last minute. I'd managed to acquire a newspaper at the beginning of the week and so I spent the evening reading it for about the fifth time. I knew every horse in every race from the sports pages. That was my latest pastime.

I'd been told that I would be travelling to Ford on the train in the custody of a prison officer. This thought excited me, as it meant I would have a few hours out of prison. It would give me a chance to taste the outside world and to recharge my desire to live and get out of prison. I didn't like the idea of being handcuffed in public, but on the grand scale of things this was a minor concern.

As I flicked through the last remaining pages of the paper, I heard the jangling of keys. I kept an eye on my hatch in case the officer was coming to see me, but I'd learned over the course of the past week not to raise my hopes too much so I didn't move from my position on the bed. Amazingly, he came to my hatch. He was a short man with a shaved head and several tattoos on his arms, which he made no attempt to hide. He was athletic and had a flat nose. He looked as though he could handle himself.

'Alright, mate,' he said, in a strong cockney accent. 'I've been sent up to tell you you'll be going on the train with me in the morning. We'll be getting off early so make sure you're ready.'

Even though I acknowledged this straight away, it did amuse me a little. Whether I was ready or not was completely out of my hands. Nevertheless, I nodded and smiled as I realised that my time at Armley was almost certainly going to end.

There was now very little that could stand in the way of my transfer to Ford. The officer who was transporting me was here, I wasn't relying on prison transport and I was going alone, so there would be little administration for the officers. The work had been done to instigate my transfer. Surely nothing would go wrong this time? I tried to hold back my feeling of elation, but it was impossible. I sprang from my bed. I was in good spirits and I'd imposed a rule of never writing letters when I was feeling negative, so I spent the next hour or so writing maniacally. I wrote to my parents and my sister, as I was missing my nephew. I desperately wanted to write to my nan, but I couldn't because we'd kept the fact that I was in prison from her.

By the time I'd finished writing, it was dark outside. I walked around my cell for ten minutes or so just to loosen up my legs. Being caged in the cell for a week had taken its toll and I ached from head to toe as, one by one, each muscle began to waste away. I was determined that I would use Ford as a means of improving this situation, before my release. What would the inmates at an open prison make of me?

It was dark outside when an officer came to my hatch and woke me.

'Get yourself in the shower. I'll be back in five minutes and then we're out of here. Okay?' It was the same officer with the tattoos. His attitude seemed different today – he was less friendly, more officious.

'Yes, sir,' I said, as a means to reassure him that however desperate I was, I would never consider trying to escape, or cause him any problems.

I ran down to the shower block alone. It was quiet again and so I didn't have to subject myself to the shampoo torture in my eyes. I had a relatively leisurely shower, then ran back to my cell and waited for the officer. I gathered my things together and sat and waited for about twenty minutes with my cell door wide open. Not only did I have my book, but I also had four tea bags, a phone card, several letters, some paper and a pen, and my little booklet from the chaplain.

Footsteps approached. I took one last look around my dark, dingy, depressing, numb cell. I felt nothing other than acute relief that I was being released from it. The depth of these feelings made me realise just how much I thoroughly loathed the place.

'Bet you won't miss this shit hole, will you?' the tattooed officer asked, his sympathetic tone having returned. I stared into the cell and privately thanked God for delivering me from it safely.

The journey began as he slammed and locked the cell door, this time with me on the outside. The echo down the corridor seemed louder than ever.

After signing a few forms, I was ready to leave. The officers wished me well for the rest of the sentence and they told me they hoped I would keep my job in the police, as I didn't deserve a dismissal. I thanked them and followed the escorting officer towards the door leading to the yard. As it opened, the fresh air hit me immediately. I took deep breaths; my first breaths of clean, unspoiled air for over a week. It was a bitterly cold day and I pulled my jacket around me. We headed towards the large gate. On the other side of this gate was a civilised world, a world which was only a matter of feet away, but which still seemed like miles.

Three officers who were huddling in a little office by the gate came out to greet the officer whom I was with. One of them was carrying a pair of handcuffs. My escorting officer looked at me. 'Now then, son. You know you're in bother if you leg it, don't you? I don't give a shit what you do, but you'll get two years if you leg it, and it won't be in a five star prison like Ford, either.'

'I've no intention of legging it,' I said, teeth chattering in the cold.

'Right, we'll forget the cuffs then.' This was an unexpected bonus.

The gate opened. The first thing that struck me was the

queuing traffic on the main road as people went to work. To them, it was the normality of just another day. For me, it was radically different. How I yearned to be one of the weary-looking people waiting in the cold to go to work. A day at work seemed like a real luxury to me now. I was jealous of their freedom. Once my nightmare of prison was finally over, I would never take liberty for granted again.

We waited outside for the taxi to take us to the station. With precise timing, and as if this were the start of a meticulously planned operation, it arrived, billowing smoke from the exhaust as it did so. The officer told the taxi driver to take us to Leeds train station. I bowed my head as, for the first time, my imprisonment was causing me considerable embarrassment and I didn't want the driver to see me. He was obviously quite used to these jobs, though, casually smoking a cigarette as though he hadn't a care in the world.

The taxi ride was short but mesmerising. I have never been absorbed in my surroundings so much in all my life. It was still very early, but the heavy volume of traffic into Leeds city centre starts early and so there was plenty to see. I must have looked like a child in a sweet shop with five pounds to spend. I didn't know which way to look. Queuing traffic is enthralling to watch when you've just spent the last eight days staring at the same four dirty walls. The three of us remained silent for the duration of the journey. I still hadn't worked the prison officer out and I think he thought the same about me. Running away never crossed my mind. Even if it had, I would have been unable to do so as I hadn't managed to eat at all in Armley and I'd lost almost two stones in weight in just over a week. I was fatigued, weak and feeling rather ill.

We arrived at the train station. It was unbelievably busy. The noise from the announcements seemed louder than I'd ever experienced before. People hurriedly went about their business; most of them with glum expressions on their faces as if the effort of getting out of their nice warm beds to face this ice-cold air and hectic journey to work seemed too much to bear. *How dare they look so miserable?* I thought. They had no idea what misery really was.

The officer didn't let me wander more than a couple of feet away from him and if I ever made a sudden movement, he tensed up ready for the chase. This became so blatant that, after having collected our tickets and walked to the relevant platform, I reassured him that an escape was not on my agenda. I also told him that, having had responsibility for people in custody as a policeman, I understood how he was feeling. This seemed to act as a pressure release as he immediately increased the gap between us to something a bit more natural.

We began to talk as we waited for the train and after I had explained the full circumstances of how I had come to arrive in prison, he seemed to warm to me. His name was Phil. As we talked more, he handed me his mobile phone.

'Here, call your mum and dad. Tell them what's happening.'

A free phone call was unexpected and very exciting.

'I'm going to get a paper. Don't go anywhere, will you?'

I knew the consequences if I tried and Phil knew I wouldn't risk a longer sentence. He *was* being very generous in allowing me to have this bit of freedom, though. 'I'll stay here, Phil. Cheers,' I assured him.

Picture the scene: it was about eight o'clock in the morning and there I was, standing on a busy platform at Leeds train station in my suit, holding a mobile phone. What could have looked more normal? But what was going on inside my head was by no means in keeping with my appearance, I assure you. For five minutes I didn't move. It was as though my feet were stuck to the floor. Finally, the train arrived and we took our places. Everything seemed bizarre to me. I'd forgotten about prison already. I was enjoying this moment too much to spoil it by looking back. I knew that my fascination with watching people eating sandwiches, drinking coffee, or simply doing some work on their laptop computers, was only a product of the complete boredom and desperation I had just endured. If anyone had seen my infatuation, they would have thought I was weird, but I couldn't help it.

The journey to London seemed to be over in minutes for me, but Phil commented on how arduous it had been. He was being fair with me and I really liked him. We had a whole hour at Victoria Station because the train to Littlehampton was not due for another hour. The day was getting better. Phil once again afforded me the ultimate freedom. We arranged a rendezvous point where we were to meet ten minutes before our next train.

I had £4 for my lunch, just enough to buy myself a cup of tea and a tuna sandwich. I sat down and pretended I was just another commuter. It felt brilliantly liberating. I tucked into my sandwich in a manner that gave away the fact I hadn't eaten in days, savouring every bite. I swilled big mouthfuls down with my tea. I must have looked a sorry sight. I almost vomited as the food landed in my empty, sore stomach. One of the waitresses came up to me and politely asked if everything was okay with the food. I felt like telling her I was a prisoner in transit and that she had no need to ask. Instead, I just looked at her and said, 'It was the best meal I've had this week.' I chuckled to myself as she gave me a vacant look. She didn't understand. Why should she?

I looked around the station as I wiped my mouth with a serviette. I wanted this time to last forever, but I knew I had to prepare myself for the shock of arriving at HMP Ford. I tried to visualise how the prison would be. Would my cell be as destructive as the one I had just left behind? Its inertness had destroyed my spirit. I prayed for something better, but knew that there was only so much that God could do. I overheard two of the staff behind the counter moaning to each other about their long working hours and low pay. If only my problem was so inconsequential. I realised, though, that it was unfair of me to disregard the problems of others just because mine seemed so much more serious. So I stood up and thanked them for their hospitality and waited for Phil just next to a florist's stall. He arrived almost instantly. My time was up and the institutional routine was to begin again. This had felt like the most precious fifty minutes of my life and it was a highly significant lesson to me about the meaning of freedom.

I don't remember exactly how long we were on the train. All I recall is feeling incredibly depressed about leaving Victoria Station behind. I began to feel annoyed that I hadn't run away whilst I had the chance. The weather complemented my feelings as the grey clouds thickened and the wind drove the rain hard against the windows of the train. The carriage was almost empty. I was miles away from home and I didn't know when I would be allowed to see my mum and dad again. The feeling of detachment and loneliness was almost crippling and, though I absolutely hated it, the thoughts of suicide entered my head again. I stared out of the window, completely uncaring of anything around. Phil was watching me. I didn't care what he thought. The horrible, destructive feelings were with me again and there was nothing I could do to stop them. The world passed by outside and no one gave a damn about me. My eyes filled with tears and I shook my head from side to side. At least I'd been near to Mum and Dad when I was at Armley. Down here, I had nothing.

I spent the rest of the journey in this awful state, my emotions spiralling down into a well of self-pity.

The world around me floated off and left me as we arrived at Littlehampton Station. I wanted to float off, too. I was bound for prison and there was no way out of it; I was mentally and physically trapped.

Phil climbed into the waiting taxi next to me and with unusual vigilance. His eyes were fixed on me. 'Are you okay, Mick?' he asked.

'Not really. It's a bloody long way, is this place.'

I was glad that the taxi ride was short. In a little while, we pulled up outside Ford Prison. The first thing which struck me was a hanging basket full of beautiful flowers. It was very quiet. The building appeared quite modern, unlike Armley, and I saw that there was practically no physical barrier at the gates other than a traffic pole, rather like the ones you see in car parks. There was nothing to stop a prisoner from walking out.

Phil escorted me into the building and took me to the booking-in desk. This time there was just one prison officer present. He was in his early fifties and looked ready for retirement. He slouched in a chair and our presence took some time to persuade him to turn his eyes away from a portable television which he was watching intently. He looked at Phil, then looked at me, without altering his posture.

'This one's from Armley, DK8639,' said Phil, placing a small file of paperwork onto the desk.

This provoked a reaction of annoyance from the officer as he eased himself gently out of his chair. He took another large sip of his drink, had a quick drag on a cigarette and then walked across. Expecting me to be familiar with the routine, he pointed to an area of the room, which had been partitioned with a shabby-looking curtain. He didn't say anything and I didn't know what he wanted me to do.

I glanced across at Phil, who told me to go behind the curtain and strip off my clothes. As I was doing so, I listened to the older officer chatting to Phil from behind the curtain. He was talking about a recent result of Southampton's in the Premiership. I was amazed. I was standing here stark naked and all this officer was doing was talking about football!

The situation had gone on for a good five minutes when I decided to put my boxer shorts back on. I peeped around the curtain. 'What would you like me to do now?' I asked. I was worried that this might annoy him, but I'd waited long enough and I was troubled by his lack of interest.

'Oh, come out here,' he ordered.

I walked out and, having made one quick visual assessment of me, he shouted through a little hatch, 'Medium, please.'

Within seconds, the hatch flew open and a working inmate produced a pile of clothing. The prisoner looked at me with little interest, but I knew that I had to pretend to be one of them so I smiled at him and he nodded back. I then knew immediately that he, and probably the rest of the inmates, too,

didn't know that I was a policeman. Upholding my false identity had begun and it was down to me whether or not I blew it.

The officer passed the clothes to me. This time I would be
wearing an old jogging suit. The top was bright maroon and
the bottoms were a piercing blue. One leg hung beneath my
heel whilst the other only made it halfway down my shin. To
finish it off, I had to wear my own footwear, which consisted of
a pair of smart, black suit shoes, as they had run out of prison
issue footwear. This resulted in making the tracksuit look even
more pathetic and it was very degrading.

Once again, my belongings were placed into a box and put
away in storage This time, though, it would be for a lot longer.
The officer asked me to sign a few pieces of paper. I think this
was to confirm what had gone into storage and also that I was
going to conform to the prison rules. I signed another piece of
paper accepting that I knew the consequences of an escape
from custody. The officer then took me to another door.

I thanked Phil and said goodbye, then I walked through the
door and was amazed by what I saw. There was a cricket pitch
immediately in front of me, with three or four prisoners tend-
ing to the grass. Scores of accommodation blocks were dotted
around the place. Each block looked big enough to hold about
twenty people. They were more like wooden huts than cells.
The place was dominated by a baleful silence. The feeling of
oppression was undeniable. How would I fit in I wondered. I
had no idea. Now, mild panic added itself to my depression. I
was unable to speak, as my whole face seemed to freeze.

'Wait here. The induction orderly will collect you in about
five minutes,' said the officer with a hint of relief, as he was now
able to go back to his television. He walked back through the
same door and left me standing alone in the cold, clutching my

pile of clothes and a towel. I noticed a large sign on the back of the door. It was a warning for prisoners not to knock on the door in any circumstances.

For a few minutes, I watched the prisoners on the cricket pitch. Just as the litter collectors at Armley had done, they huddled together and chatted whilst smoking cigarettes. I saw a well-built prisoner on the horizon. He came walking towards me carrying a file underneath his arm. He spoke to the prisoners on the pitch as he walked by; they all laughed together. His demeanour was different and I could tell just from his gait that he was not a violent person. He was clean looking and, as he got closer, I noticed that he had a rather intellectual look about him. I was about to meet my first white-collar prisoner.

'Bunting ... DK8639?' he enquired, rather effeminately. His voice was far gentler than his dominating appearance. He was well spoken and I was already intrigued to know more about him. Questions raced through my mind.

'Y-yes,' I stuttered.

'Follow me, please.'

We walked around the cricket pitch and headed towards one of the accommodation blocks. He enquired if I'd had a pleasant journey down. He was behaving more like a receptionist of a hotel welcoming an important guest, than a prisoner welcoming a new inmate. I found the whole situation bizarre, especially as it was such a total contrast to Armley.

I looked into each block as we passed. The inside horrified me. There were sixteen beds in each one, separated only by a small partition. The thought of spending my life with fifteen other prisoners terrified me. What if they found out who I was? They would kill me, I was sure of it. I looked around for the reassuring sight of a patrolling prison officer. There were none.

There didn't need to be, as this was a category D prison. I was probably the only person in here who would be looking for their presence. Without them, I was on my own, this time without the 'luxury' of a secure cell to hide in.

I yearned for this security now, feeling increasingly anxious with each step. However, my anxiety eased as we stepped into one of the smaller blocks, where a prison officer sat behind a desk reading a newspaper. It seemed that my arrival had been anticipated and planned as efficiently as the journey down.

'Stand here,' he instructed, pointing to a black spot painted on the floor.

I had barely got into position when a blinding light flashed. My second prison photograph had been taken without me even expecting it. In seconds, the picture spewed out of the camera. Without saying a single word, the officer laminated the photograph then promptly tied some string to it and placed it around my neck.

'Keep that with you at all times, failure to do so will result in a seven day nicking.' His tone was quite obnoxious. It must be a trait of reception officers to be like this, I thought, remembering the officer who had booked me in at Armley.

'Right, follow the orderly and he'll show you to your dorm,' he said, as if my arrival had been an inconvenience. He sat down and started reading his newspaper again. I followed the orderly, who continued to be chatty towards me. I had expected the prison officers to be friendly and the prisoners to be aloof, but my first impressions of Ford were quite the reverse.

I was alarmed by the scene which greeted me as we entered my dormitory. There were about a dozen prisoners lying on their beds. These were more like the type of prisoner I was used to. They were mainly young and most of them exhibited tasteless tattoos. All but one of them were smoking rolled cigarettes. The dormitory walls were covered in graffiti and the familiar musty smell was present again. They stared at me as I entered, still clutching my clothing.

'This is your bed,' said the orderly. 'I'll be back here in about an hour to give you the rundown of the place.'

'Okay,' I replied. The prisoners continued to stare and soon began whispering amongst themselves. My feeling of isolation deepened. There was no way that I could share a dormitory with these people, but I didn't know what to do or where to turn.

The loneliness of Armley suddenly became more appealing. I had spent the whole time wanting to get to an open prison and now I was finally here, it felt even worse. My stomach wrenched once again, causing me to double over as if I were going to vomit. The prisoners laughed at me. I just wanted to burst out crying. The isolation was unbearable. I couldn't take it. I ran out of the dormitory and all the prisoners banged on the windows and jeered at me as I did so. If this was their reaction to a new arrival, then what would happen when they found out that I was a policeman? I knew that if I was seen out of my dormitory then I would be nicked, but rational behaviour is difficult when you are feeling as low as I was then.

I arrived at the prison officer's block. He was still reading his paper. He looked up, perplexed by my presence.

'What is it?'

'Sorry to bother you,' I said, 'but I really can't sleep in that dorm.'

'I beg your pardon?'

I looked around to make sure that there was no one else about. 'I'm a bobby.'

'Oh,' he said, rather bemused.

'They'll have a go in there if they find out,' I said.

'Well, there's not a lot that I can do other than let you stay with Sean. He has his own room in one of the blocks. You can stay in the block if you like.' Sean was the orderly I had seen and I sensed he was no threat to me.

'Thank you very much,' I replied, quite sorry that I'd probably misjudged him earlier.

He walked me over to Sean's dormitory. It was identical to the one I had just been in, except it was empty. Sean had his own private room at the top. He had achieved the highest possible status in the prison.

I looked in through the door. He was sitting at his desk writing a letter. His room was rather like any ordinary bedroom. He had a television, photographs of loved ones on a board and even a pair of slippers next to his bed. Prison surely couldn't get any more comfortable than this. But Sean looked annoyed at our presence.

'Sean, can we put this one in with you, please? He'll be in the dorm by himself, but he doesn't mind.' I was amazed that the officer was asking the permission of a prisoner.

'Why, what's wrong with the other dorm?'

My stomach sank once more. I prayed the officer would make something up and spare me the ordeal of being in another prison where the inmates knew my history.

'Oh, we're expecting a load from Parkhurst later. They'll be in there.'

'Go on then,' came the reluctant response.

Sean wasn't quite as friendly as he had first appeared, but I was confident I could win him over because I wasn't the usual type of prisoner and I knew that he wasn't, either. This dormitory was obviously his territory and he did not want me on it. The officer left.

'Hi Sean, I'm Mick,' I said as I approached him, holding out my right hand.

'Hi Mick,' he said reservedly.

'I know that you don't usually get other prisoners in here, but I'll be no trouble to you, I promise.'

'Okay,' he said, shaking my hand with a disgruntled expression on his face.

I put my clothes onto the first bed in the dormitory. The room was massive, which made it seem all the more empty, but this was a far better option than sharing with other inmates. Sean went back into his room. He seemed halfway to being decent and I really wanted to befriend him, as I knew that the forthcoming months were going to be tough and having him as a friend would make things easier.

I made up my bed and had a quick walk around the dormitory. I was pleased to find a relatively clean shower at the top. It looked normal. Sean's shower gel hung from the shower rack. I decided that some of my next canteen money would have to go on some shower gel. I found a notice board and began to scrutinise every poster on it. I was aware that there were several head counts every day in category D prisons, the times were posted on the board. I had to be standing to attention by the door of the dormitory at 9 a.m., 1 p.m., 6 p.m. and then the final check of the day at 9 p.m. You weren't allowed out of your dormitory after the last count. Any prisoner seen breaking this rule was automatically locked in one of the few cells at Ford and, the following day, transported back to the prison from where they had come. I needed a watch.

I had to laugh to myself when I saw various anti-bullying

posters on display. Ford prison contained murderers, armed robbers and rapists; I doubted that a stern warning from the prison governor about bullying other inmates was likely to have much of an effect on them.

I went back to my bed and as I did so, Sean came out of his room with a file. 'We may as well do your induction here and now,' he said.

'No problem, Sean,' I replied.

He explained what I would be doing for the first week. He told me that each day I had to visit the various departments of the prison so that I could get a feel of the place and try to make the best use of my time there. I would be a working prisoner by the start of the second week and one of my tasks was to find a job in the prison. I had a number of choices: rubbish collection, where I would walk around the prison grounds all day picking up litter; farms and gardens, which would entail hard labour; education centre, but I did not qualify for this as my sentence was too short; and there were various other cleaning jobs around the prison. He told me I was unlikely to get a choice. All this was to start the following day, as it was now almost teatime. Another day of my sentence had passed.

Sean grabbed his plastic cutlery and we began the walk down to the dining hall.

'What's the food like here?' I asked.

'As prison food goes, it's very good,' he answered.

'I nearly starved at Armley.'

'I've heard it's bad up there. What brings you down here, anyway?' he asked.

'Oh, my family are down 'ere. It's just easier for the visits.' I tried to be as natural as I could, but I could feel myself going bright red so I pretended that I had something in my eye in an attempt to cover this.

He looked at me inquisitively. 'I know,' he said harshly.

'What do you mean?' I asked in panic.

'I know you're a copper.' He had a smile on his face as he said this, and it wasn't sinister.

'Where have you heard that? What a load of rubbish,' I insisted; not very convincingly, I admit.

'I saw your records when you arrived at the prison. I'm the bloody induction orderly. I know everything about you.'

I filled with dread, yet he didn't seem too bothered about it and just kept walking towards the dining hall, tapping out a beat using his cutlery.

'Don't tell anyone, will you? I'll be dead if you do.'

'Don't worry. I'll keep it to myself.' I don't know why, but I believed him. There was something increasingly mysterious about him. What did he have to gain by keeping my true identity a secret? He had the officers eating out of his hands, he had the best room in the whole prison and he had a cushy job as the orderly. He seemed to have it all.

I didn't get the chance to say more about the issue, as another prisoner approached Sean to accompany him for the evening meal. Sean seemed completely unaffected by our conversation. I followed him and the other prisoner like a lost sheep as we walked into the dining hall. I was desperate to ask him once again not to say anything, but he simply kept on chatting. He took large strides and so, every so often, I found myself having to skip in order to keep up with him.

In the dining hall I had my first experience of hundreds of inmates together in one room. Sheepishly, I walked to the end of the queue. There were about forty men waiting, carrying their personal issue cutlery in their pockets. Everyone had a tray, too. I seemed to have lost Sean in the crowd but I hoped that everything would be okay as I gradually got nearer to the food. Kitchen work was highly sought after in the prison because the working hours were long and so this made the time pass quite quickly. For this reason, the prisoners who managed to get jobs here usually tried their best with the food. Some of them were actually training to be chefs in the prison education department. When I finally reached the front of the queue, I chose shepherd's pie. If it was anything to judge them by then they had been taught well – it smelt good.

I looked around for a table with the least number of prisoners on it, then sat down and began to eat slowly, keeping my head down so as not to appear confrontational to anyone. I had no idea where Sean had gone to, but I really needed him as I felt very uncomfortable. As I tentatively forked some more food into my mouth, I felt a tap on my left shoulder. I swallowed the food and braced myself for a thud on my head. It didn't come. I kept my head low and turned round. Standing behind me was the very first prisoner I had met at Ford, the one in the booking-in area giving out the prison clothing.

'Alright, mate?' he asked in his strong southern accent.

'Hello.' Although I was astonished by his friendliness, I didn't let this distract me from thinking that he might have had a hidden agenda. He was tall, thin, about thirty. His hair was black and scruffy and his hard-featured face suggested he'd had a tough life. His fingernails were filthy and his hands soiled with tobacco. I was immediately defensive.

He placed his tray on the table and sat down next to me. 'You're the one from Armley, aren't you?' he asked.

'That's right, mate,' I replied, trying not to sound as intimidated as I felt.

'Why are you down here, then?' he asked, with a rather suspicious tone in his voice.

'My family live down here.'

'You've been fucking lucky to get your move for that. How long have you been inside?'

'A while,' I said, trying my best not to give anything away.

To my surprise, the prisoner held out his hand. 'I'm Ryan, anyway,' he said.

'Mick,' I said, shaking his hand.

There the conversation ended for about five minutes as he shovelled his meal into his mouth. He hardly chewed the food. It was as though he hadn't eaten in months. I ate at my own pace. Gravy slowly dripped from Ryan's chin, but this went unnoticed as he began to eat several slices of dry bread. I looked around the hall. Everyone seemed to adopt Ryan's eating style, making me realise that I was already beginning to show I was different as I ate with comparative finesse. I tried to deliberately spill some food down myself in an attempt to fit in. All this achieved, though, was to highlight my edginess and it was greeted by a few titters from some prisoners sitting opposite me.

'You'll be alright in here,' Ryan said. 'You just need to eat quicker. You can't keep other prisoners waiting in here.'

'Oh, cheers,' I replied. 'I'll remember that for tomorrow.'

I noticed that Ryan had taken four extra slices of bread and had placed them into a little plastic bag. I looked at them. 'The nights are long here, especially when you're hungry. They don't mind you taking a few slices of bread, so long as you don't rip the piss,' he said.

He stood up and it seemed natural for me to follow, as I had lost Sean some time ago. We walked towards the exit door. The prison officers sitting around the edges of the hall kept a watchful eye on me. Either they knew I was a policeman and were wondering why I was hanging around with another prisoner, or maybe Ryan was a troublemaker and they were making sure that I didn't follow his lead.

I didn't know what to do or where to go, and so I followed Ryan. He turned and looked at me.

'What happens now, Ryan?' I asked subserviently.

'We have to be at our beds for the six o'clock head count. I'll be in the snooker hall straight after, if you wanna meet up,' he said, as he began to run towards his block.

'I'll see you in there then,' I replied, as I walked towards my dormitory, perplexed by yet another prisoner. There was a biting chill in the air and I was underdressed for the conditions and so I began to run, too.

Sean hadn't arrived back at the dormitory yet and so I was alone, which pleased me. I sat on my bed and took a look at my photograph hanging around my neck. I looked sick. My face was pasty and drawn and I looked miserable and frightened. Armley had done this to me in just eight days. I lay back and thought that I couldn't have stood it much longer in Leeds, but I was feeling equally uneasy at HMP Ford. What was Sean's motive for not telling people that I was a policeman? Why was Ryan being so nice to me? How would I survive the next four months?

Chapter 15

On the Bins

The cold wind penetrated the gaps in the ill-fitting dormitory windows. The curtains blew around so much that I systematically checked that each window was shut. And unfortunately they were. It was going to be a cold night ahead. I put the remaining scraps of paper that I had left over from Armley on my desk. The rest of my possessions were in a transparent prison issue carrier. The partition board next to my bed was covered in writing. I tried not to read it as my surroundings were already depressing me. I saw an old poster of a motorbike over one of the other beds. I have never been into motorbikes, but looking at this was a more favourable option than reading the filth covering the walls. I stuck the poster up next to my bed.

Sean arrived as I did it. 'Was the food okay for you?' he enquired in a friendly way.

'Yes, better than Armley, thanks,' I replied, still a little puzzled at his hospitality. He was a far cry from the typical Armley prisoner. He had a presence about him, but it was a respectable presence. And for some reason even the nastier prisoners seemed to respect him. I still dared not ask him what he had done to get a prison sentence.

'Can you mop the floor in here?' he asked politely. I must have looked surprised by the request. 'It's my responsibility to keep it clean in here and so you'll have to do your bit.'

'No probs,' I said.

He showed me where the mop and bucket were and I got to work. I would have given my right arm to have had such a task at Armley and so I whistled contentedly as I mopped. After about five minutes or so, he came out of his room and stood at attention by his door. 'Get to your bed,' he yelled, as the shadow of a figure walked past one of the drawn curtains.

The prison officer entered and made a joke with Sean, who once again seemed very much at ease with the system. The officer then approached me. The peak of his cap was down to his nose.

The officer held a clipboard out in front of him and looked puzzled. He turned to Sean. 'I've only got you on the list for this dorm,' he said.

'Bunting will be with me till he's done his induction,' Sean replied.

It didn't even seem to cross the prison officer's mind to question Sean and, with a quick stroke of the pen on the page, he left. He didn't even acknowledge my presence. Sean went back to his room and I quickly finished mopping the floor so that I could go and meet Ryan.

The bell rang, which signified the end of the head count. Prisoners darted in all directions from the dormitories. I didn't appreciate why they were rushing. I walked in what I believed to be the direction of the snooker hall. At this time, I had mixed emotions: I was very apprehensive about integrating with the prisoners, yet I was pleased to have the freedom to be able to walk around. Such freedom would cease if word got out about me being a copper and so I continually rehearsed my cover story in my head. I did worry about Sean having seen my records and that I might be walking into his deliberate trap, but I had to take the risk.

About ten minutes later, having visited several wrong locations, I found the snooker hall. I entered cautiously. There were six tables and the room was packed with inmates, all of whom seemed to be smoking. I could hardly see the other end of the hall because of the tobacco smoke. I spotted Ryan and he waved me down to him. There were about eight inmates all standing around the table with snooker cues. One by one, Ryan introduced me and one by one, I shook their dirty hands. It probably seems arrogant but I hated the pretence. The one prisoner who stood out most to me was a man called Bruce. He was only about five feet eight inches tall, but he was about the same width and it was lean tissue. His nose was flattened to his face and he had tattoos on both cheeks, one of which was a picture of a dagger slicing into his skin. He was quiet and didn't make a show of his hard features and this, I knew from experience, was something to be wary of. He almost crushed my hand when he shook it. He looked into my eyes as he did so and his facial expression told me that he regarded himself as the boss. I had no desire to disagree as I pulled my hand back, stretching my fingers in order to relieve the pain. Here was one man who must never find out that he had just shaken the hand of a policeman.

The game began and we each took our turn to take shots. I kept close to Ryan, though I don't know why because he was probably as dangerous as them all. The topic of conversation was not one I was familiar with, as everybody talked about the first crime they were going to commit when they got out. In order to maintain my cover, I pretended that I was going to do something as well. I told them that I was in prison because I'd seriously injured a man in a disturbance in a pub and that as soon as I was released, I was going to finish the job properly. In reality, the first thing I was going to do was attend my disciplinary hearing in front of the Chief Constable and make representations to keep my job as a policeman. My story was met with enthusiasm and my new-found friends seemed to respect my tenacity. I felt, however, that I was digging a deeper hole for when they eventually discovered the truth. I had to keep up the pretence for as long as I could, though. The game continued and I found the lack of any other topic of conversation rather strange.

After about an hour or so, Ryan decided to go to the television room and he asked if I wanted to go with him. I certainly didn't want to stay with Bruce and his gang. Ryan was my safest bet in a wholly dangerous situation. As we walked towards the television room, he began to ask me more questions about why I had been transferred to the south coast. I began to feel he was suspecting something. I told him the story about my family living in the south and after a few more probing questions he dropped the subject.

We entered the television room. It was pitch dark. There were a few moans as we walked in. 'Close the fucking door,' came from more than one inmate. Every so often, the room was illuminated as a bright picture came on the television and I saw that there were very few seats remaining as a lot of the prisoners were using two to put their feet up.

I decided it was safer to stand than to ask for a chair, but I was at odds as to where to put myself as I thought that wherever I stood I would have been in someone's way. The familiar musty smell was present again. I looked around the room, more interested in my surroundings than the television. Fortunately, there were a couple of inmates who looked different to the stereotypical hard-featured, tattoo-covered prisoner. I would have to rely on blending with them to maintain my non-police guise – I was sure I didn't look like a routine criminal and certainly didn't feel as if I belonged. I knew someone would pick up on this sooner rather than later. The pressure was mounting. It was a different but equally unpleasant pressure from that of Armley. The protection of my cell there increased in its appeal as I anticipated someone in the room finally realising who I was. That would be the end for me; there were no prison officers in the television room.

There was a chorus of hushes from the inmates as the opening beats to the *Eastenders* theme music came on. This was obviously why the room was so full. There was absolute silence apart from when newcomers entered, when they received the same brusque welcome. I didn't feel quite so paranoid after this and sat on the floor to watch the programme. Ryan sat with me. Funnily enough, I was in prison at the same time as *Eastenders* characters Matt and Steve were facing trial for murder. The room filled with boos each time a policeman came on the screen. I joined in. I had to. It was horrible. Steve, on the other hand, received a rapturous cheer every time he appeared. Well, he would, wouldn't he? He was the 'baddie' and so were the guys in here with me.

The programme went on and I had terrible recollections of my trial and how unfair it had seemed. It is hard to say clearly how I felt about it because I believed in strong punishment for offenders, but I really held very little respect for the judiciary any more. I still feel like this today and I suppose I always will.

As soon as the end credits began, there was a big rush for the exit. Ryan explained that there was another television room for ITV and that there was probably something on which they all wanted to watch. The best seats were up for grabs, hence the rush. I clambered to my feet and waited for the room to empty, then wandered off with Ryan.

It was a bitterly cold night. The sky was clear and there were hundreds of stars. The sea breeze was piercing. Ryan and I wandered around the cricket pitch and he began to talk about his girlfriend and how badly he missed her. He had been in prison for just over three years and had another four months remaining. I don't know how I could have coped in a situation like this for three years. I was finding *my* sentence hard enough. He sat on one of the benches, bowed his head and remained silent. I was in no state to offer him any kind of support because I was feeling just as bad. I simply stood next to him and waited for his moment of contemplation to end. Eventually, he looked up at me and told me that he had bought a small jar of coffee with his canteen money and asked me if I wanted a cup before the nine o'clock head count. After that, we would be required to stay in our dormitories until the next day. Ryan knew that I wouldn't get my canteen money until the following day and I had nothing to eat or drink in my room. I was beginning to like him for his compassion. Feelings of guilt manifested within me, as I knew that he would have felt differently if he'd known the truth about me.

On the short walk back to his cell we met another of his friends, Scott. Scott had been in prison for a long time. I never found out exactly how long, but I once remember him saying that he had spent more time in prison than out – and he was only in his early thirties. He spoke openly about why he was there. I don't want to say too much because it would be dangerous for me if he recognised himself in this book. However, he was quite graphic in his explanation of the way he had killed and mutilated someone who had got in the way of one of his drug deals. It still shocks me to think that I sat in Ryan's room drinking coffee with this man. I got the impression Ryan did not really want to be friends with Scott, but was too intimidated by him to say anything. My own fear was mixed with intrigue.

Scott had a scar from the corner of his right eye down past his ear. The list of people who must never find out about me continued to grow. Ryan sat in silence. His wall was covered with cards from his girlfriend and he proudly displayed photographs of his two young children. I knew Ryan was different from Scott and I wanted Scott to leave. Instead, though, he stayed and began asking me awkward questions about the reason for my imprisonment and my immediate transfer. He knew the prison system well and understood that getting a transfer to an open prison usually took longer than the eight days I had been at Armley. He had figured that there was something different about me.

'So why did you get this cushy number straight away?' he asked.

'Cos of my family,' I replied, feeling wholly invaded and slightly annoyed.

'Were you shagging the fucking governor up there or something?'

'Don't be fucking stupid!'

'Well, I don't know what it is, but there's something about you that stinks.'

'It's fuck all, mate. You know what the prison authorities are like with the prisoner welfare lark. That's all it was.'

He seemed to accept this and drank his coffee, slurping every mouthful. He looked across at Ryan and smirked. The moment he finished his coffee, he rolled a cigarette and mixed it with cannabis. He lit it and stood up. 'Right, I'll leave you two boring fuckers to it then,' he sneered. He opened the door and walked down the corridor openly smoking the cannabis joint.

Ryan shuffled down his bed and kicked the door shut. 'What a fucking wanker,' he said, rather too loudly for comfort. I said nothing, but I agreed with him.

We spent the next half hour or so discussing my forthcoming induction week. He told me the jobs to volunteer for and the jobs to avoid. To be honest, my only aim during the first week was to see the Home Detention Curfew department, to find out if there was any possibility of me being released early on the tagging system. I wasn't bothered about which job I got because thinking about it made things seem too permanent and I couldn't allow myself to think that way. We made arrangements to meet again the following day and I left for my dormitory just before the 9 p.m. head count.

Sean was already in his room and I heard the sound of some action movie on his television. He was lucky. The wind was even stronger and colder than before and the room filled with a sinister howling. I saw a light flickering outside and Sean immediately opened his door and stood just outside his room. I stood at the end of my bed. The prison officer entered. He wore an overcoat zipped right up to his nose, which was red with the cold. He struggled to take a glove off as he ticked us both off the list. 'Thanks, fellas,' he said, turning to brave the inclement weather once again.

Sean didn't speak to me this time. He went straight back in his room and closed the door. I decided to have a shower. I appreciated the freedom of being able to do this, it was a very welcome luxury. I still had about five units left on the phone card from Armley and so I decided that I would phone Mum and Dad just before I went to bed. Having the freedom to use the phone in the dormitory, without having to book the call with an officer and waiting to be let out of your cell to make it, was equally luxurious. I placed my phone card under a pillow on one of the other beds. I didn't think Sean would steal it, but I was taking no chances.

The cold temperature in the shower room intensified the steam from the piping hot water. It was a real struggle to get out, but when I finally did, my skin was bright red from the heat of the water and I felt thoroughly clean for the first time since entering prison. I dried myself and got dressed. It was too cold to go to bed with nothing on.

Sean came out of his room. 'I'm watching *Patriot Games* if you want to watch it?' he invited.

'I'd love to. Thanks, mate.' This was unbelievable.

I told Sean that I was just going to make a call to Mum and Dad and that I'd join him as soon as I'd finished. It was an ideal time to ring them because I was feeling better than I had done all day. The call seemed to last for only a few moments as I tried to reassure them I was okay. Hearing their voices and imagining them at home upset me again, but I didn't dwell on it, and after I'd said goodbye to them, I went straight into Sean's room to watch the film.

I was amazed by what I saw when I went in. There was a carpet on the floor and he had been afforded brand new UPVC windows, which kept the room warm and draught-free. There was a little heater mounted on the wall, too. The room was decorated neatly with posters and photographs of family and friends. With natural curiosity, I inspected them closely. Several featured Sean in black tie attire mingling with rich and famous people. One photograph grabbed my attention more than any of the others. It showed him hugging a very famous male pop star. I tried to hide my astonishment, but I hadn't known anybody like this before and Sean's apparently glamorous lifestyle on the outside captivated me.

'Oh, I've known him ages,' he said, without prompting. 'He's a real sweetie. We only split up last year, just before I got sent down.' Sean said this in a matter-of-fact tone. He wasn't boasting about his liaisons with the rich and famous; in fact, it all seemed quite mundane to him.

'Wow, this is amazing,' I said, and I could hold back the inevitable question no longer. 'Why are you in here?' I asked.

He scowled at me. I had broken the rules, but the pictures I'd seen of Sean confirmed to me that he was special. He was not a stereotypical inmate, nor was I; I thought this common ground would enable us to talk a little. I was beginning to realise why the officers were treating him with such respect and why he had a room that would have made a pleasant spare room in anyone's house. I spotted a huge pile of phone cards but didn't say anything about them.

He turned the television off with a sudden flick of the remote control and rolled over on his bed to open a drawer. He pulled out dozens of photographs. 'Look at them,' he said.

He lay back on his bed as I looked at each photograph with renewed fascination. I must have recognised at least fifteen different celebrities. They all hugged Sean and looked very happy in his presence. I asked the question again. 'What did you do, Sean?'

'I got greedy.'

'What do you mean?'

'I had, still have, I think, a really good job in the city. I'm on, like, three hundred and twenty grand a year with all the trimmings. To cut a long story short, I saw a chance to avoid the tax man and keep all the money. I couldn't resist it and I got caught. It's as simple as that.'

'Bloody hell!' I said.

'I've known these people for years. I hang out in some well-established wine bars in the West End. It was getting silly. I was drinking three or four bottles of champagne every night. Something had to give. I think prison has saved me in a way. I've already lost four stone in here.'

He must have been massive before he got to prison!

He put the pictures away and smiled at me casually. He flicked the remote control and the film recommenced. My concentration had gone, though, and all I could think about were the stars in the photographs. Our lives outside the prison were worlds apart, but inside, our dissimilarity from the other inmates was a uniting factor. Before I knew it, the film had finished. He turned the television off and I went back into the main dormitory. I was grateful that he hadn't mentioned my job again.

The dormitory was much colder than Sean's room and so I curled up in bed wearing all three of the issue jumpers I had been given upon my arrival. The windows rattled in the wind, drowning any other sound and giving the dormitory an eerie quality. As I thought of how far I was from home and how long I had to maintain this false identity, I began to feel low again, but I was grateful that the evening had passed relatively quickly and drama-free. There was still a long way to go, but I remained confident that Sean wouldn't tell anyone about me.

Once again, I found that the hours dragged by and the frustration of not knowing the time was a nasty reminder of my stint at Armley. It began to rain and the force of the wind drove it hard onto the windows. The roof of the dormitory began to leak and the sound of splashing water compounded my irritation. I shut my eyes and tried desperately to sleep. I knew that the long, lonely nights were the most likely time for depression to strike again and I was determined to prevent it.

Suddenly, I saw the light flickering outside again and, with no attempt to keep quiet, the night-duty officer opened the door and walked into the dormitory. I pretended to be asleep and lay motionless. I could sense him walk right up to me. I wanted to open my eyes, but I defied my instincts and kept them shut. He shone the torch directly into my face. I found this rather odd, but I didn't react. He walked off and I opened my eyes slightly. I watched him hold some kind of electrical device to a painted dot on the wall. It made a ringing sound as if it were an electrical register. He then left, making an equally inconsiderate exit as the door slammed shut. I reminded myself of where I was and tried not to let it get to me. I eventually dozed off in the cold and wet weather of the south coast.

I had an early start the following day, as the induction routine began for me and several other prisoners who had been transported over from Parkhurst Prison. Attending breakfast wasn't compulsory, so I decided not to go. I wasn't hungry. My first appointment was an induction meeting with the acting governor of the prison. This was to be held in an unoccupied dormitory next to the one where I slept. There were several prisoners already present when I entered, all laughing and joking together. The long journey to HMP Ford from Parkhurst had obviously united them. They made no attempt to acknowledge my presence so I pulled up a chair and sat down, hoping that someone would speak to me and end the uneasy feeling. I spent the next fifteen minutes waiting for the governor to arrive, unacknowledged by any inmate in the room.

Several of the group boasted of crimes they had got away with. They showed no remorse and once again openly talked about their next planned 'job'. Prison was like a break between crimes for these boys, rather like you or I would take a weekend away after a week at work. To anyone reading this book who believes prison rehabilitates offenders, I can say that, in my experience, it usually doesn't.

The door swung open. An old man entered. He was small and his hair was silvery white. He had the butt of a cigarette in his mouth and he turned round and threw it out of the door as he walked in. As he blew out the remainder of the smoke from his lungs, I heard gasps of desperation from the cigarette-starved inmates. Despite this man's non-threatening appearance, his character changed the instant he spoke. He ordered us to stand. His voice was deep and loud and the tone was confident and non-fearful. His eyes panned the room and, one by one, he looked us in the eyes with an angry expression. He walked to the front of the room and pulled up a chair to face us all. There was no doubt that he had great authority and only a fool would cross him.

'I'm Mr Shaw, the acting governor of this jail and I am here to lay some ground rules for your time here.' His voice deepened and his expression intensified. 'As you will all be aware, the regime here is far more relaxed than Parkhurst, or whichever jail you have come from. If you step one foot outside the gate, we won't waste our time stopping you, you can go. But you will get caught and, believe me, you will never get a jail like this again. All I ask is that you screw your loaf, do the work, get your head down, do your bird and get out when you are due to get out. If there is any sign of alcohol or drugs, then it's a straight nicking and you are out. If you play the game, then your time here will be easier than any other jail you've been in. If you fuck up, then I'll fuck you up and make you wish you'd never met me. Is that clear?'

No one dared to speak.

'*Is that clear?*' he shouted.

One by one, we all softly said, 'Yes, boss.' In the space of about three minutes, he had asserted his authority on us all.

He got up, pulled another cigarette from his packet, put it in his mouth and walked out of the room before lighting it outside.

As he walked away, some of the prisoners muttered, 'Wanker', whilst others just gesticulated with their hands. I found it quite amusing – they all made sure that he didn't see or hear them. I spent the rest of the day with this group. By far the most useful part of the day was the visit to the prison library. I became a member and was instantly freed from my reliance on Tony Adams. I took three books back to my dormitory and went across to Ryan's room before tea. He was sitting writing a letter, but when he saw me and realised what time it was, he immediately picked up his plastic cutlery and stood up. 'Tea time already?'

'Are you coming across?' I asked, feeling more familiar with the routine now.

'Yeah. How's it gone today?' he enquired.

'Just had the governor's welcome and the library today. Not done much really,' I said, keeping my thoughts on the group from Parkhurst to myself.

We walked towards the queue for the dining hall. The doors were never opened early. We planned the evening and decided to meet in the TV room after the meal. When we eventually got in for tea, I was again pleasantly surprised with the quality of the food and ate the largest meal since I'd been in prison.

I had £7 to spend in my canteen allowance and, as soon as the bell went following the 6 p.m. head count, I ran to the room where I could obtain my goods. It seemed like a massive amount for me to spend. Once again, there was a long queue. Eager prisoners waited for the shutter to lift so they could purchase their supplies of tobacco and other luxuries. Other prisoners hung around the queue, waiting for debts to be paid in tobacco.

I had been waiting in the queue for about forty minutes and I was slowly but surely approaching the top, when a man walked in and barged his way straight to the front. The inmates before me must have been waiting for the best part of an hour and so the arrogance and aggression of the newcomer caused inevitable anger. One of these inmates took hold of the man by the throat and, without saying a word, head-butted him square on the nose, causing a loud popping sound as it shattered, spraying blood onto the walls and floor. There was a big cheer from everyone. The man wiped the pouring blood from his nose on his sleeve. He looked at his assailant and suddenly thrust his elbow across into the side of the man's head. The assailant fell to the floor, his legs buckling. He was dazed, but determined not to lose face. He got to his feet and what ensued was undoubtedly the bloodiest battle I had ever seen, as the men traded blows, using their fists, elbows and heads as weapons. Each blow that landed resulted in a horrific cracking noise from the other man's head. Two inmates went to stand guard at the door to keep a watchful eye for officers, as if it were rehearsed. The man serving behind the counter carried on as though nothing was happening. He was too scared to even acknowledge that the fight was taking place.

After a couple more minutes of gratuitous exchanges between the men, the man with the broken nose could take no more and he remained on the floor, nursing his injuries. The other man returned to his place in the queue, shouting, 'That's what happens if you try to push in front of Macca!'

The embarrassed and injured aggressor left empty-handed. Macca was bleeding from a wound on the side of his head, but he didn't seem bothered about it. My turn to be served eventually arrived and I quickly purchased six pounds' worth of phone cards. I used my remaining pound to purchase peanut butter and a packet of digestive biscuits. You can't imagine how much I valued these two normally trivial items.

My next task was to get a job. I had been quite impressed with the demonstration in the kitchen, but I knew that with weapons readily available, asking for such a job could be fatal if the truth about me ever came to light. The only other job which vaguely appealed to me was in the education block, but I was automatically barred from this due to the short duration of my sentence. As it turned out, I was given my job on my third day at Ford.

The tour around the prison on the first few days seemed pointless, because I was given no choice of job. My task for the foreseeable future had already been decided for me. It was to empty the bins and collect the rubbish around the prison building and its grounds. I would be expected to cover the full extent of the prison grounds and rid them of any rubbish that had collected there. My day's work was to commence at 8 a.m. and finish at 4 p.m. I was told that the working week was from Monday to Friday, with weekends off. My rate of pay was £1.20 per day. I had been reduced to the lowest of the low and my contempt towards the judiciary returned without much prompting. However, I tried to remain positive and each time I thought back to my incarceration at Armley Prison, I realised I was better off at Ford.

However, I received some bad news at the end of the week. The final head count of the day had taken place and I was chatting to Sean in the block when he suddenly informed me that I was being transferred to another wing. I had settled reasonably well in the dormitory and Sean posed no threat to me at all. Even though the conditions were hard in there, it was preferable to moving to a wing where I would be mixing with inmates. I pleaded with him to make representations for me to stay with him, but he told me that my induction week was over and the other inmates would suspect something if I stayed on there.

Luckily, something happened on the Saturday afternoon to distract me from the bad news. My mum and dad had travelled the length of the country just to see me for a two-hour visit. I had spent the whole morning looking forward to it. It had seemed like an eternity since my transfer from Armley, though in reality I had only been at Ford for three days and it had been just six days since my last visit from my parents.

The visiting hall, unlike the other buildings at Ford, was quite pleasant. The chairs were soft and there was a carpet on the floor. Once again, Mum and Dad looked exhausted. I wasn't sure whether this was due to the five-hour journey, or because they were living with the fact that their son was in prison for something he hadn't done. It was good to see them, though.

I tried to convince them I was okay, but I couldn't hide my bitter disappointment about my impending transfer to another wing on the following Monday. We joked about my new job on the bins. Once again, in complete contrast to the general speed at which time seemed to travel inside, these two hours seemed like two minutes. They promised they would be back the following Saturday. This provoked a mixed reaction inside me. I was glad they were coming again, but one week was another lifetime and I also knew that surviving another seven days unnoticed wasn't going be easy, especially on the new wing.

We said our goodbyes and I walked out of the hall past a long queue of suspicious officers. Just when I thought I was through, one of them pulled me aside and made what he thought to be a thorough search for smuggled articles. With my police training, I knew that the search he had just performed was useless and had I wanted to smuggle anything in, I could quite easily have done so. I ambled back to my dormitory feeling rather depressed that the visit was over. I was worried about my parents who now faced such a long journey home. At least I could ring them later.

I lay on my bed and began to read. The rest of the weekend passed slowly and I read two of the books I'd taken from the library. One was *The Damage Done*, by Warren Fellows, and the other was about shark attacks. Reading was my only escape from the torturous anticipation of Monday, the start of my job on the bins and my transfer to B-wing.

I asked Ryan if he knew anything about B-wing. Frankly, I wished I hadn't, as the information he gave me increased my dread. He told me that B-wing housed many of the long-term prisoners and even though they were in the latter part of their sentences, some still had six or seven years to do. This seemed an inconceivably long time to me. Many of the depressing and destructive emotions I had experienced at Armley returned to me on the Sunday and I lay awake all night in fear of the following day. There were several occasions in the early hours of the morning when I had gone to the phone and inserted my card, desperately needing to talk to someone. This was probably the only disadvantage to having easy access to a phone. But I resisted the massive temptation to ring home.

Officers made three checks on me during the night and each time they shone the torch into my face. Each time I pretended to be asleep. I had time to reflect on things and it on was this particular night that I actually realised the gravity of my situation, as I thought about my career in the police. Up until then, I had had neither the energy nor the will to give anything in the outside world much thought (apart from my family, of course). I considered the outcome of the disciplinary hearing which I would have to face. I tried to remain positive and I hoped that the force would see the injustice of my conviction and have the spirit to back me up. At least I would be out of prison by the time I'd learn my fate and that was always going to be a positive aspect to the hearing. For now, though, I had to concentrate on my new job, the job of emptying the bins and collecting the litter at HMP Ford.

Next day, I missed breakfast once more. My stomach had shrunk quite considerably as a result of the malnutrition and therefore I found that one good meal a day was plenty to keep me going. I now had the added benefit of my peanut butter and, using the bread I scavenged from the dining hall, I could eat at will.

I really didn't want to leave the dormitory and I was afflicted with nausea. Reluctantly, I packed my things together and with shaking hands put them all into my plastic bag. It didn't take long as I hadn't acquired many possessions. My pile of letters had grown considerably, though. Some days I had received up to ten letters from family and friends. Every time I'd gone to the collection point at lunchtime, the officer had made a point of telling me how popular I seemed, due to the consistently high volume of letters.

Naturally, letter collection was my favourite time of the day and was one of my only pleasures in my prison life. As soon as lunch was finished, we had ten minutes to go to the hut and collect our mail. I used to run back to my room and read each letter intently, gently floating off into the outside world for the half hour or so that it took me to read them. I found the letters from unexpected people very heart-warming and I often couldn't stop myself from crying. I was a desperate man in a desperate situation and the emotional response that these letters produced reaffirmed this to me. Having said that, I couldn't have got through without them, though. My time in prison really did teach me the high value of a simple letter. Knowing someone cared about me was a source of great strength and I hope that everyone who sent me a letter during my time inside realises how much I'm gratefully indebted to them.

I tidied my bed and left for B-wing. Even though it was only at the other side of the cricket pitch, it seemed miles away from the shelter and security of my dormitory with Sean. I hoped that this was going to be the final upheaval before my release. My strength was being drained every time I had to rely on it to get me through another ordeal. The emotional battering I had taken had left me very weak in a number of ways.

An attractive-looking female prison officer waited for me at the entrance to B-wing. Despite her natural good looks, she appeared stern. I understood her need to be like this and treated her with the appropriate respect. Nevertheless, her responses were short and abrupt and this alienated me from her. She marched me to my room. The familiar dilapidation was evident. There were huge flakes of paint hanging from the wall; there was a large, sticky coffee stain on the bare floor; the bin was full and smelt obnoxious. When I pointed out the mould on the mattress, she simply told me to turn it over and advised me it would be in my best interests not to moan about such trivial things.

I thanked her and she left. The door was wide open and because there were another seventeen rooms on the landing I decided to close it as I felt exposed and vulnerable. There was little activity on the landing, though, as everyone seemed to be at work for the day. I made the room as homely as I possibly could by pinning some photos onto the wall, then left for my first day's work on the bins.

The job specification wasn't complicated. As I reported at the desk, the officer simply handed me a black bin liner and a pair of old gardening gloves. He told me to walk the grounds and if I saw any litter to pick it up and put it in the bin liner. I didn't know how I would last an hour doing this, let alone a full day, or four months, but I thanked him politely and went on my way.

As I made my way to the reception gate, I saw Ryan going to work. He looked at the bin liner and grimaced. 'They didn't give you the bins, did they?' he asked in horror.

'I don't mind,' I answered and I was telling the truth. All I really cared about was seeing the Home Detention Curfew department so I could get a release date.

I walked around aimlessly. Occasionally, I'd see an empty crisp packet swirling around in the wind and would chase it and put it in my bag, but the hours passed as slowly as they had done in my cell. I was cold and wet as the rain penetrated the so-called waterproof coat I'd been given. I didn't dare go indoors. I would surely have been nicked if I'd been caught and so I carried on walking in the pouring rain, getting wetter and wetter and more dejected with each raindrop. I looked forward to the lunch break and the chance to read my mail. My thoughts wandered once again as I tried to imagine the world outside. I wondered how my colleagues had reacted to my sentence and tried to imagine them all at work. But being a policeman seemed a distant memory now as I carried on walking and tried to find the empty drinks can that was making a din as it rolled around in the wind. I was as lonely here as I'd been at Armley and I was beginning to feel as bad as I'd ever done because an end to my trauma seemed nowhere in sight.

I looked for Ryan at lunchtime but couldn't find him and so I ate alone. Sean was eating with a group of inmates I didn't know. The room was full of maybe three or four hundred prisoners. They all seemed friendly with each other. Even though I didn't really want to associate with the prisoners, I felt envious of the fun they were having. The prison officers saw me as just another prisoner and so, once again, I was trapped in a lonely land as I tried to assume an identity. I learned over time that the only way to handle my isolation was by switching off completely.

I ate what I could and sprinted to the mail hut. 'DK8639 please,' I said eagerly.

'Popular again,' he replied, handing me the biggest pile of letters that I'd had to date. There must have been at least a dozen of them.

'Thanks,' I said, as I dashed out of the hut and made my way to my new room. There was only twenty minutes of the lunch hour remaining. I wasn't quite so lucky on this occasion, as the landing was busy with prisoners who were also on their lunch break. Smoke billowed out of some of the rooms as large groups got together to play cards. Each room went quiet as I passed.

'Ooh, here's a new one!' a camp, sarcastic voice came from one of the rooms. Laughter followed.

'Come here,' said the voice again. This time it was assertive.

I didn't want to get off on the wrong foot with the people on my landing so I walked back to the room. A tall man stood at the door. He made exaggerated homosexual gestures, blowing me a kiss and taking a deliberate look at my backside. I wondered whether to take an aggressive stance, but decided it was better just to walk away. The room contained four or five prisoners, drinking from a large bottle of whisky. They roared as I walked off. I'd never felt so uncomfortable.

'Mmm, Vivien, he's ever so young,' said the same man, towards another room.

Incensed, I slammed my door shut, to which I got the inevitable reaction from the group. I was unable to lock my door from the inside, so I pushed my bed up to it to prevent anyone from getting in. I pinned a small towel over the glass panel in the middle of the door, as I knew they'd all want to look in at me. All I wanted to do was to read my letters in peace.

I climbed onto the bed and sifted through them to find the one with my mum's writing. I knew it would be there, she never failed to write to me on any of the days I was in prison. I hastily opened it. She had written the letter before the visit, but had posted it anyway, so I'd have it to read on the Monday. She told me that she expected that by the time I read her letter I'd be feeling low because the visit had passed. I was feeling down for other reasons, too, but her perception of my feelings was uncannily accurate. She countered the negative by pointing out the positive side of things – that two more days of my sentence would have passed by the time I received the letter, meaning that the end was nearer. Her words of love and support once again brought tears to my eyes, but with the giggles from the inmates just outside my room, I knew I shouldn't let my feelings show. I frantically wiped the tears away, but for each one that I wiped away, another two rolled down my face. I carefully folded the letter and washed my face in cold water. It was no good. The more I thought of home, the more the tears came.

'He's in here, Vivien,' said the camp voice once again. He was now at my door. He knocked quietly. 'Don't be shy, let us in.'

I decided that it would be in my best interests to play the game and so I hid my letters, moved my bed, and opened the door.

'Awwww, have you been crying?' he said, trying to touch my face. He had gone too far and invaded too much of my space. I pushed his arm away.

'Fuck off,' I whispered to him.

I knew that if I didn't assert some kind of authority now, then the rest of my time on this landing would be hell. He looked rather taken aback and walked back to the room where the others were. Once again, I slammed my door shut and burst out crying as I held my mum's letter to my chest. My time on this landing was not going to be easy. Through no fault of my own, I had got off to a bad start with the inmates on my wing. There was nowhere else to hide; this was it until my release.

Chapter 16

Anyone for Cards?

The routine for the head counts was slightly different on B-wing. Everybody had to stand outside his door so that the officer could walk up and down the corridor and make sure everyone was present. On my first head count there, the last thing I needed was another verbal battering from prisoners on my corridor, so I decided that if anybody had a go at me, I would challenge it. It was a gamble, but my experience as a policeman was that most bullies tend to back off if you stand up to them. So I washed my face again and braced myself as I opened the door.

The corridor was lined with prisoners. There was one person missing, however – the person from the room opposite mine. As I stood outside my door, everyone stared at me, smiling mockingly. Yet again, I felt extremely isolated. However, this was a time when I simply couldn't show any sign of weakness and so, one by one, I looked them all in the eye. Some looked away, others tried to outstare me. The only way I was going to get any kind of respect on this corridor was by earning it. I already knew that the men here had each spent many years in prison and so they were all hardened to the regime; I wasn't.

The stares continued. Then a man walked in; he *oozed* authority. The corridor went quiet the instant he appeared. He was quite short but very stocky, in his mid-forties. It was easy to see that he had trained to quite a high level in the past, as he had kept a lot of his muscle bulk and tone. He was wearing knee-length shorts, a T-shirt and flip-flops. And he was draped in gold – most of his fingers carried a huge chunk and he wore several thick neck chains. He strutted up the corridor, smiling at everyone as he did so. No one dared to move or speak. He approached the tall man – the same man who had goaded me earlier – and slapped him full in the face with the palm of his hand. He said nothing as he did this and the tall man didn't react. He continued up the corridor towards me and stood at the door opposite mine. He looked at me. To say that I felt intimidated is an understatement. He rummaged around in his pocket and pulled out a pile of phone cards. There must have been fifty or sixty of them. He took one from the top of the pile and offered it to me.

'There you go, kid. I'm Kirk.'

I didn't want to take the card as that would have amounted to a debt and debts are to be avoided at all costs in prison. But I didn't want to offend him, either. Everyone watched.

'No thanks, Kirk,' I replied. 'I've got some. I've just had my canteen.'

Kirk threw the card at my feet. 'Take it,' he insisted.

I bent over to pick it up. 'Thanks then,' I said, not really knowing what to do for the best.

He wandered further up the corridor. Occasionally, he stopped and spoke to a prisoner and an item would exchange hands. There was no doubt that Kirk was running this corridor and maybe the whole prison, even. I didn't know whether it was a good or bad thing that he occupied the opposite room to me.

At that moment, the officer arrived and he quickly strode up and down the corridor with his clipboard. Kirk casually meandered back to his door. He smiled at me in defiance of the officer's presence. The officer said nothing to Kirk and, with several ticks on his sheet, he left. Everyone darted into his room and as soon as the bell went we all left for work.

Collecting litter in the pouring rain suddenly became more appealing. Anything was better than being on that landing. I knew that returning after tea would be unpleasant and I dreaded to think what it would be like after the nine o'clock head count, when I had no means of escape. I thought about the tall man and Kirk. I hadn't worked Kirk out yet, but I was very wary of him.

I headed to Ryan's room and we made our way over to the queue for tea. I asked him about Kirk and he seemed cagey in his answers. One thing I remember, though, is that he made it clear that everyone in the prison feared him. He told me that it would be to my cost if I crossed him. Apparently, Kirk had killed several times in his life and he had told me he would kill again if he felt justified in doing so. Having seen him and his obvious status in the prison, I believed it.

We ate tea and I collected several slices of bread so that I could have my peanut butter sandwiches again later. Once again, we arranged to meet after the head count but he didn't want to come to my room. I was suspicious of this but I said nothing. Keeping my head down at Ford was proving to be a lot harder than I had first imagined.

I returned to my room. The tall prisoner had just had a shower and was parading up and down the landing completely naked. I tried not to look at him but he made this impossible, as he synchronized with my movements when I tried to walk past him. Eventually, I got past without any words being exchanged but I knew that I would have to choose my time to shower very carefully. I noticed that Kirk's door was wide open and I could just see the bottom half of his legs on his bed. I heard him snoring. I couldn't ever imagine me getting to sleep with the door wide open, but that was because I was never going to have the status that Kirk had in prison.

I went into my room and shut the door, then lay on my bed and waited for the head count. I must have dozed off because I was suddenly awoken by a thudding sound on my door and was alarmed to find an angry-looking prison officer standing there when I opened it.

'Sorry,' I said, rubbing my eyes.

He scowled at me and carried on. Kirk laughed. I couldn't work out whether he was being malicious or not. I hoped he wasn't and I laughed along with him.

As soon as the bell rang, I ran across to see Ryan. Once again, he was writing a letter and I sensed he was missing his girlfriend even more than usual. He made me a cup of coffee and we began to talk. He told me about his life outside prison. All my replies were fictitious and as Ryan became more sincere and open, I felt more and more guilty. I debated whether or not I should come clean with Ryan. He seemed okay. He even seemed trustworthy. Here I was, telling all kinds of lies to a man who was telling me his life story with some feeling. I liked him. He told me that he had been imprisoned for a deception from his bank for £20,000. He had never been in trouble prior to this. I maintained my story about the pub fight but still pondered whether or not to tell Ryan that I was a policeman. Time ran out before I had made my decision – the final head count was fast approaching. I genuinely did like him and I felt that my dishonesty was unfair. We shook hands and I left, anticipating with dread my reception on the corridor.

I was enraged at what faced me when I got back. The door to my room was wide open despite the fact that I'd locked it. There was a heavy stench of urine and it was apparent that my sink had been used as a toilet. I immediately threw my toothbrush in the bin, as that was on my sink and was soaked in urine. There was no way that I would ever use it again. I used my fingers to clean my teeth for the rest of my time in prison because I couldn't afford a new brush, owing to my limited canteen budget and my large demand for phone cards.

I decided not to let the others become aware of my disgust, so I went down to the shower block to collect some bleach and began to scrub my sink. The inmates had obviously been monitoring my movements as they all converged at my door, laughing at me as I cleaned up after them. I was furious, but once again I laughed along for reasons of damage limitation. I resented them all but I didn't allow myself to let it show. I dreaded to think what they'd be like if they ever found out about me. My decision not to tell Ryan was finalised at this point – I knew that living with the guilt was by far the safer choice.

The inmates, including Kirk, tapped at my door frequently. 'Come on, Mickey, open up. It's me, Kirk.' His tone was sarcastic and I knew he was trying to intimidate me in front of the others. He was being very clever, though, because on the surface he was being pleasant to me and this actually compounded his nastiness.

Reluctantly, I opened the door and he came in, closing it behind him. He sat on my bed, knowing that his blatant invasion of my personal space was frightening me. He was still wearing his T-shirt and shorts. He had a strong suntan – I don't know how he managed it because he'd been in prison for so many years. He sat back and smiled, flicking through my letters in silence. I filled with panic as I tried to remember whether any of them had made any reference to the fact that I was a policeman, and snatched them off him. This angered him and, for the first time, I witnessed why he commanded the respect that he did in the prison; his face changed from being placid and happy to furious. He looked ready to kill.

'Kirk, they're private,' I said submissively. 'Please don't look at them.'

Once again he just smiled at me. And fortunately he made no attempt to look at them again.

'We're playing cards after the head count. I'll see you in my room straight after, okay?' he said.

'It's okay thanks, Kirk, I have a few letters to write.'

'Mickey, you need to lighten up. I'll see you in my room in half an hour.'

He put his arm around me and squeezed. He possessed unbelievable strength and I felt the air being forced out of my lungs. His face went bright red yet he continued to smile. I began to feel even more intimidated. 'Okay, I'll see you later,' I conceded.

The head count was brief. Everyone was present and the officer was on the corridor for only a matter of seconds. Before I had had the chance to retreat into my room, Kirk grabbed me and escorted me into his. There were several chairs and a small table ready for the game. I really didn't want to be there but knew I had no choice. He was being very forceful and if I tried to get away, I knew things would get nasty. He took hold of me by the top of each arm and ushered me to the chair at the far end of the room. This meant that once everyone else had taken their seats, my exit was blocked. I was terrified, but I dared not show it as Kirk continued to be outwardly pleasant to me.

He opened a drawer. There was a large bottle of vodka, a bottle of Bacardi and two bottles of whisky. 'Fancy a drink, Mickey?' he asked.

'No thanks,' I replied. There was no way that I was going to have a drink. Being caught would have inevitably meant a nicking and a trip to the nearest category A or B prison. I'd take a beating first, even from Kirk. Nevertheless, he poured it and handed it to me.

'Go on, take it,' he insisted.

'No, really. I don't want it,' I said, even though I was terrified of the repercussions.

'You fucking ungrateful bastard,' he said, in an exaggerated East End accent. He drank my drink in one gulp and breathed out heavily after it had gone down. I sat and waited for the others, knowing I'd been set up and aware that something was going to happen.

One by one, prisoners entered the room. They all joked with Kirk and ignored me. There were six of us in all and the cards were dealt.

'Do you know how to play Scabby Queen, Mickey?' Kirk asked.

'No,' I replied. I did know, really. I had played it in my schooldays. It's where you deal all the cards evenly between players and you pick cards from each other on a rotational basis. Each time you get a matching pair, you get rid of that pair. The person left with the Queen of Spades is the loser and then has to pick a card from the pack at random. The number on that card is the number of strikes which the loser receives on the knuckles from one of the other players.

The game got underway and everyone quietly took cards from each other. One by one, the pairs were put on the table and one by one, relieved players dropped out of the game as they had got rid of all of their cards.

'So how long are you with us, Mickey?' Kirk asked, carefully taking one of my cards.

'I got four months.'

There was no point in lying. The room erupted with laughter. Kirk looked at me with piercing malevolence. I knew that everybody else on the corridor had much longer sentences and I also knew that I would be resented for having such a short one.

'Four fucking months?' exclaimed one of the other prisoners. 'You're a fucking shit and a shave.'

'I'm sorry?' I said, baffled.

'He means once you've had a shit and a shave, then you're out of here,' Kirk explained. I couldn't think of an appropriate response and so remained quiet for fear of annoying them.

The game continued in silence but I suspected they all knew the result of the game already. More players left the game, having got rid of all their cards and finally it was down to Kirk and me. I had two cards left, one of which was the Queen of Spades. Kirk had one left and if he picked the other card from me, that would make his pair and I would be the player left with the Queen.

He eyed up my cards, completely at ease. I willed him to take the Queen.

'It doesn't bother me if I lose,' he said. 'I love pain.' With this, he took a razor blade and made a short cut on his forearm. It bled profusely. He smiled as he casually took my Three of Clubs, leaving me with the Queen. My stomach sank. I knew they were going to hurt me, especially now that they were aware of the short duration of my sentence. Kirk licked the blood from his arm, staring into my eyes as he did so. He fanned out the cards for me to take my pick. 'Pick a fucking high one, you cunt!' he shouted.

I hesitated, hoping for a two or three; that wouldn't be so bad. I took hold of one of the cards and pulled it out. Everyone looked on eagerly. I flipped it over. 'Oh shit,' I muttered; I had picked a nine.

Kirk stood up and pulled the belt from his trousers. The buckle was massive. I looked on in disbelief. 'Oh, did we forget to mention this bit?' he said as the others laughed. 'You get the belt, not the cards. This is fucking prison after all.'

The exit was well and truly blocked off and other inmates from the landing had gathered at the door to watch my punishment. I couldn't believe what was happening. Anyone would think that they knew I was a policeman. I stood up, held my right fist out and braced myself. Kirk slung the belt behind his shoulder with the buckle end loose. This was going to do some real damage. He stared into my face and tensed up as he swung the belt. The buckle slammed hard onto my knuckles. The pain was excruciating. I pulled my hand away. It swelled up within seconds and was bleeding with the first shot. I put my injured hand under my armpit to try to relieve the pain. Everyone in the room grimaced, but laughed too. Kirk gestured for me to hold my hand out again. He repeated each strike with the same brutality, resulting in agony for me and the same merriment from the spectators.

After I had taken nine blows, he allowed me to leave the room temporarily. Tears were streaming down my face and the knuckles on my right hand had swollen to such a degree that my fingers went cold, as the circulation had been stemmed. The whole of my hand went blue. I really thought that I had broken bones. I bathed my hand in my sink with cold water. Kirk came in. His demeanour had turned once again as he showed concern for me. I hated him and wanted to do something to protect myself, but there was nothing that someone like me could do to such a powerful figure as Kirk. After ten minutes or so I was coaxed, against my will, to take part in the next game. It was exactly the same as before as Kirk and I were the last two players remaining, duelling it out to prevent the belt to the hand. I lost. This time my left hand took the battering, but luckily I had picked a three so the injury wasn't as severe as the first, even though Kirk had rounded up the number of blows to five just for good measure.

I was allowed to leave after this game and I closed my door and tried to finish off a letter which I'd started earlier. Even though I'm left-handed, I was still unable to write due to the pain, so I got into bed instead and turned off the light in the hope that it would detract any further attention away from me. At this point, I decided to make a visit to the Home Detention Curfew Department the following day, to explain my circumstances and to see if they could speed up the process of my release on a tag. I knew the plan could backfire, but I was so miserable I didn't care.

Surprisingly, I slept quite well despite the noise on the landing. I was aware that the other inmates in Kirk's room had been drinking heavily. I couldn't understand their mentality, because officers made several checks on every landing and there was a real risk of being caught. I figured that they didn't have too much to lose and the threat of a three week addition to the end of a fifteen year sentence was no deterrent and was worth it for the pleasure of alcohol. In any case, I don't think that there was an officer in the jail who would have dared to nick Kirk.

I woke up rather late the following morning with only ten minutes to report for work. I swilled my face and got dressed. I fingered a small amount of toothpaste around my mouth and left my room, having hidden my phone cards down a split in the wood on my wardrobe door. I knew locking my door was futile so I decided not to bother. I hoped that this would reduce the interest level in my room and its contents. I had burnt six or seven letters which had given a hint of my occupation.

The day was much the same as the previous one. I spent hour upon hour walking around the ground clearing up after dirty inmates. It was degrading. I wouldn't have joined the police service had I known that I could have ended up in prison for using what I considered to be an appropriate level of force on a violent criminal, and in self-defence. I hadn't even injured him and here I was, in prison. I focused my thoughts on my future and how I was going to turn the situation around upon my release. I planned exactly how I could rebuild my police career. The thought of dismissal didn't seem a realistic possibility to me. It wouldn't happen.

The lunch hour couldn't come quickly enough and I rushed straight to the Home Detention Curfew office. I rang the bell tentatively and a lady in her early thirties greeted me. She was wearing civilian clothing and didn't have the appearance of a prisoner officer. She was kind-faced, which came as a welcome change from what I had been used to.

I asked if I could speak to her in private. She looked concerned and led me to a private room. She was very polite, which again came as a welcome change, offered me a seat and sat opposite me. She listened intently as I told her that I was a policeman and described how I had come to end up in prison, and that I was struggling to cope.

She noticed my bruised hands and her face filled with horror. 'Have you had that because they know you're a policeman?'

'I don't think so,' I answered. 'I think I'd be dead if they knew that.'

She inspected my injuries. 'Wait here,' she said. I found her concern refreshing. She was my only hope of getting out of prison early. I put my face in my hands and sighed as I tried to hold back the tears again.

There was a hint of urgency in her step as she returned to the room carrying some paperwork. She began to fill in a form. 'I think it's wrong that you are in prison,' she said sympathetically. 'If we fill these HDC forms in now, it will speed up the risk assessment that you'll have to undergo before we can release you on tagging. You'll pass the risk assessment.'

'What's that?' I asked.

'It's just things like previous character and do you have a fixed address to live in and that kind of thing.'

'Oh yeah, I'll be okay with all that,' I said enthusiastically.

'Once you've been risk-assessed, we can fix a release date. I'll do my best for you,' she said, as she thrust the form my way for me to sign.

'Thank you very much.'

'No worries. Come back here to see me in seven days and I'll hopefully have some news for you. My name's Viv.'

'Thanks, Viv, I really appreciate it. I'll see you next week.'

I collected my mail and ran back to my room, ready to face anything that they were going to give me on the corridor of my wing.

Surprisingly, there was nobody about so I decided it was a good time to get a shower. I went into the shower room for the first time. There were six open showers and I pressed the button and switched one on, then got undressed quickly. The water trickled out. It was quite cold but I wasn't in a position to be fussy. I hastily got in, and it immediately took my breath away. I must have only been in the shower for about a minute but it was long enough to get clean. As I pulled my clothes back on I noticed a mop in the corner. There was an airing cupboard opposite the showers and the inside of the door frame made an ideal place to hide something. I carefully took the mop head off, which left me with the long stick. I figured this would make a good weapon if I needed to defend myself, so I opened the airing cupboard door and balanced the mop handle on top of the door frame. Just as I planted my weapon, I heard voices on the corridor. I dashed back to my room, feeling clean and refreshed. There, I read my mail in relative comfort at last.

The rest of the week dragged even more than usual, as I was desperate to see Viv again and find out if I was going to be getting out early. By Friday, I had collected more litter than you could possibly imagine. Even to this day, when I see litter blowing about in the wind I have an instinct to grab it. I walked around in the usual biting cold air, eagerly awaiting my parents' visit the next day.

I distinctly remember queuing for tea on that Friday. I had met up with Ryan as usual and we'd arrived quite early, so there were only about a dozen inmates in front of us. At the front of the queue was an old man who always seemed to get there first. He looked pale and weak and I knew that his crime must have been serious, otherwise an alternative punishment to prison would have been found for him. He was, however, extremely vocal and openly made racist comments in front of a black prisoner. Perhaps he thought that his frailty would protect him from retribution. Whatever, he seemed completely ignorant of the potential consequences of what he was saying. He rolled a cigarette and he could barely get it into his mouth, his hands shook so much. He boasted about murdering a paedophile ten years earlier, explaining how he had befriended his victim some months prior to the murder. When he had found out that the man was a convicted paedophile, he had waited for him to fall asleep in his flat one night and had then thrust a kitchen knife through the man's heart, killing him instantly. He was remorseless and told us all that it was his right to rid society of such evil. The ferocity of his crime was in complete disparity to his physical appearance.

That night, I managed to escape the torture of the cards. Kirk was busy writing letters, meaning I was off the hook. I used the time wisely and wrote six letters myself. It was the best night I had had on the landing and so I went to bed in relatively high spirits.

The usual Saturday morning routine ensued and I even managed to watch the first hour of *Grandstand* before the visit. Things seemed to be settling down a little. Maybe I had endured my initiation on the corridor and had survived and so was now accepted. But then again, maybe I was being overly optimistic. One thing that I did know was that nothing mattered on Saturday morning, because I had a two-hour escape to come in the form of normal conversation with Mum and Dad. I made my way back to my wing and as I did so I bumped into Ryan, who was also having his visit at the same time.

'Have a good one,' he shouted across the cricket pitch.

'Thanks, mate, and you.'

'Are you going like that?' he asked, referring to my prison clothing.

'I've no choice, mate. I've got nowt else to wear.'

'I'll lend you some of my gear if you want.' Ryan had had a considerable amount of his own clothing taken into prison. This is the right of inmates in category D prisons.

I ran across to him. 'That'd be great,' I said. It would be nice to wear normal clothing for a change. We went to his room and he passed me an old tracksuit top and some rather shabby-looking jeans.

During the visit, I spent the whole of the two hours trying to hide my right hand from Mum so that she didn't see the bruising. It was considerably better than it had been, but the swelling was still noticeable. I tried to keep things as positive as possible and I enthusiastically told them about my meeting with Viv. They were elated about the possibility of an early release.

As usual, the end of the visit came all too quickly. This time, though, we were more upbeat and their departure wasn't quite as desperate as the others had been, as we anticipated the news of my release date. However, I still returned to my corridor feeling dejected that I had to get through yet another week before I would see them again. I knew that anything could happen in a week and I knew that if Kirk and the others had their way, which they inevitably would, then I would have some more bruises by their next visit.

I got changed and took Ryan's clothes back to him before returning for tea. Once again, we went together.

'Have you heard the news about Scott?' Ryan asked.

'What about him?'

'He's been nicked for drugs. The screws sprung him for a piss test a few weeks ago and it came back positive. He's back at Pentonville.'

I didn't express my pleasure at the news, but it meant that one of my threats had been removed; it was a small mercy, and a welcome one.

I stayed in my room for the remainder of the evening. Things were generally quiet on the landing before the final head count, as prisoners were taking the last opportunity of the day to watch television or do some training in the gym. I had wanted to train, but my body was still too weak and there was always the potential for trouble in there so I decided to stay away from the gym for the full duration of my sentence. As I walked down to the toilet, one of the other prisoners arrived back on the landing. I only knew him as 'Scouse', for obvious reasons. He was a quiet lad and looked very young. He hadn't been involved in the card game and I hadn't really had much contact with him at all. He carried a large ring binder, containing a considerable amount of paperwork.

'Hello,' I said as we passed on the landing.

'Alright, mate,' he replied. 'What are you up to?'

'Not much tonight,' I said.

'Do you fancy a cup of tea?' he asked.

'Okay, thanks.' I saw this as a rare opportunity to make another friend.

His room was remarkable. The walls were covered with posters of Bob Marley. He had a stereo system that must have been worth several hundreds and he had his own bedding and a beautiful rug on the floor. There were several mathematics textbooks plus a few plants on the windowsill. Scouse had made his prison life as comfortable as he possibly could.

I flicked through one of the books. 'What are these for?' I asked.

'I'm in the final stages of my maths degree.'

'That's good. Have you done it all inside?'

'Yes, I've been in for fourteen years now.'

For a man who only looked to be in his early twenties, this shocked me. 'How old are you then?' I asked.

'Thirty-two. I got sent down when I was eighteen. I should be out in about nine months.'

I couldn't imagine what he could have done. He looked clean-cut and was obviously very intelligent, yet he had spent all of his adult life in prison. I sat down and he passed me my tea. We chatted about our plans for the future and, once again, I found myself telling more lies to someone who I didn't really want to deceive. He told me that he hoped to start a career and new life. He seemed so normal, yet I was guarded, as I knew that no man could spend all this time in prison without suffering adverse effects.

'I don't know what I'm gonna do on the out,' I said, trying to keep things as vague as possible.

'Can't you do something like this?' he said, referring to his degree.

'I don't think I've got what it takes.'

'I used to think that about myself, but I did it. I thought my life was over when I killed John.'

'You killed a man?' I asked.

'It's not as simple as that, but John died, yes.'

'What happened?' Once again, I was breaking unwritten rules by my questions.

'John was my best friend. We'd been out drinking and when we got back to my place he told me he'd been sleeping with my girlfriend.'

'Shit.'

'I told him what I thought of him and asked him to leave. As he walked out, there was like this surge of anger and I had to do something to him. I couldn't control it.'

'What did you do?'

'I picked up a house brick which had come loose from the front step and I followed him up the drive and rammed the brick into the back of his head.'

'Was that game over then?' I asked, feeling a little uneasy by the calm manner in which he was telling the story.

'Not straight away. He fell to the floor and his eyes just stared at me. He looked lifeless, but he was still moving. He began to breathe more quickly and then he had a fit. It all ended when blood started to pour out of his mouth, nose and ears. I knew he was history. I rang for the ambulance and got lifted by the Old Bill that night. I've never been out of custody since.'

I sipped on my tea, feeling rather numb by what I'd just heard. He got up and watered his plants as though he'd just told me what he'd watched on television the night before.

He turned and looked at me. 'Has that shocked you?'

'Yeah.'

'Murderers are not all big hairy monsters. I just lost my temper for thirty seconds and got unlucky. I'll never do it again. It could have been a cut to the head, but it wasn't. He died. It's the luck of the draw.'

He went on to tell me how he had received death threats from John's family for the duration of his sentence, so before he could be released he would have to change his name. Also, he would have to start his new life away from Merseyside for fear of revenge attacks. Even though Scouse was, on the face of it, a brutal killer, I couldn't help but like him. He made no attempt to hide what he'd done and made no excuses for it, either. He wasn't remotely bitter and he'd accepted his sentence and done his time. It was obvious that he was going to try to make a success of his life after his release.

I wandered back to my room somewhat amazed that I had found myself liking a convicted murderer. My mind was opening up from the tunnel vision I had inadvertently developed in the police service. I still see this as positive effect of my going to prison. I haven't lost sight of the fact that some prisoners are thoroughly evil, but I have to say now that there are other prisoners who don't by any means fall into this category.

The new week got off to a very bad start. I had spent the whole of Monday morning psyching myself up for possible good news from Viv. However, when I went to see her, I was told that she was off sick and probably would be for the whole week. The anguish that this news brought me resulted in yet another bout of extreme depression. I had built my hopes up all week for the good news, only to be faced with yet another week of uncertainty. Once again, I was unable to eat and I started to lose weight at the same rate I had done at Armley.

The week dragged on and so did the long hours spent in the cruel weather collecting litter. Every moment was spent thinking about my release, but it had become so intangible that I was filled with panic. Looking back, these were my worst times in prison. At Armley, I had had the feeling of hope as my transfer to another prison loomed. This had given me a focus. But at Ford, I felt that I had no hope at all and losing the focus that I'd had at Armley was soul-destroying. Time becomes your worst enemy and four months is an unimaginably long time when you are desperate.

I tried not to show my feelings the following Saturday at my next visit. I had had the worst week imaginable and the thoughts of suicide had frequently crossed my mind again. My mum tried to hide her disappointment about my release date but I could see the despondency in her eyes. We all tried to remain positive about the forthcoming week, but we had done that the previous week and everything had turned out totally negative. The weeks were painfully long and I didn't know how many more I could take without being given a release date. One thing that I simply can't convey to you by mere words on a page is the slowness of time in prison. It was this, and the living in constant fear, which was destroying my spirit.

I woke up on the Monday feeling a little happier as I antici-pated my meeting with Viv. I wasn't entirely sure that she was going to be there, but I knew she'd been off for a week and I had a gut feeling that she would be in her office again. I had been made to play cards once again and this had resulted in more swelling to my right hand. This was unimportant com-pared with my meeting, though, and I was used to the constant aching in my hand by this time. I had even stopped feeling angry about how I was being treated, because I knew that I'd have the last laugh when I walked out of prison. However, I knew that I couldn't let the others know about the possibility of my tagging because that would inevitably lead to jealousy and more beatings.

I found myself looking over my shoulder as I made my way to Viv's office. I was delighted to see that she was back at work and even more overjoyed when she greeted me as warmly as she had done before.

'I'm sorry about last week, Michael,' she said, as she ushered me through to a private room.

'No problems,' I replied.

'Really?'

'Well, if I'm honest, it nearly killed me not knowing, but I'll be alright. You can't help being ill.'

'Well, I'm afraid it's neither good news nor bad. There's been no reply from the risk assessment board but I'll chase it up this afternoon. Come back and see me on Wednesday. I should have something a little more definite for you then.'

The disappointment physically shook me. I opened my

mouth but no words would come and I could only let out a deep sigh. Two more days of uncertainty was a lifetime in my state of mind, and there was no guarantee of success.

Viv allowed the quiet moment to last for a few seconds before she spoke. 'I'll get you an answer, Michael. Just hang in there.'

'It's bloody hard. I just never seem to get anywhere.'

I felt incredibly oppressed by the weight of the judicial and penal systems. Once again, I questioned the system which had done this to me. All I had done was my job. I had removed a violent man from the street and I had got badly hurt in the process. The system was now treating me with a ferocity equal to that with which he had attacked me. My eyes filled with tears of frustration, which I wiped from my face. As I did so, she noticed my hand.

'Who did that to you, Michael?'

'It's nothing,' I replied. A swollen hand would have been the least of my worries if I'd told her that Kirk was the culprit.

I spent the next couple of days walking around in a daze. I was beginning to find it difficult to function properly and even the simplest of tasks had become a chore. I had even lost interest in my mail, as I no longer wanted reminders of a world I thought I was never going to get back to. Once again, I seriously considered suicide; it seemed like a quick and permanent solution to my suffering.

Indeed, I almost couldn't be bothered to see Viv on the Wednesday. I no longer had the energy to take more bad news and I anticipated nothing else. That morning, I lay on my bed motionless and tried and failed to get up to go and see her. I had even been off the bins for a few days as I was feeling so depressed. I didn't want any contact with anyone and I hadn't even seen Ryan since the weekend.

There was a knock at my door, unusual in prison. Respect of privacy wasn't high on the list of prison ethics and I had come to expect people to just walk into the room whenever they wanted, both prisoners and officers. I opened it expecting a stampede of prisoners but it was Viv. She looked shocked by my appearance.

'How are you doing, Michael?'

'Fine,' I replied.

'Can I come in?' she asked.

I was rather embarrassed, because I liked her and I didn't want her to come into the room and see what I had been reduced to. Nevertheless, I couldn't turn her away. She made a point of leaving the door wide open and she had a panic alarm in her hand.

I looked at her inquisitively, as if to ask her for the answer to the question of my release. She gave me it by way of a big smile. My relief was as definite as my disappointment had been before.

'Thank God!' I exclaimed. 'When?'

'Monday, October the eleventh.'

'That's only two weeks away!'

'I have some things that you need to sign as soon as possible. Do you feel up to it?'

Yes, I certainly I did; I had just experienced an instant cure to my depression. I bounced to my feet and accompanied Viv to her office. My guard had dropped and for these few moments, I didn't care who saw me with her. This proved later on to be a big mistake.

The paperwork was laid out on her desk when we arrived. She really had worked hard for me and when I saw the mounds of work, I thanked her. She told me that I'd be held on a Home Detention Curfew from my release date up until Monday, 8th November. I would be electronically monitored and I'd have to remain in my home between the hours of 6 p.m. and 6 a.m. This was a small price to pay for my release, no question. The formalities were completed and I had to consciously hide my delight from the other inmates over the following days.

However, the following Sunday night still haunts me today. Call it unlucky, or call it what you will. The events of this particular night were either bad luck, or a deliberate attempt by the system to make an example out of a policeman. Whichever you think it is, I hope you will forgive me for feeling a little paranoid about it.

The weekend had gone very well. The visit from my parents had been superb, as we were now able to count down the days to my confirmed release date. I was still maintaining my 'disguise' and there wasn't long to go before my release, so I shrugged Kirk's bullying tactics off. I was mentally stronger than I'd ever been since I'd been inside, and I was feeling able to stand up to the other inmates.

That evening, I'd gone to bed relatively early and had spent a few hours reading. The usual commotion was taking place on the landing but I'd been left alone. There was another drinking session going on in Kirk's room when I fell asleep at around midnight. Once in a while, I was woken by the officer's torch in my face but I was getting used to that as well by this time.

However, on this particular night the torchlight remained in my face and I began to come round.

I sensed that my door was wide open and I heard whispers in my room. Not knowing whether it was a dream or reality, I sat up suddenly. The light in my room came on and I found four officers standing over me. Two were going through my drawers and the other two were just watching. I felt very confused.

'Get out of bed, Bunting!' shouted one of the officers.

'What's going on?' I mumbled.

'Get out of bed,' came an equally discourteous command.

I had gone to bed without any clothes on and so I had the embarrassing task of getting dressed in front of the disdainful officers. I couldn't believe their demeanour. They were behaving in quite the opposite manner to the officers at Armley, who had generally afforded me and the other prisoners some respect.

I finished getting dressed and one of the officers took hold of me by the top of my arm and pulled me sharply. His grip was so tight that I felt a throbbing in my swollen hand. I was completely compliant. He continued to jerk me around, hurting my arm.

'Will you fucking well stop manhandling me!' I said firmly. All four officers appeared surprised by what I'd said.

'I don't know what's going on, but I'm a fucking copper,' I continued. 'I'll comply with anything you want me to do. Just stop pushing me about! There's no need. I'll do what you say.'

The officers had obviously had no idea that I was a policeman and the man released his grip immediately. They looked at each other, puzzled.

'I'm sorry for swearing but there was just no need for that,' I said, trying to make my peace and keep as good a rapport as was possible.

'It's okay. We have to be firm. We get some right dickheads in here,' replied the officer who'd shaken me.

'I know, mate. I used to bring them to you. What's all this about?' I asked, still alarmed.

'You've been randomly selected to provide a urine sample for drugs testing,'

'This is crazy. I've never touched any drugs in my life. I don't even bloody well smoke,' I said.

'As we say, it's purely random.'

At this, I was marched out of the wing to a part of the prison I hadn't been to before. When I entered, I was surprised to see that I'd been taken to what looked like a laboratory. I was the only inmate present. One of the officers passed me a small sample bottle. He told me that if I couldn't provide a sample within four hours, then it counted as a failure to provide and would result in the same action as if I'd given a positive sample. Fortunately, I had no problem in providing the necessary sample within minutes.

The bottle was sealed and I was informed that I could go back to my room. Suddenly, the implications of what had just happened hit me. I began to panic as I thought that the impending results of the urine test might impede my early release. I turned to one of the officers.

'Will this affect my release date next week? I'm due out on a tag.'

'I don't know, to be honest. I wouldn't have thought they'll let you out of here until the results are in.'

'How long will that take?'

'Four to six weeks, depending on workload,' he answered.

I couldn't believe it. Just as I thought I'd taken all the bad news I was going to have to take, he told me this. I needed to see Viv urgently. She would know whether it would affect my release or not. I would have to wait until she started work, though, and that meeting would be crucial.

I walked back to my room, extremely anxious, my heart racing. Just when I thought I was getting on top of things, the system had delivered yet another killer blow to me. I didn't know whether I could recover from this one. It was totally unexpected and that made it all the more painful. I vomited into my sink as, once again, my future hung in the balance as precariously as my mental state. Ford was proving tougher than Armley to endure.

Chapter 17

Watching the Clock

The rumours were rife on the landing the following morning and Kirk wasted no time in entering my room to ask why I'd been required to provide a urine sample. The explanation that it was a random test didn't provide the prisoners with the necessary level of entertainment and so several false stories circulated on the wing. This was all meaningless to me, though, because I was so traumatised by the fact that I could no longer look forward to my release.

I spent the day looking for Viv. I even risked a nicking as I completely abandoned my litter collection duties. Her office was locked up at lunchtime and there was no sign of her in the afternoon, either. It felt like a horrible conspiracy against me. The despair was insufferable. She was the only person who could help me. Where was she? I picked at my tea but was unable to eat as I resigned myself to the fact I was going to have to spend yet another night of grave uncertainty.

Kirk was waiting for me on the landing when I returned. He looked angry. Everyone else was conspicuously quiet. 'I've been waiting for you, Mickey,' he said threateningly.

'Oh hi, Kirk.'

'We know all about you,' he said.

I turned to run. There was no way that I could face him but another two prisoners wielding planks of wood blocked my exit.

Kirk laughed. 'Come here,' he ordered.

I ignored him. I was going to stand up to him this time.

He walked up to me. 'Why didn't you tell us?' he asked quietly and not unpleasantly. He was at his most dangerous when he pretended to be nice.

'Tell you what?' I asked.

'You're leaving us next week, aren't you?'

I filled up with relief as I realised that he hadn't been referring to me being a policeman.

'No. I got piss-tested, didn't I?' This was actually my saviour now, as it wouldn't have crossed his mind that a policeman would have been tested for drugs in prison. It was now acting as a camouflage to my true identity.

'It makes no difference. They can't keep you in for that unless it comes back positive.'

I was unsure whether to believe him, but I agreed anyway.

'You were going to leave without saying goodbye, were you?'

'I haven't had it all confirmed yet,' I said. It was the first thing I could think of saying.

'You're fibbing, Mickey,' he said.

He took my arm and began to squeeze until it felt hot with a friction burn. Only that morning a prison officer had grabbed the same arm. I was getting it from all ends. I pushed Kirk away.

'You're feeling a bit brave, aren't you, Mickey?' he said disapprovingly.

'Just let go, Kirk. It hurts.'

He complied but I knew that it was because he'd chosen to and not because I'd told him to. 'I'll see you later,' he warned.

I rushed to my room and closed the door. Everything was going wrong again. I had no real hope of an imminent release and I feared that violence towards me would increase as the long-termers discovered that my Home Detention Curfew was, at least, being considered.

I sat and wrote a couple of letters. The first one was to Gary, my tutor constable; we'd always remained good friends. I told him that I feared that Kirk was going to use some form of extreme violence against me and that if he did, I was going to use all the force necessary to prevent him. I had written the letter as a means of defence, should I face any problems with the authorities for being involved. If anyone knows about the tenuous nature of using self-defence as an argument against a charge of criminal assault, then it's me.

I wrote a similar letter to Samantha, a girl I'd joined the police service with. The effects that my letters would have upon the recipients didn't enter my mind. With hindsight, I think that it was probably a bad idea to write them but rational thinking wasn't exactly one of my strengths at the time.

Just as I'd sealed the envelopes, Kirk entered my room once more. I was deliberately less subservient this time but he was unperturbed by my show of strength. He sat on my bed while I remained seated on the chair. There was a prolonged silence as we stared at each other.

'I really like you, Mickey,' he said finally. 'You've got character. You're doing well to survive in here.'

I responded guardedly as I didn't want to fall into another of his traps. 'Why the fuck do you keep beating me up, then?' I said, trying to sound as humorous as I possibly could, but in actual fact being deadly serious.

'Have I ever hurt you?' he asked, trying to sound innocent.

'Look at the state of that.' I showed him my bruised and swollen hand.

'That's just a game. We all get that from time to time.'

'Well, I haven't seen any of you lot get it since I've been here.'

He removed his belt and passed it to me with the buckle swinging. He held out his fist. 'Go on then, Mickey. It's all yours.'

'No, I don't want to.'

'Do it!' he shouted.

Even this felt intimidating. If I didn't do it, then I was disobeying his order and if I did, I'd probably hurt him. As a compromise, I half-heartedly swung the buckle round on to his fist. It didn't hit him full on, but that was what I had intended.

'Fucking do it,' he demanded, as he braced himself again. This time I did and he just smiled through the pain. 'Again!' he shouted. I repeated this several times until Kirk had the same amount of swelling that I had. He kissed his fist, winked at me and walked out of my room. Kirk was pure bloody evil.

I knew that I'd have to watch my back even more from this moment on. Even though he'd made me hit him, I knew he'd turn it around so that it was now his turn again to attack me. I prayed that I only had a matter of days left in this real life hell.

I went to Viv's office every day, only to be faced with the same sight. Her door was locked and it was apparent that she hadn't been in for the whole week. There was nobody there to ask and I got progressively more anxious as the days passed. I didn't see

Ryan as much now, as I'd decided that my best course of action was to keep as low a profile as possible. I knew he'd suspect something about me if he found out that I'd been offered my HDC so soon after my arrival. He had waited over six weeks for his own risk assessment and therefore I didn't want to talk to him about mine. One thing I can tell you about most prisoners is that they're not stupid. They're very quick to suspect when something is amiss and I had no doubt about Ryan's sharpness.

Completely to my surprise, as I was walking around the cricket field on the Friday evening resigned to the fact that I would not be getting out on the Monday, I saw Viv. She was hurrying along with a file under her arm but this was no deterrent to me – I chased after her. She hadn't seen me but as she heard my footsteps approaching, she turned round.

'Viv what's happening? I've been trying to get to see you all week.'

'What's wrong?' she enquired.

'I got pulled for a urine test last week. I was wondering whether that meant I would have my HDC withdrawn.'

'Oh Michael, I'm sorry, I had no idea. There's no problem with your tag. You're leaving at eight o'clock on Monday. They can't stop that unless it comes back positive and you know that it won't, so you're out of here.'

I almost collapsed to the ground with joy. 'I can't believe it. I really thought that I was going to have to stay in here until the results of the test were out.'

'No, it doesn't work like that,' she replied, seemingly amused by my naivety.

'What do I have to do on Monday, then?' I asked.

'I'll be working on Sunday but you need to go around the various departments like the library and the stores and get your discharge card ticked off by each department so that we know we have everything back from you before you leave. I'll go through it all with you when I see you on Sunday. Come to my office at nine o'clock.'

'I'll be there at ten minutes to,' I joked, as I realised that I really was getting out of prison and that I only had one more weekend of prison life to endure.

My elation was halted slightly as I saw Kirk across the cricket square. He purposely looked at me and winked as if to let me know he'd been watching us. I knew that my weekend wasn't going to be easy on the landing but I no longer cared. Even another beating would be insignificant now.

'See you later then,' she said.

'Have a good weekend and I'll see you Sunday.'

'Just so you know, Michael, everyone in the office thinks it's a travesty that you were even charged, let alone put in prison.'

'That means a lot to me. It's not just me that thinks I was stitched up, then?'

'No. They've made an example of you because you're a bobby, but God knows what their motives were.'

I sprinted back to my room to get a phone card so I could tell Mum and Dad the good news. Their elation was obvious. I had two visiting orders remaining for the month and that meant they could visit on both the Saturday and the Sunday. They decided to stay in a local hotel for the weekend so that they could meet me at the prison gates upon my release on Monday. Nothing was going to stop me getting out now. All that remained was for me to deal with Kirk's antics over the weekend and I knew that there would be some, as he also anticipated my release.

There seemed little point in writing any more letters to my family and friends after this news, because I would be home before the letters got there. But such was my joy that I couldn't stop myself and I spent hours on that Friday evening writing to people who had kept in touch with me. Occasionally, I'd hear whispering outside my door as inmates deliberately made it obvious that they were planning something. For the first time in a month, I wasn't scared. Looking back, my complacency was misplaced and naive.

I decided that I would have a shower reasonably early that night. Most of the inmates left their doors open whilst they occupied their room, so quite a few people saw me walking down the corridor with my towel and pathetic bar of soap. The shower block was empty but the window was wide open and was swinging in the wind. I closed it in an attempt to keep some warmth in because it was bitterly cold. I turned the shower on and got undressed as the water warmed up, this time to a bearable temperature. The whispering started outside the shower block. I still wasn't unduly concerned as my jubilation at the good news was dangerously masking any potential fear.

Then the door flew open and Kirk and two other prisoners walked in, completely naked. They got into the showers next to me. Kirk stared at me and sarcastically looked me up and down with exaggerated facial expressions of desire. The other two inmates were in hysterics as they pretended to have a shower. I turned my back to the wall and kept cleaning myself. Backing down in this situation was not the right thing to do.

Kirk approached me and gently put his forearm across my throat. 'Right then, Mickey,' he said, reverting to his menacing expression.

There was too much skin-to-skin contact for my comfort and so I thrust my knee into the side of Kirk's thigh, which immediately disabled him. He limped back a few paces, which was just enough for me to get to the airing cupboard where I had stored the broom handle. I grabbed it.

'Fucking do it then, Kirk!' I shouted. 'Come on!' I continued. I was consumed with fear, but I knew I had to show that I was prepared to go down fighting this time. The difference between protecting oneself and getting into trouble for fighting is a very fine and undefined line in prison.

'Mickey, Mickey,' he said calmly, 'we're only playing.'

He wrapped himself in his towel and limped towards me. 'You'll fucking pay for that, you northern cunt,' he whispered.

That's when I knew that his chance to really hurt me had passed. I know from experience that the people who warn you of what they're going to do to you are far less likely to actually do it. I believed I'd won the battle against Kirk and I walked slowly back down the corridor and got dressed in my room with the door wide open. I had stood up to Kirk and so nobody bothered me this time.

This incident did distract my thoughts from my release somewhat and I have to admit that even though I felt a little more confident about the weekend ahead, I was still very scared by what had just taken place. My temporary drop of guard could have been costly and so I decided to try to forget about

Monday until it arrived. After all, I still had two full days of prison life to survive.

I didn't hear from Kirk or any of the prisoners again that night, despite the fact that I had left my door open. They had either got the message that I was going to stand up for myself, or they were planning their next attack for later. I spent Saturday morning getting my room ready for the following day. I was probably premature with my preparations but excitement had taken over. It was the second Saturday of the month and that was toilet roll day, meaning that I would have to queue with up to a hundred prisoners to be issued with toilet rolls. Each prisoner received only two rolls per month and for this reason they were viewed as a useful currency. Even though I had some left and I would be going home on the Monday, I decided to collect mine all the same. You never say no to anything that's free in prison. In any case, I would give them to Ryan or Sean before I left. I was sure they'd appreciate them and I wanted to show my gratitude to them for what they'd done for me.

We were all very upbeat on the visit that afternoon. My mum and dad were staying close to the prison so saying goodbye wasn't so hard this time.

On the Saturday night I met an inmate who had fascinated me from the moment I first met him. I had very rarely walked to the top end of the corridor; I had never had the need because my room was only midway up. On this occasion, I had gone to look out of the tall window that was situated at the top. For some reason, the landing was very quiet. Unusually, most of the doors were closed but I could hear groups of prisoners in each room. Something was going on but I didn't know what and as long as it didn't affect me, then I wasn't too concerned.

One door was open, however. I tried not to look in but it was impossible not to, as I heard several clocks ticking. I saw dozens of timepieces ranging from a valuable looking grandfather clock to tiny watches with faces the size of a fingernail. I had seen the inmate before but he never seemed to associate with the others. His room looked more like a little workshop. He was sitting at his desk, which was cluttered with small tools and various parts of watches and clocks. He had a light strapped to his forehead and a magnifying glass over one eye. He seemed to sense me watching and stopped what he was doing.

'Hello,' he said, in a broad Lancashire accent.

'Another northerner?' I said.

'Yes, lad, I'm from Bolton.' He looked to be about fifty years old and appeared very respectable. He had several suits hanging up in his opened wardrobe and there must have been at least twenty ties, too. He must have been inside for a long time just by the look of his room.

'I'm from Leeds,' I replied.

'I know you are. You're going home on Monday, aren't you?'

'Yes.'

'Back to Leeds?'

'Yes.'

'What are you going to do?'

'I'll have to look for a job, I suppose.'

'You seem like a good lad. I've been watching you in the visiting hall. Don't mess up again, will you?' He spoke quietly and he seemed genuine. I had never seen him in the visiting hall.

'I won't ever end up inside again. I've learned my lesson,' I said, maintaining the pretence.

'Good lad.'

'When are you out?' I asked, feeling rather at ease in his presence.

'I have eight weeks to do.'

'How long did you get?'

'Life,' he replied, turning a screw in the back of a clock.

'Oh shit,' I said involuntarily. 'How long have you been in?'

'I'll have done exactly twenty years when I get out.'

Such a long sentence in prison defied my comprehension. How had he coped? He seemed so together.

'What are you gonna do?' I asked, entering the room.

'I'm getting day releases from prison at the moment and I have a clock repair shop in Littlehampton. I'm going to set up full-time when I'm out.'

'That's good,' I replied.

'Well, I've nothing to go home for so I thought I'd try again down here.'

Our conversation was interrupted as all the clocks struck the hour with a chorus of chimes and rings. He smiled at me. 'I never get any sleep in here,' he said.

We carried on talking for some time. I asked him why everyone was keeping a low profile on the corridor. He informed me that one of them had instructed his wife to buy a number of Chinese takeaways and throw them over the security fence. One of the prisoners had collected them and so most of the men on my landing, at this time, were tucking into the culinary delights of Chinese cuisine. Their nerve astounded me but it made me realise how Kirk had managed to smuggle in his bottles of alcohol. I said my goodbyes to the man and went back to my room.

I didn't have any problems on that particular night and I

woke up on Sunday feeling elated that I had only one more night to endure in prison.

I spent the morning returning prison property to the various departments and by lunchtime, my discharge card was fully signed up and ready. For the first time since coming into prison, there was absolutely no doubt in my mind about my release. I anticipated a jubilant visit that afternoon but I was still worried about the 'prisoner discharge' procedures that would be implemented on the landing that night.

My last day in prison passed quickly and I had my final meal with Ryan. In a strange way, I was sorry to leave him. He had asked me for my telephone number and my shame surfaced once again as I deliberately gave him a false one. I couldn't allow myself to be traceable once I was out of prison, as I knew that the truth about me would eventually circulate. I'd been lucky, because Sean had kept the secret for the full duration of my sentence. I dread to think of the consequences had he not done so.

After tea, I went over to Ryan's room and gave him a book of stamps which I had remaining. His eyes lit up as if I had given him a cheque for a million pounds. I shook his hand, gave him a hug and we said our farewells. He thought we were eventually going to meet again on the outside. I knew that I'd never see him again, but I'll never forget him.

My next stop was Sean's dormitory. He was watching television. He looked weary as I entered. I told him that it was my final night in prison and I thanked him unreservedly for the secret that he had kept from all the other inmates for the whole of my time at Ford. He remained typically cool and wished me well for the future. He also wished me well for my disciplinary hearing with West Yorkshire Police. If you had told me that a prisoner would be supporting me in my quest to keep my job as a police officer, I would have thought you were joking. This was yet another example of the unpredictable world I had lived in for five weeks. We shook hands and I left.

As I walked back to my room, I knew that it wasn't going to be an easy night on the landing. To a certain extent, I was resigned to a beating of some form, but I wasn't prepared to put up with too much. I knew that it was going to be the prisoners' objective to provoke me into some wrongdoing so as to jeopardise my release, but they would have to do something fairly drastic for this to happen. I took my final walk around the cricket pitch and looked up into the clear sky. The stars were still waiting for me. I entered my room and, to my amazement, everything was exactly as I had left it.

The inevitable last game of cards started just after the final head count. Kirk 'invited' me to play. I didn't even try to resist as I thought that this would be counter-productive for me, as the prisoners would get me somehow. At least this way I presumed I was getting it all over with.

For the first time since I had been on the wing, the game was played fairly and I didn't lose a single one. This puzzled me. I was allowed back to my room at about midnight. Still my apprehension remained and I knew that something was bound to happen, but I just didn't know what. I entered my room and cautiously began to get undressed. I climbed into bed and, to my horror, felt something wet and sticky as my legs slid down between the sheets. I immediately jumped out of bed, yelling out as I did so. I looked down and saw that my legs were covered in white paint. I looked in my bed and saw that it had been filled with emulsion and human excrement.

I was rather annoyed but in another sense I was also relieved, because if this was my send-off, then it was rather tame. I went over to the sink and washed as much of the paint off as possible. Once again, I heard whispering just outside. Their attempts to cover up their laughter were poor as they watched me washing my legs. I turned my light off and crouched down behind my door. Occasionally, I heard the patter of footsteps and more whispering. This went on for hours, well into the early morning and I became frightened and exhausted by their determination. I knew that my door would burst in at some point and so I moved to the other side of the room, waiting for the inevitable to happen. Then the quietness ended abruptly. One of the doors further down the landing slammed shut and I heard maybe five or six prisoners running towards my room. There was no knock and I had deliberately left my door unlocked so that they wouldn't have to damage it to get in.

Four men barged in, wearing black masks with eyeholes cut out of them. One grabbed me and threw me onto the bed whilst two others threw a sheet around me and held me down by pulling tight on each end of it. Two men began punching me in the stomach, causing me to choke. Paint splattered from my bed, going all over the walls and on the floor. The sheet became tighter as I struggled to get out, restricting my breathing. This produced such a surge of strength that I tore the sheet with my bare hands, then punched one of the men in the face, which temporarily grounded him. It was difficult to see exactly what was happening because it was dark. Another man entered my room and threw a bucket of ice cold water over me. And then they ran out, laughing. It was over.

I was relatively unscathed, even though I was paddling in an inch of water and nursing bruised ribs. My fear had been that blades were going to be used, but I had been spared this. I turned on the light and saw that the bucket of water was in fact urine, but I wasn't too bothered, I had survived prison. Paint was splattered on the walls and floor. The bedding was ripped. The room was a mess.

One by one, I heard the doors slam as the inmates finally went to bed. Despite the fact that I had just been beaten up, I felt remarkably good. Walking down the landing to fetch a mop and bucket, I felt euphoric and free.

I cleared up the mess into the early hours. Birds were singing and dawn was breaking before I'd managed to get anything like clean again. I folded my sheets in such a way that the damage would go unnoticed when I handed them in. I was shattered, but overjoyed, too: the next bed I would be getting into would be my own at home.

I had quite a lot to do before my actual discharge and I wasted no time in doing it. I handed the remaining items of prison property into the stores and reported to the discharge office. I was escorted back to my room and an inspection was made. My early morning clean-up operation had actually made the room cleaner than when I'd first arrived. The officer ticked the sheet and I was taken back to the discharge office. I would never have to go back on that wing again.

I sat and waited. The bench was hard and cold. There was only one other prisoner getting out with me. His head was down and he looked rather upset.

'What's up?' I asked, puzzled by his misery.

'I don't want to get out. I like it here,' he said.

'You what?'

'It's good food here. It's free, isn't it?' he said.

'Yes, but I'd rather be home, mate,' I said, trying not to get too involved with the conversation.

'Are you on the tag?' he asked.

'Yip.'

'You're mad. Why leave this place for home?'

I didn't even entertain answering the question. His name was called and he walked through to collect his belongings. He shook my hand. 'Good luck, mate,' he said.

'Cheers, and you.'

I was left alone in the small waiting room. This was to be my last ten minutes of loneliness. I could sense Mum and Dad waiting outside for me and I couldn't stop smiling, something which I hadn't done for a long time. It made my gaunt face ache. I tried to think back to what I had just been through, but my mind protected me and wouldn't allow me to. It was as though it had all happened in a former life and all I could think about was walking out of the gates.

My name was called. I was handed my clothing and I quickly changed, occasionally being interrupted to sign yet more forms. They could have handed me anything to sign; I just wanted out. The officer gave me £46 and I was told that I had to be home before 6 p.m. so that the HDC officer could come to my home to fit the tag around my ankle and install the accompanying box of electronics in my house. He shook my hand and winked. 'Well done, lad,' he said.

I fastened my belt and hung my tie around my neck. I picked up the black bin liner containing my belongings and threw it over my back. Another officer unlocked the door and I was faced with the outside world. I didn't know what this world had in store for me and I didn't care, even about whether or not I was going to keep my job. I closed my eyes, took a deep breath and stepped outside. I wasn't completely free, but boy, did I feel it.

I saw my mum and dad waiting on the other side of the road. I tried to look at the prison behind me but my head refused to turn. I never, ever want to see that place again in my life. I crossed the road, dropped my bag and ran to the car. Mum hugged me whilst Dad put my bag into the boot of his car. Then we got in and began the long journey home.

I had done my time. Only God knew what the future held for me from this point onwards, but prison had taught me that whatever my future held, God would be with me every step of the way.

Part III

Michael Bunting
after Prison

Chapter 18

Life on the Out

They say that time is a great healer. I wrote this chapter in 2007, ten years since the incident and eight years since my release from prison. I would say that, in my case, 'they' are wrong.

I remember the day I was released as vividly as the knife attack at Armley and the card games at Ford. It was the moment I'd waited thirty-three days for. That may not sound long, but when you're a policeman doing time, thirty-three days feels like life. The journey from the south coast back to Leeds took almost five hours. Dad drove without a break so as not to miss the six o'clock deadline. I was to spend the next five weeks with a large plastic box fixed around my ankle, monitoring everything I did. I was still a policeman.

With two hours remaining, Dad took me to the local super-market. The prison service had given me the money, and I intended to spend it. I'd never received anything from the state before, and I felt a little guilty. However, the luxury of being able to buy what I wanted meant I entered the store with child-like enthusiasm. It's difficult to describe the feeling I had as I went in; something that had been so basic and meaningless before had now become the focus of my elation.

I sauntered around the aisles, completely infatuated by the food. I spent ten minutes or so just walking aimlessly. My parents wandered behind me. I remember Mum was clutching a few ten pound notes, so I knew that I could exceed the £46 if I so wished. I must have looked a sight. I was wearing a creased suit with the shirt out and unbuttoned at the top. I was also looking gaunt and undernourished. I had lost over two stones after all. I kept on repeating the words, 'thank you', in my head. I'm not sure who I was talking to, but given the religious reali-sation that I'd experienced in prison, I suppose it must have been God. God had truly played a huge part in my survival, and even though I'm not a deeply religious person, I still think back to the chat I'd had with the chaplain in Armley Prison. I think I'll always believe that God exists in some form.

My first significant experience after being released came as I was leaving the supermarket. As I made my way to the exit doors, I saw something that immediately grabbed my attention. It raised an issue in my mind that had always been there before, anyway, but this encounter brought it to the forefront, which is where it has remained to this day. I saw a little boy of maybe eight or nine years of age. His legs were restrained in an extended position in a rather elaborate-looking wheelchair. His wrists were secured on the armrests in a similar way. His head was held upright by a large strap around his forehead and his eyes rolled uncontrollably. I assumed he was blind, and he was wearing two very large hearing aids. He salivated from his mouth, which was wide open. For a reason I'm still not sure of, I squatted down in front of him and said something. I can't remember exactly what it was, but it was something like 'Alright, lad?'

He made a groaning sound and seemed to gain control of his mouth for a second or two as a smile appeared on his face. The woman who was pushing the wheelchair said nothing, but smiled appreciatively at me for a few seconds. His body had become momentarily rigid and I sensed his excitement as she pushed him away into the store. This chance encounter, just hours after my release from prison, didn't mean a great deal to me at the time. It would become more significant as time went on.

Walking into my house was another strange experience. It didn't really feel like home, yet I'd lived there for years. Balloons filled the living room and there were neatly arranged vases of flowers everywhere. It was perfectly tidy. My mum had obviously spent hours cleaning. This made me feel out of control, which angered me about my situation. I was grateful to Mum, though, and, ultimately, the joy of being home was my prevailing emotion.

Eating my first meal that evening was interrupted by the arrival of the Home Detention Curfew staff. The euphoria of being released powerfully overrode any negativity this caused but, nevertheless, having two strangers walking through every room in my house to install the electronic tagging equipment was not the nicest way to spend my first evening out of jail. They were a little bewildered by my situation, and we began chatting about how I'd ended up in prison. They seemed sympathetic and even said that if they'd had any choice in the matter, they wouldn't have tagged me. They were duty-bound, though, and duly fastened the cumbersome thing to my left ankle. It felt degrading and unnecessary. I wasn't permitted to leave my house between the hours of 6 p.m. and 6 a.m. until further notice; if I were to do so, an alarm would be activated and I would be arrested and placed back into a high category prison with no questions asked. Being tagged was a small price to pay for getting out of prison, though.

Three or four police cars arrived on my drive that evening as my colleagues came round for a cup of tea to welcome me home. I made them a drink, to a wave of tongue-in-cheek jibes about me being an ex-con. I laughed along with them, but the stark truth of the matter was that my future was in the balance.

At that point, 11th October 1999, I was still a police officer. My salary had been frozen and, as the rules of the force state, I wasn't able to seek alternative employment or claim benefits. It quickly became apparent that I needed money from somewhere. My mortgage payments mounted and I began to struggle with my bills. The pressure intensified very quickly. It was a different kind of strain to being in prison, but nonetheless it was difficult to deal with. My jubilant mood after getting out was thwarted within days by this unexpected feeling of financial panic. I'd already lost my freedom and my career and I'd got a criminal record; losing my house would have been the final straw. I began to understand why some habitual criminals seek sanctuary in the prison system.

I kept trying to make contact with senior officers to address the limbo that I was in. I didn't want handouts; I just wanted to know where I stood. Twenty-six months had gone by since I'd been attacked and now the pressure seemed to be increasing again. I'd built the court case up in my mind and saw its conclusion as an end to the worst two years of my life. This had been a naive view and, in a way, a dangerous one. I began to feel really low and I'd spend ages just sitting in my living room alone, gazing at the large device around my ankle, surrounded by red-lettered bills.

The officers rarely returned my calls, which compounded my problems and increased my feelings of isolation. The suicidal thoughts I'd had in prison soon returned and I'd spend hours thinking of the easiest way to kill myself. I never really thought I'd do it, but it was a comfort to know that ultimately I had control of my destiny. The little boy I'd met at the supermarket played his part on these darker days, and thinking of him helped me through. In fact, I think of him to this day.

Financial salvation came from my parents, who loaned me a substantial sum of money to prevent me from having my house repossessed. This may sound like the answer to the problem; however, the guilt I felt about borrowing such a large amount seemed as bad as losing my house. They'd only just retired and there was no guarantee of them ever getting the money back. Who'd employ an ex-con who'd been dismissed from the police? My only hope was that I wouldn't get the sack.

Slowly, I began to concentrate on the future. I knew that there was to be a disciplinary hearing, but I didn't know when it would be. Just as I had fought to acquit myself during my trial, I would go to my disciplinary hearing in a fighting spirit. I knew there were several convicted police officers serving with West Yorkshire Police, and so I had some hope that, given the circumstances of my conviction, I wouldn't get sacked.

Realistically though, I had to prepare for an unfavourable

outcome. If I lost my job, the dream was over. If only I hadn't been sent to that call on 24th August 1997. If only I hadn't been attacked in the way I had. If only I hadn't used force to defend myself. If only Sergeant Milburn had supported me and not my assailant. All these things did happen, though, and another lesson in my life was learned: you can't change the past. The only way to deal with it all was to think about a new career and start writing about what had happened.

Using some old notes I'd made in prison, I sat down and began writing on a cheap A4 pad using a pen I'd used to do my reports with as a policeman. I'd write for hours at a time, just committing my experiences to paper. I didn't really think I was writing a book; it was just great therapy for what had become an unexpectedly difficult period after my release. Within just a few days, I had pages of writing and scribbles. It was only when Tim came round one afternoon that these notes became something more substantial.

I'd left the pad on the table in the living room, and I heard him flicking through the pages while I was in the kitchen making some coffee. He was sitting on the edge of his chair, using his finger to scan each line as he read intently. He frowned and grimaced occasionally. My presence went completely unnoticed, as did the coffee I put on the table for him. He just kept reading. After a few more minutes, he put the pad down. He looked flabbergasted, yet intrigued, and we started discussing in detail what happened in prison. Several hours passed and Tim ended up flippantly remarking that the notes would make a good book. Even though I didn't take his suggestion seriously at first, the idea to write *A Fair Cop* was born.

I spent the next few weeks rearranging the notes I'd made into a sequential format. It gave me great focus, which distracted me from my troubles. It was just what I needed, not only to keep me busy, but also as a way to handle the stress. *A Fair Cop* became my initial salvation from the most desperate time in my life. It also gave me the desire to face my future head-on and to start making decisions about my career based on the assumption that I'd lose my job.

I'd been interested in sport and fitness since watching *The Incredible Hulk* in the late seventies. I was always amazed by Lou Ferrigno's awesome physique. I'd exercised from an early age and joined my first gym at sixteen. I sometimes ran forty miles a week. I knew that writing the book wasn't going to pay the bills and so I'd devote a couple of hours a day to researching courses in the fitness industry, which seemed the logical way to progress my career, given my high level of interest.

I found out that my tag was to be removed at midnight on Sunday, 7th November 1999. I enrolled onto a three-month, full-time diploma course in fitness training and sports therapy which was due to start in my home town on Monday, 8th November. This was a perfect way to try to rebuild my professional life. It came as a blow, then, when I received a letter from the police stating that my disciplinary hearing was to be heard on Tuesday, 9th November, the second day of the course. However, I began my diploma as planned on the Monday, having spent the previous month at home writing my book for around eight hours a day.

The hearing on the Tuesday did nothing to restore my faith in some of the higher echelons of the police service. My experiences up to this point had prepared me to expect little or no sympathy from Assistant Chief Constable Smith and his two colleagues. I did, however, have a glimmer of hope that they would see that what I had done on the night of Sunday, 24th

August 1997, had been no different to what police officers do every day, up and down the country. We (the police) deal with the most socially unacceptable people around, and we usually encounter them at their worst: when they are drunk or high on drugs, agitated and violent. Dealing with them is never simple. That is how it will always be. This didn't seem to help much, though, and I was dismissed from the force within twenty minutes.

I remember driving back to the course after the hearing. I loosened my tie and looked at myself in the rear view mirror. My recovery from prison had been slow, and I still looked incredibly emaciated. I'd been eating pretty well, but the thoughts of the hearing and the financial pressures had clearly taken their toll. Now, the bitter disappointment of losing my career in the police service would add to the strain, but I was determined that this was to be a turning point. I'd spent over two years at the mercy of the judiciary and senior West Yorkshire Police officers. I'd been unable to have any control of my life, so I felt unexpectedly free as well. Again, the little boy in the supermarket came to mind and I drew strength from him. Succeeding in a future career was the only way I could envisage recovering from this latest devastating setback, so I was keen to do well on my new course. It was at this point in 1999 that I knew I would have to finish writing my book. I also knew that I really needed to get it published, however long it took.

It was around this time that Mum drove down to Nan's in Northampton to tell her what had been happening over the past couple of years. She lived so far away so she'd had no idea that her only grandson, who she thought was still a serving police officer, had, in actual fact, just come out of prison and was jobless. I think we'd all estimated her response to the situation wrongly. Despite the fact that she was told just a month after what would have been her and Grandpa's sixtieth wedding anniversary and it was less than a year since he'd died, she took the news very well. Her methodical approach to the situation and her belief in me were a great help.

As I wrote this closing chapter in 2007, I planned to give her a copy of my book for her eighty-eighth birthday, which was in January 2008. My other three grandparents never knew what happened to me, and I don't really know how this makes Nan feel. The fact that Grandad and Grandpa died whilst the judicial process was going on angers me. I didn't really mourn them properly and that can never change.

I'd been fortunate to have a good education, leaving Batley Grammar School in 1992 with 11 GCSEs and 4 A-levels. I successfully graduated from my sports course in February 2000. It had prevented me from working and even though my financial pressures increased further, I was steadfast in my desire to succeed.

My feelings of failure and antipathy were soon combined with obdurate hunger, so I took the first job on offer: stacking shelves at the local Asda supermarket. I was being paid something like £5.90 an hour so I needed to work long hours to make ends meet. In what spare time I had, I began setting up a sports injury clinic business. Every night, the last thing I'd do would be to spend a couple of hours writing. It was this final task of each day that gave my life real purpose, and even though no one was reading it, I took a lot of comfort from putting my thoughts down on paper.

I began researching how published authors had got their first contract and emailed everyone that I thought could help. It was the same story from all of the authors; it's hard to get published if you're unknown, but if you believe in your writing, you'll do it eventually. I took solace from the fact that the first Harry Potter manuscript had been rejected many times until it was eventually taken on. I tried to prepare myself as best I could as I kept on writing. I hadn't realised the enormity of the task when I'd first started jotting down the notes that Tim eventually suggested should be turned into a book.

I'd never intended to work at the Asda store for very long, but I ended up working there for several months. I was earning a regular income and I was able to put my efforts into setting up the business and, of course, doing the two hours of writing every day. I wasn't ashamed of my new job, in fact I was proud of my resilience, but it was hard to see people who recognised me: people who knew me as the 'dedicated young policeman' – words that had been used to describe me in a newspaper report after I'd been sent to prison.

The feelings I got simply fuelled my ambition, and I began to withdraw from people in a bid to secure a virtuous future for myself. Isolation soon took hold. I found socialising too hard, as my friends would openly talk about police work and the latest office politics from the department where they worked. In fact, even just seeing a police car made me feel uneasy and still does. Once again, the nights merged into days, as I found sleeping too difficult. I'd lie in bed feeling my heart thump in my chest, my eyes wide open. I'd go to work increasingly disorientated, unable to function in even the most basic tasks. Work on the new business became a struggle and, more importantly, any progress with my writing was halted. I'd been relying on this as my escape, but the complexity of my situation even seemed to take this away from me. The vicious cycle I was in felt very oppressive.

Facing people became more difficult each day, and I wanted above all to stop working until I was okay. However, I knew this would have the reverse effect and so I decided to carry on. I'd arrive each day with a feigned smile. Inside, though, I was falling to pieces. How wrong I'd been to think that my troubles would end as I walked through the prison gates.

It became obvious that the way I was feeling was how it was going to be for some time. I spent months stuck in the same routine. My drive had temporarily deserted me, and I didn't seem to be going anywhere. I woke up one morning and received a letter from the police pensions department stating that I wouldn't be entitled to my pension contributions. One of the reasons I'd joined the police at nineteen was because I wanted to retire early with a good pension. The realisation that this had also been taken away from me was a blow, but it was probably a blessing in disguise. My motivation had returned.

Fighting my desire to withdraw, I began to drive the business again and spent every spare moment doing presentations in sports centres. My sports injury clinic started getting busier and my reputation began to grow. I took a job as a fitness instructor, and even though I'd had stability at Asda, I was gaining experience in the industry I'd trained to be in. I was also getting more customers for my clinic.

The £3.74 an hour was a difficult pill to swallow, though, so I began writing again and my book gradually began to take shape. In September 2001 – in fact, the very day of the Twin Towers atrocity – I started as a fitness manager at another health club. The money wasn't brilliant, but it was a promotion that would undoubtedly fill a hole on my CV. It was also salaried, which meant I was able to re-mortgage the house and pay Mum and Dad back the money they'd lent me. This was the first achievement since my release that registered in my mind as a significant step forward. It also took away the guilt of having borrowed my parents' retirement money. Things were on the up, but it had taken almost two years from the time I got out. I was still struggling with money, but my progress was tangible.

There were always setbacks, though. My mind still struggled with the integrity of the judicial process to which I'd been subjected. I tried to imagine where I'd have been if I hadn't lost my job in the police. Negative thoughts were never far from my mind, so I threw myself into my new management role with zeal. It wasn't a very demanding job, but I was learning new things and I was left to do it my way, which I liked.

The next six months were productive. I made a number of changes to the way the health club was run and this was received well by the members and staff. The stability of the job gave me time to focus on writing, and I was back to doing at least two hours a day. My clinic continued to grow, and I found myself struggling to fit everything in. I thrived on this feeling, as it was the complete opposite of the failure I'd felt initially. I'd never stopped training, but I was back in the gym with a vengeance, and I was beginning to feel fit again. At the end of 2001, I was even featured in several national fitness magazines as a 'success story' from the course I'd been on.

I knew that complacency was an enemy, though, and I had many sleepless nights along the way when something had happened during a particular day to upset me. It could have been the smallest thing: seeing a police car whiz past with the blues on, or seeing a clip of *The Bill* on a TV trailer. These may sound like pretty small things, but the effects they had on me made me realise just how vulnerable my mind still was. I never told anyone about how I felt, and it must have appeared that I was happily building a new life for myself. The reality of the matter was that I was still having occasional thoughts of suicide, as I just couldn't seem to shake off the demons from my past. I got used to the disparity in my feelings and I became apt at covering them up. The negativity became a permanent feature of my deeper psyche, but it also became my driving force. The determination outgrew the desperation.

My developing strength was constantly being tested. There seemed to be a deluge of police programmes on the TV, just when I could have done without them. There were constant reminders about my past job every day. I'd meet the occasional person who would judge me purely on the fact that I had a conviction. Given my perceived injustice of how I got it, and the fact that I pride myself on being a law-abiding person, I found this challenging. I still meet this type of resistance now, and it still bothers me: another reason to get the book published, I guess.

But then, in December 2001, just a few days after I'd been on the back page of one of the sports magazines, I got my biggest break of all. I'd seen a job advertised as a lecturer. It was with the company through which I'd got my qualification, so I thought I'd apply. It was a speculative effort, I thought. I didn't have any teaching qualifications and I'd only been in the industry for two years, but I spent four days meticulously filling out the form. I found myself writing pages in a desperate attempt to explain why I had written 'yes' in the *Criminal Convictions* section and why I had written 'dismissed' in the *Reasons for Leaving Employment* section. A momentary decision I had taken over four years earlier still defined me. I just hoped that whoever read it would see the reality of the situation.

I sent it off and hoped. It was obvious that any job I ever applied for again would be the same. There would never be any escaping the past and the injustice of what happened to me would be there forever. The deep despair this caused resulted in some of the most creative writing I'd done up to that point.

It came as a huge surprise when I was invited to an interview within a week. I initially thought there'd been a mistake, but when I rang to confirm my attendance, the woman was expecting my call. This was amazing: just what I needed. I spent the next fortnight preparing to give a lecture on the anatomy and common injuries of the knee-joint to an osteopath, a chiropractor, a chartered physiotherapist with twenty years experience and the managing director of the company. Even though I'd not got the job yet, I considered this to be another step forward.

The whole day was daunting. Dad, unremitting in his support for my recovery, drove the 250 miles to the small office in Wiltshire where the interview was to be held. I can't begin to imagine what effect my initial downfall has had on my parents, but this long drive was typical of their endeavour to help me. I used the four-hour journey time to do my final bits of preparation.

Christmas 2001 was another defining moment in my recovery process. On Christmas Eve, I was delighted to be offered the job as a lecturer. The salary was better than when I'd been a constable, and this was important to me. It wasn't so much the money, but more the fact that it showed my renaissance was real. It will come as no surprise that I accepted the job, and I remember to this day the comments made by one of my interviewers about my conviction. He was overtly critical of how I'd been treated and said that the police's loss had been his gain. This professional acceptance was yet another step taken on the ladder of my psychological recovery.

I began the role in February 2002 and, because of the intensive level of studying required to get me to teaching standard, progress with my book was slow. I wasn't too bothered, though. I knew I'd get back to it one day, but securing my new job had become a priority. It took over twelve months to fully settle into the role. Teaching is a huge challenge, but massively rewarding and the purpose in my life had been restored. There was little time for despondent indulgences and, despite occasional minor setbacks, I rarely dwelled on the past in this busy period of my life. The thought of completing my book was a source of real excitement, even though I wasn't actually writing at that time.

I was finally able to start writing properly again in 2003. I'd qualified to the necessary level within my job and I was comfortable in the role. I'd done bits on the book, but never really got going with it. A double-page piece about me in the *Sunday Times* in 2002, followed by a radio interview on BBC Radio Scotland, served as a motivation to get the book finished, so I got back down to the thankless and lonely task of sitting at my desk in the spare room writing the closing chapters. I used the notes that I made in prison, but I'd remembered everything, anyway. I shall never forget.

By 2004, the first draft of *A Fair Cop* was complete. The joy of finishing this lengthy task, that had so irksomely been interrupted by the necessity to build a new career, was quickly ruined as the arduous task of editing began. I knew that I was a long way away from sending the finished manuscript out to publishers, and so the lengthy correction process began. It became apparent that several edits would be needed. It's a lonely job being a writer; it's even lonelier being an editor. This job took a further two years, as the pressures of work and being sent all over the UK eroded the time I had available to concentrate on the book.

In 2006, I set up my website, *www.afaircop.co.uk*. I didn't really think that people would look at it, so I was surprised when the BBC contacted me, wanting to do another radio interview. This was to be the first of many. Newspapers began taking an interest in my case and I began to build a sizeable media page on my website, as I was featured in several of them. The public support grew, as did the traffic on my website. It helped when people left supportive messages, as the upsetting task of talking about what happened over and over again began to take a hold. The anxiety I'd experienced in the first few years came back, as the distraction of work was replaced by the constant focus on my case. I began to feel depressed again and it was only the support of my girlfriend, Rachel, whom I'd met in 2005 at work, which kept me going. She understood everything about me: she'd grip my hand if I saw a police car; she'd stand up for me whenever my case was discussed. She even sat up night after night listening to me read my book out loud in an attempt to get another opinion on it. Quite simply, she has become my rock.

I needed her more than ever after I'd been interviewed on Radio 5 live on 21st August 2007. That was the first time I'd been openly attacked on air. Both the presenter and the guest, a public interest lawyer, seemed unsympathetic to my cause. I remember the lawyer saying to me that I should have 'negotiated' with my assailant: the man who I'd just described live on air as repeatedly punching me about the head in a sustained assault whilst in drink. I asked her to explain to me how I should have negotiated with him, and I quickly realised I was gaining the upper hand in the discussion when she was unable to answer the question. The response on air was overwhelmingly in my favour, as rank-and-file officers called the show to support me.

I've had much support over the past ten years from a whole cross-section of people, ranging from politicians to journalists and university lecturers, and most of all, of course, from friends and family. My website gets hits from all over the world. I'm still disillusioned about what happened, but I am hugely grateful for what I have now. The little boy in the supermarket taught me that in 1999, and Rachel teaches me it every day.

Since his conviction, Michael became a qualified lecturer and worked for seven years in this role.

He opened a sports injury clinic in 2000 which runs successfully to this day.

Michael now works as a Restorative Justice Co-ordinator which focuses on working with victims of crime and helping offenders to take responsibility and change their behaviour.

His book is being written into a screen drama.

His case has recently been referred to the Criminal Cases Review Commission.